Kitchens

KITCHENS
The
Culture
of
Restaurant
Work

GARY ALAN FINE

UNIVERSITY OF CALIFORNIA PRESS
Berkeley · Los Angeles · London

University of California Press
Berkeley and Los Angeles, California

University of California Press, Ltd.
London, England

© 1996 by The Regents of the University of
California

Library of Congress Cataloging-in-Publication Data

Fine, Gary Alan.

    Kitchens : the culture of restaurant work /
Gary Alan Fine.
       p.   cm.
    Includes bibliographical references and index.
    ISBN 0-520-20077-2 (alk. paper). — ISBN
0-520-20078-0 (pbk. : alk. paper)
    1. Kitchen—Social aspects. 2. Cooks—Social
life and customs.
    I. Title.
    TX653.F57   1995
    305.9642—dc20   94-49673
                                     CIP

Printed in the United States of America

9 8 7 6 5 4 3 2

The paper used in this publication meets the
minimum requirements of American National
Standard for Information Sciences—Permanence of
Paper for Printed Library Materials, ANSI Z39.48-
1984.

    The publisher gratefully acknowledges permission to reprint parts of several chapters of the present work:
    Chapter 1: Reprinted from *Current Research on Occupations and Professions* 4 (1987): 141–158, "Working Cooks: The Dynamics of Professional Kitchens," by Gary Alan Fine, with the permission of JAI Press, Inc., Greenwich, Connecticut.
    Chapter 2: Reprinted from *Social Forces* 69:1 (1990): 95–114, "Organizational Time: Temporal Demands and the Experience of Work in Restaurant Kitchens," by Gary Alan Fine. © 1990 by The University of North Carolina Press.
    Chapter 6: Reprinted from *American Journal of Sociology* 97:6 (1992): 1268–1294, "The Culture of Production: Aesthetic Choices and Constraints in Culinary Work," by Gary Alan Fine. © 1992 by The University of Chicago. All rights reserved.
    Chapter 7: Reprinted from *Theory and Society* 24/2 (1995): 245–269, "Wittgenstein's Kitchen: Sharing Meaning in Restaurant Work," by Gary Alan Fine. © 1995 Kluwer Academic Publishers. Reprinted by permission of Kluwer Academic Publishers.

To Graham Tomlinson
and Hans Haferkamp,
their absence lessens my life,
my sociology, and my table.

Contents

Preface

Eroticism is the most intense of passions while Gastronomy is
the most extended. . . . Although both are made up of combinations and connections—bodies and substances—in Love
the number of combinations is limited and pleasure tends to
climax in an instant . . . while in Gastrosophy the number of
combinations is infinite; pleasure, instead of tending toward
concentration, tends to propagate and extend itself through
taste and savoring.

—*Octavio Paz*

Gender roles ensnare us all. In the early years of my marriage, when
my wife and I were graduate students, she did the housework. When,
at last, we both obtained "real jobs," she insisted that I assume more
responsibilities. Like many males who share household tasks, I chose
those that permitted the most freedom, creativity, and personal satisfaction: I decided to learn to cook. Of all chores, cooking seemed least
onerous. But, even so, that justification was not sufficient; I needed a
rationale to avoid "wasting" time in the kitchen—transforming life
into work, just as my work was leisure. As a sociologist interested in
art, I could learn to cook and observe professional cooks, a group that
had not been examined ethnographically. I cannily transformed household chores into professional engagement. My cooking skills expanded
to where I enjoyed eating what I had cooked: no small achievement in
view of those first hot, harsh evenings at the stove.

Finally I had learned enough that I would not be thought hopelessly
and laughably inept if I shared space with professional cooks. At that
point I took a giant step from my kitchen into the "real world" of the
food production industry. I decided to learn how students learn and
are taught to cook professionally. I received permission from two
state-run technical-vocational institutes in the Twin Cities metropoli-

tan area to observe their cooking programs. I was accepted, even welcomed. I attended one almost every day and became reasonably profi-
cient in the skills that entry-level cooks must acquire, becoming socialized to the tricks of the trade. I developed a theory of the development
of occupational aesthetics.

My experiences at these schools led to restaurant kitchens. I was
welcomed cordially and hopefully, and I was given access that permitted me to explore organizational culture and structure, grounded in interactionist and interpretivist sociology. My informants were convinced that the world outside the kitchen walls did not understand
their working conditions and did not appreciate their skills or the pressures and troubles they experienced. They believed that the public
thought of them as drunken and loud, as bums. Most cooks were
pleased that a fair academic outsider would tell the truth about them
or would at least experience their working conditions.

It is widely accepted in the kitchens of academe that there is no one
truth. While my views are my own, I hope to present one set of truths
about cooks that will be close enough for them to recognize, even if I
don't mirror what any one of them believes. I hope, like Paul Stoller
(1989), to capture some of the sensory conditions of work and provide, to borrow his title, "the taste of ethnographic things," not among
the distant Songhay of Niger but among the cooks of Minnesota.

My observations in trade school—collegiums bureaucrats now label
"technical colleges," mirroring a desire to professionalize everything
(Wilensky 1964)—taught me how the children of blue-collar workers
become socialized to a career that demands knowledge of arenas of
cultural capital ("taste") to which they have not been exposed. Yet,
these data ended at the job market: what did these young men and
women do when actually employed by an industrial organization? My
observation of four restaurant kitchens allowed me to find out. In each
restaurant I spent a month watching, taking notes, asking questions,
and, when needed, stringing beans, washing potatoes, and performing
minor chores. I was never a cook, but I was, occasionally, an empty
pair of hands. In each setting described in the appendix, observations
were supplemented by in-depth interviews.

As a matter of "field ethics," I ate those dishes that cooks graciously
placed before me to demonstrate their culinary virtuosity, to celebrate
my role in their community, and, perhaps, by forcing me to accept
their hospitality, to make it more difficult to criticize them. I gained
about ten pounds during each month that I spent observing. The two

months' interval between each month of observations permitted me to acquire a critical perspective on the data and work myself into shape. Those scholars who choose research projects of which others dream must face a cordial professional jealousy; these collegial critics forget the long hours, the sweat, and the filth: it's a dirty job, but I challenged myself to do it.

Sociologists and friends assisted me in shaping this research by providing ideas, comments, criticism, or simply fellowship as I talked and ate. Specifically I thank Howard S. Becker, Harold Bershady, Charles Bosk, Terry Clark, George Dickie, Robert Faulkner, Priscilla Ferguson, William Finlay, Joseph Galaskiewicz, Wendy Griswold, Jay Gubrium, Hans Haferkamp, Janet Harris, Mark Haugan, Lori Holyfield, Thomas Hood, Sherryl Kleinman, Michal McCall, Richard Mitchell, Harvey Molotch, Richard Peterson, Charles Stevens, Robert Sutton, Doris Taub, Richard Taub, Graham Tomlinson, and John Young. I am grateful to colleagues at colloquia at Harvard University, the University of Pennsylvania, the University of Chicago, the University of Georgia, and Emory University for challenging me on critical points. Pam Chase and Cathy Rajtar helped to transcribe the interviews quoted in this volume. Hilda Daniels, Gloria DeWolfe, and Clara Roesler helped in typing the manuscript, particularly before the time that I acquired word-processing skills. I am grateful to the Center for Advanced Study in the Behavioral Sciences for providing an environment in which I could complete this text, and grateful for financial support provided by National Science Foundation grant SBR-9022192. Warm appreciation is also due to my wife, Susan, and sons, Todd and Peter, for sometimes eating what I cooked. I am deeply grateful to Naomi Schneider and her colleagues at the University of California Press for providing a hospitable home for this volume.

As is customary and right, I reserve my special thanks for those individuals I cannot name, who let me intrude into their lives and kitchens. I hope that I have managed to capture a taste of their tasks and the environment in which they labor.

Palo Alto, California
September 1994

Introduction

What is patriotism but the love of the good things we ate in
our childhood.

—*Lin Yutang*

Food reveals our souls. Like Marcel Proust reminiscing about a
madeleine or Calvin Trillin astonished at a plate of ribs, we are entan-
gled in our meals. The connection between identity and consumption
gives food a central role in the creation of community,[1] and we use our
diet to convey images of public identity (Bourdieu 1984; MacClancy
1992). The routinization of feeding is one of the central requirements
of families (DeVault 1991) and other social systems. The existence of
profit-making organizations to process and serve food reveals something crucial about capitalist, industrial society. As is true for mills,
foundries, and hospitals, the growth of restaurants—the hospitality industry—is implicated in the economic changes in the West in the past
two centuries. Given their ubiquity and our frequency of contact with
them, restaurants represent the apotheosis of free-market capitalism,
production lines, a consumption economy, and interorganizational
linkages. The production, service, and consumption of food is a nexus
of central sociological constructs—organization, resources, authority,
community, rhetoric, gender, and status.

Yet, for all their potential allure, restaurants have rarely been studied sociologically (but see Whyte 1946; Gross 1958; Hannon and Freeman 1989). Cooks, despite continual, though mediated, contact in our
quotidian lives, are invisible workers in occupational sociology.

While wishing to capture the flavor of this work environment, I
have equally salient theoretical aims. I wish to present an organiza-

tional sociology that is grounded in interactionist and cultural concerns, but does justice to the reality of the organization and the equal, insistent reality of the environment outside the organization. Alan Wolfe (1991) labels my generation of organizational ethnographers the "new institutionalists" (see Dimaggio and Powell 1991). These scholars look behind the generalizations and abstractions of institutional theory to examine how institutions operate in practice. While I first heard the term used by Wolfe, the moniker captures part of the impetus for this volume. Through my ethnography I present a perspective that accounts for features of the organizational literature (e.g., Scott 1992) while remaining true to the lived experiences of workers who labor behind the kitchen door. An interactionist approach need not eschew organizational and system constraints, and can address the political economy. In the past two decades, while embracing the basic precepts of an interpretivist perspective, I have confronted questions that had often been left to structural sociologists.[2] This book explores several features of organizational sociology, providing some basis for future research.

The font of my analysis is the negotiated order perspective: that approach to the interactionist understanding of organizations pioneered by Anselm Strauss and his colleagues from the University of Chicago, such as Donald Roy and Howard Becker, some three decades ago (Colomy and Brown 1995). Strauss's studies of psychiatric hospitals (Strauss et al. 1963; Strauss et al. 1964)[3] are classics and contribute to an ongoing research project (e.g., Corbin and Strauss 1993). The most detailed treatment of this approach, which expands it beyond the confines of a single work setting, is found in Strauss's *Negotiations* (1978), in which he develops a theory of organization and structural negotiations. While Strauss did not emphasize the impact of external forces and social constraints in shaping trajectories of work and did not provide a single detailed case, his theory provides a base for any interactionist examination of organizations. Strauss is at pains to explain the flexibility within organizations and the conditions under which this flexibility is likely to appear. Others have expanded the negotiated order approach (Maines 1977; Fine 1984), examining it in a variety of empirical arenas (see Farberman 1975; Denzin 1977; Kleinman 1982; Levy 1982; Lynxwiler, Shover, and Clelland 1983; Hosticka 1979; Mesler 1989) and demonstrating how negotiation pervades a range of organizational and institutional environments. The negotiated order approach represents one of several theoretical apparatuses that at-

tempts to link micro- and macroexplanations. It provides an understanding of how interaction emerges from structure and, in turn, how
interaction becomes structured (Busch 1980, 1982): how the effects of
interaction become patterned, creating social structure (see Fine 1991;
Sewell 1992). Erving Goffman remarks:

> All the world is not a stage—certainly the theater isn't entirely. (Whether
> you organize a theater or an aircraft factory, you need to find places for
> cars to park and coats to be checked, and these had better be real places,
> which, incidentally, had better carry real insurance against theft.) Presum-
> ably, a "definition of the situation" is almost always to be found, but those
> who are in the situation ordinarily do not *create* this definition, even
> though their society often can be said to do so; ordinarily, all they do is to
> assess correctly what the situation ought to be for them and then act ac-
> cordingly. True, we personally negotiate aspects of all arrangements under
> which we live, but often once these are negotiated, we continue on mechan-
> ically as though the matter had always been settled.
>
> (Goffman 1974, pp. 1–2)

As Goffman indicates, a consequential reality exists to which people
pay heed, even when negotiating around the edges. People are able to
define situations, but these definitions have consequences. For organizations, ecology, political economy, and authority hierarchy have this
character. Micronegotiations that are so compelling to interactionists
are organized by an obdurate, enveloping reality. To understand persons and their settings, we must oscillate between their "free" acts and
the larger environments in which these actions occur. Anthony Giddens (1984, p. xxvi; see Collins 1981) notes: "The opposition between
'micro' and 'macro' is best reconceptualized as concerning how interaction in contexts of co-presence is structurally implicated in systems
of broad time-space distanciation—in other words, how such systems
span large sectors of time-space." Several critical assumptions under-
gird the development of the negotiated order perspective. First, in this
view all social order is negotiated order; that is, it is impossible to
imagine organization without negotiation. All organizations are composed of actors, and even when we do not focus on their actions, they
can subvert or support structural effects. Second, specific negotiations
are contingent on the structure of the organization and the field in
which the organization operates. Negotiations follow lines of power
and communication, and are patterned and nonrandom. Third, negotiations have temporal limits and are renewed, revised, and reconstituted
over time. The revisions may occur unpredictably, but the revisions

themselves are often predictable post hoc if one examines changes in the organizational structure or ecology. Negotiations are historically contingent. Fourth, structural changes in the organization require a revision of the negotiated order. In other words, the structure of the organization and micropolitics of the negotiated order are closely and causally related (Herzfeld 1992). Strauss writes: "The negotiated order on any given day could be conceived of as the sum total of the organization's rules and policies, along with whatever agreements, understandings, pacts, contracts, and other working arrangements currently obtained. These include agreements at every level of organization, of every clique and coalition, and include covert as well as overt agreements" (1978, p. 2). Although this passage does not address the historical contingency of the negotiations, the ongoing and consequential character of these understandings is crucial. Strauss's later work (1991) on articulation and arcs of work attempts to bring temporality into the negotiation process.

Within a "negotiation framework," two broad issues are crucial: (1) How organizational, economic, and environmental constraints affect choices and behaviors of workers in their daily routines—how "life worlds" are colored by constraints (Fine 1991). How structure affects culinary doings—the mundane experience of the occupation. (2) How all occupations involve a concern with "quality" production, and how these aesthetic standards are negotiated in practice. As I describe in chapter 6, all art is work, and all work is art. A delicate balance exists between action and constraint—what in other sociological venues is labeled the problem of agency and structure (e.g., Dawe 1978; Archer 1988; Fine 1992a). Before discussing each theme, I situate my analysis in the history of restaurants.

THE DEVELOPMENT OF RESTAURANTS AND CUISINE

If restaurants didn't exist, they'd have to be invented.
Because a restaurant takes a basic drive, the simple act
of eating, and transforms it into a civilized ritual—a
ritual involving hospitality and imagination and satisfaction and graciousness and warmth.

—*Joe Baum*

Gastronomy has a distinguished pedigree, a history as lengthy as human political and economic history, but not always as well documented. Food has long been produced by "specialists" outside the family in "civilized society" (Mennell, Murcott, and Otterloo 1992).[4] The ancient Greeks wrote of cookery as art (Bowden 1975, p. 2), and some suggest that the Chinese were concerned with "cuisine" at nearly the same period (Anderson and Anderson 1988; Chang 1977; Tiger 1985) and, according to others, subsequently started the first "serious" restaurants during the Tang dynasty (A.D. 618–907) (Ackerman 1990, p. 133). The great and gross banquets of the Roman Era and early Middle Ages are well known (Mennell 1985; Elias 1978; Wheaton 1983). By the Middle Ages cookbooks existed, street foods were sold to the public, and kings and nobles employed chefs to run their kitchens. Some medieval chefs such as Taillevent were famed throughout courtly society.[5] If they were not as esteemed as artists, they were still ranked above craftsmen.

Cooking was not accorded equal status in all nations at all times ("Cook's Interview: Anne Willan" 1985, p. 19; "Cook's Interview: Richard Olney" 1986, p. 22); and France and China (and, according to some, Italy) are reputed to have established a "true" aesthetic, or court, cuisine. It has been a commonplace that English cookery and French cuisine differ substantially, much to the disadvantage of the former (e.g., Charpentier and Sparkes 1934, p. 131)—a difference that has existed for centuries (Mennell 1985, pp. 102–33)—although whether it is a function of national character, class structure, geographical organization of the nation-state, agricultural production, weather, or some other cause is a matter of contention. French cuisine has not always been considered the foremost in Europe, however. In the sixteenth century, Italian cuisine held that distinction. The change in national reputation is attributed to the 1533 marriage of Catherine de' Medici to Henry II of France. As queen, she brought with her some of the finest Italian cooks, and French cuisine was established by these new immigrants (Bowden 1975, p. 6).

Political movements and economic concerns contribute to culinary migration, just as they are associated with other migrations. An unanticipated consequence of the French Revolution was the emigration of some French court chefs to England (Bowden 1975, p. 8). A latent benefit of the end of the American war in Indochina was the influx of Vietnamese cooks to our shores, infusing urban restaurant scenes. Likewise, the new wave of immigration to American shores by Chinese nationals has produced a flowering of restaurants (Epstein 1993, p. 50). In fact, the American restaurant scene has benefited from waves of third world migration, bringing cuisines, cooks, and many minimum-wage kitchen laborers. Migration moved west, as well as north and east: French tax rates, coupled with the growth of American culinary sophistication (and salaries for top chefs), have impelled French chefs to seek employment in American kitchens.

Court cuisine was well established by the late Middle Ages and the Renaissance, but it was not until centuries later that the restaurant as modern, Western diners would recognize it appeared. Inns, teahouses and coffeehouses, caterers, cabarets, and taverns have long served food for a price (Brennan 1988), bringing dining into the public sphere, but it was not until 1765 that the first "restaurant" was established in Paris (Willan 1977, p. 85). With attention to the preparation and serving of *meals,* these restaurants were more specialized than previous establishments that served food, and they explicitly addressed the status needs of their clientele (Clark 1975, p. 37).[6]

In the aftermath of the French Revolution, these establishments grew in number and importance as courtly cuisine declined. Prior to the French Revolution, fewer than thirty restaurants operated in Paris; some thirty years later three thousand restaurants dotted Paris (Clark 1975, p. 37). They served a *grande cuisine* but one available to all with financial resources. Restaurants in Paris and other cities benefited from the population influx into urban areas. While restaurants were not created in direct response to political and social changes, these changes facilitated their development. In the last two hundred years, restaurants have altered from a respite for the rich to a bastion of the middle class. Restaurants meet a combination of aesthetic, status, and entertainment needs—although the means in which these needs are met has changed with circumstances.

The first restaurant in London was established in 1798 (Bowden 1975, p. 19), and in 1831, Delmonico's opened in New York, arguably the first full-fledged American restaurant, certainly the first sanctified with a French chef. For much of the nineteenth century the name "Delmonico's" epitomized American haute cuisine (Root and de Rochemont 1976, pp. 321–22).

The spread of restaurants was a consequence of the agricultural revolution, the desire for mass feeding in urban areas, and the needs of the elites for quality food in status-conferring surroundings without the necessity of employing their own cooks (Symons 1983, p. 39). Thus, symbolic issues merge with the structure of the political economy in fostering this industry. The prosperity of postindustrial Western soci-

eties, particularly in the last few decades, has provided a fertile breed-
ing ground for new restaurants. This prosperity is both a cause and a
result of changes in global markets: with the ability to obtain culinary
items from all over the world at all times at prices that consumers can
afford, the possibilities of food preparation multiply (Zukin 1991, p.
209).

Jane and Michael Stern (1991, pp. 133–37) date the birth of an
haute cuisine orientation to the opening in 1941 of Le Pavillon in New
York, in part as a function of those intellectuals who wanted to appear
cosmopolitan by disdaining traditional American food, in part as a
function of international migration, and in part as a function of expan-
sions of markets for prestige goods. By the 1950s, this New York establishment began to spawn imitations across the nation, and within
twenty years of its opening, it was regarded as old-fashioned (see Levenstein 1988, pp. 206–7). The haute cuisine trend continued into the
culinary boom of the 1970s (Levenstein 1993, pp. 214–15), as exemplified by the opening in 1971 in Berkeley of Alice Waters's *American*-
inspired Chez Panisse. The food critic Craig Claiborne (1982, p. 146)
notes that along with a change in attitudes came increased prosperity:
"Hundreds and thousands of people who a dozen or twenty years ago
had to think twice before going to some small French bistro for their
coq au vin or beef *bourguignonne,* now find it financially feasible to
visit restaurants that are relatively luxury-style to sup on the *nouvelle*
and traditional cuisine." With the growth of environmentalist and
globalist ideologies, nouvelle restaurants have become ideologically
compatible with the aging of sixties' radicals and their incorporation
into the cultural establishment (e.g., Waters 1990). Indeed, Chez
Panisse opened as an outgrowth of the homemade meals that Alice
Waters had served Berkeley radicals (Belasco 1989, p. 94). The Berkeley restaurant scene pays heed to the maxim that you are what you eat,
your cuisine is your politics, and food is an " 'edible dynamic' binding
present and past, individual and society, private household and world
economy, palate and power" (Belasco 1989, p. 5). The restaurant culture of Berkeley represented the epitome of a "gourmet ghetto."

Yet, while the importance of ideological and cultural considerations
in the development of new styles of restaurants may be emphasized,
economic forces must not be discounted. As noted, an international
market of foodstuffs developed with changes in transportation, agri-
culture, marketing, and refrigeration. Further, the development of a
market for gourmet food as a form of consumption is part of the gen-

trification that has altered the urban landscape of many cities (Zukin 1991, p. 202); gourmets reside in cultural zones. This gentrification affects not only the customer base of these establishments but also its labor base, as many servers are recruited from the artistic "critical infrastructure" found in cities (Zukin 1991, p. 206). The fixed costs of restaurants are also affected when previously impoverished areas of the city are rediscovered by entrepreneurs, such as restaurateurs, who attempt to provide novel experiences for their customers who strive for the latest and most status-enhancing culinary experience. The successive popularity of various cuisines over the past two decades (e.g., Cajun, Thai, Ethiopian, Tex-Mex) has led some to suggest that the restaurant scene is as subject to trends as the art world. The culinary avant-garde grazes on.

Yet, any perspective that emphasizes the pinnacle of the restaurant industry at the expense of the vast majority of restaurants that cater to middle- and working-class eaters is deceptive. Many restaurants are not part of national chains but are small, local establishments, serving food only modestly different from that served in customers' homes. Other market niches provide Americanized "ethnic" cuisine—notably Chinese, Italian, and Mexican. Some ethnic restaurants have two menus, one for fellow members of a particular ethnic group and one for those outside it (Epstein 1993, p. 54). Among restaurants the growth of franchises is of the greatest economic significance: from White Towers in the 1920s (Hirshorn and Izenour 1979), linked to urban transport systems, to suburban fast-food establishments in the 1950s, dependent on the growth of highways, to the recent franchising of family-style and thematic restaurants found both in urban enclaves and suburban malls (Finkelstein 1989).

ECONOMICS AND RESTAURANT WORK

To understand the kitchen as a social world, we must consider it as an institutional environment. This institution consists of the industrial section of the American economy involved in the preparation and serving of food to customers: the "restaurant industry" (Hughes 1971, p. 298),[7] part of the "hospitality industry" (Olesen 1992). Restaurants are integral symbols of a free-market economic system. It was not by chance that many of the early battles over integration occurred at southern lunch counters, as eating establishments were a readily available public arena of American capitalism. Indeed, restaurants are so linked to free-market capitalism that socialist nations quickly become known for the poor quality of the food they present to diners. When a socialist country begins to move from a planned economy, the restaurant business is one of the first arenas in which the development of an entrepreneurial market economy is noticed. In the early stages of Soviet perestroika, the quality of the small, private restaurants that appeared in Moscow impressed Western journalists. Within the American context, state action can be profound. The imposition of Prohibition in the United States was said to have destroyed many fine dining establishments, constituting what the journalist Julian Street described in 1931 as a "gastronomic holocaust" (Levenstein 1988, p. 183). In fact, Prohibition did not so much destroy public eating as change it, aborting the spread of French cuisine in this country, served in luxurious restaurants and aimed at well-to-do males, and replacing those establishments with more modest "American" ones, catering to women and families.

Competition among restaurants represents, in some respects, an ideal type of a true free-market system in that capital barriers to entrance into the market are relatively modest, large numbers of entrepreneurs compete, and consumers make choices with relatively little pressure. In the pure free-market system (e.g., in which cost alone determines consumption choices), products are fully fungible: all food is interchangeable. Obviously this does not apply to the restaurant industry, as establishments strive to insure product differentiation separate from price and convenience. Restaurants strive to differentiate themselves in cultural *meaning* as well as cost. The possibility of such differentiation creates a highly competitive market with numerous niches.

The dominant industry trade group for this segment of the economy is the National Restaurant Association, which, in conjunction with state trade associations, represents a quarter of a million restaurants. Many others operate that are too small or choose not to be represented by this giant association. For instance, in the city of Chicago there are some 8,000 eating establishments. Even if we ignore lunch counters and fast-food establishments, most large metropolitan areas sport several hundred restaurants. According to 1987 census data, 330,000 eating places employed nearly six million workers with a payroll of $36 billion and sales of nearly $150 billion (*Statistical Abstracts 1990*, p. 769). This industrial segment represents the largest employer of young people between 16 and 19 years of age. The National Restaurant Association estimates that sales of food equaled nearly 5 percent of the

United States Gross National Product in 1982. In 1977, restaurants accounted for 8.8 percent of the money spent in all retail establishments (Zelinsky 1985, p. 53). On a typical day more than 77 million customer transactions occur in the food industry, and 78 percent of all families report eating in commercial food-service establishments on a regular basis. This gigantic industry comprises numerous small firms, each tightly interconnected with a network of large corporations (food producers and suppliers).

From one perspective, all these eating establishments compete with each other, but from another this is deceptive. Within a market a restaurant draws customers from different regions, choosing its market niche or segment. A restaurant differs from others in the distances that its customers will travel to eat there. A local restaurant (e.g., a family restaurant that is part of a chain, a locally owned café, or a diner) has a customer base that resides or shops near the restaurant—a small catchment area. When my family and I desire a simple Mexican meal or to eat in a cafeteria, we choose a restaurant within a mile or two of our home or near to where we happen to be at the time. We are unlikely to drive across town, because we perceive that these restaurants are equivalent—we are unwilling to incur significant costs (in money, fuel, or time) for no measurable difference in quality. In contrast, when we choose a restaurant for dim sum or for haute cuisine, we may travel great distances. These restaurants are not fungible with others, because of the unique qualities associated with them. The more interchangeable a restaurant, the smaller the area from which customers will be drawn.[8] Fungibility is an asset for a chain (if the chain itself can differentiate itself from other chains) in that advertising can be cost effective in promoting all franchisees or for a restaurant with few competitors, such as small-town restaurants. Yet, it becomes a disadvantage when attempting to convince customers to select one restaurant over another if greater costs are associated with that selection. A French restaurant seen as "nearly identical" to all other French restaurants will likely not succeed financially. The organizational ecology of restaurants is complex and dynamic, but, perhaps more than most industries, demonstrates the fruitfulness of an ecological orientation to organizational life (see Hannon and Freeman 1989), because the effect of external considerations is readily apparent.

Because of the relative ease of market entry (low start-up costs and relatively few institutional barriers), restaurants provide a compelling model of free-market capitalism. The fantasy of "Hey, guys, let's open a restaurant" is almost feasible (e.g., Miller 1978). While successful restaurants are likely to have a sufficient capital reserve to cover the expected losses during the first year, compared to other industrial sectors the restaurant industry is not capital intensive. In addition, changes in bankruptcy laws make exit costs relatively modest. Restaurants have a short life expectancy, with some claiming that 20 percent close within a year and that half close within five years.

Beyond its profit potential, operating a restaurant has cultural value (Miller 1978). Being a restaurant owner is appealing to those with cultural capital or an entrepreneurial spirit. Operating a restaurant provides a basis for the symbolic status the owner can gain in the community, as well as the privileges of owning one's own business. Unlike the owner of most industrial enterprises or small businesses, a restaurant owner can both make an aesthetic and personal statement while differentiating the business from others.[9] For many entering this industry, particularly those whose establishments aim at the trend-conscious, upper-middle-class consumer, the status and glamour of control, coupled with the satisfaction of seeing one's aesthetic vision put into practice, is as important as the income. The following decision to enter the restaurant business is a dramatic example:

> Dr. [Hilary] James [a psychotherapist] had always been very interested in good food and, while still a medical student, had been famous among his friends for his excellent cooking. After he had qualified and begun to practice, he found that he was not satisfied with the London restaurant scene; he did not like the food, the service, waiters in dirty tail-coats nor the necessity for customers to dress up if they wanted to go to a restaurant. He had become very fond of the little informal restaurants in the South of France which offered very good food in an atmosphere devoid of any pretension and so, egged on by the enthusiastic encouragement of his friends, he decided to open a restaurant of his own.
>
> (Bowden 1975, p. 85, see p. 123)[10]

One's cultural position, a need for aesthetic expression, and the existence of a community of supportive friends—each contributes to such a decision. While some restaurant owners have economic motives as their priority, from my discussion with upscale restaurant owners and reading the popular press, I find aesthetic concerns rarely absent. The economic organization of the restaurant industry permits businesses to be run for their cultural rewards.

This economic reality provides a backdrop for understanding the mundane doing of cooking—how the kitchen is experienced, and how that experience is revealed in action. What does it mean to cooks and chefs to be working? How do cooks cope with the challenges derived from the structure of the occupation? How do cooks structure their worktime, addressing the explicit and implicit demands of management and customers while mitigating the unpleasant components of culinary labor? This issue—the interplay of agency and structure—is addressed in the first five chapters. My treatment begins with a microsociological examination of work within the kitchen, expanding the focus into the larger socioeconomic concerns. In light of the structure in which they are embedded, in examining occupations I work from the "bottom up"—describing behavioral choices, grounded in local demands, before discussing the place of the occupation in the organization and the economy. The rhythms of work create and are created by the structure of the workplace. The experienced reality of a job consists of its patterned quality: knowing what is expected in minutes, hours, days, and weeks of work.

In chapter 1, I examine the negotiation of the behaviors of cooks, given the demands placed on them, including the negotiation of the division of labor within the kitchen. How is work in the kitchen produced among co-workers? In what way do the requirements of culinary work produce shortcuts, culinary tricks, approximations, and dirty work. In this chapter I examine the advantages and disadvantages to this work, along with the routes that lead workers into the occupation. In chapter 2, I discuss the use of time within the kitchen and the pressures that emerge from the temporal structure of the workday. How do cooks experience the Bergsonian concept of *durée* while at the stove? More than many occupations, cooking is temporally bounded, both in the microrhythms of preparing particular dishes and the longer rhythms of the workday. The third chapter focuses on the structural reality of kitchens. Here I focus on those elements that are not themselves part of cooking but contribute to the kitchen environment. What is the role of kitchen equipment in the production of food? How does the kitchen space constrain or contribute to culinary outcomes? Underlining these questions is the reality that restaurants are work communities. Chapter 4 explains the meaning of this community to the workers within it. How does the restaurant community and the expressive behaviors of those who are a part of it tether workers to what many outside this community perceive as low-paying, dirty, unappreciated labor? How do expressive culture and the development of an organizational culture affect the work of cooks? How do the expressive components of an occupation connect to instrumental demands? In chapter 5, I attempt to situate the restaurant and the work of cooks into the economic structure. How do the institutional constraints of the restaurant and the industrial components of the occupation affect the cooking that can and will be produced? How does the political economy in which restaurants are located influence the work in the kitchen, and in what ways do other organizational actors (e.g., managers, customers, and servers) impinge on the doing of cuisine?

AESTHETIC PRODUCTION

The restaurant industry involves more than the production of objects and the providing of services. Restaurant food, like all food, has an aesthetic, sensory dimension and is evaluated as such by both producers and consumers. I argue as a general principle that all products and services have an aesthetic dimension, but this dimension is most evident and self-referential in those organizations in which an "artistic" rhetoric is present. Although the aesthetic of food production and the aesthetic theory behind that production may not be as elaborate as that of photography or interior design (and certainly not as elaborate as that of the fine arts), restaurant employees care about the sensory qualities of their products.

Its location within a large industry, coupled with an explicit sense that the products are to be judged on their sensory qualities, makes a restaurant a compelling research site to examine the strains that affect workers. Linking macroconstraints with interaction, I find that aesthetic choices provide a means by which a cultural analysis informs and is informed by an organizational and economic reality.

Central to my analysis is the artistic character and definition of work, a rare concern in much social-scientific discourse. Food preparation incorporates four human senses: sight, smell, touch, and taste. Typically sound is not dramatically evident in food, but in the case of a sizzling steak, a bowl of Rice Krispies, a crisp apple, or crunchy stalk of celery, some measure of auditory enjoyment is tied to mastication (Vickers and Christensen 1980). Food involves more sensory dimensions than any other art form, except, perhaps, the "art" of love. This aesthetic richness allows vast leeway in choices of food preparation, a diversity that may have hindered the development of a formal aesthetics of cuisine: a theory of eating.

From an organizational perspective, cooks must compromise on what they serve customers. Not all dishes are economically or morally viable in a kitchen. I hope to extend the analysis of the ideology of "art," addressing the practical doing of aesthetics. The forms of aesthetic negotiation discussed are characteristic of all occupations. All—or at least most—occupations display a sense of the aesthetic, sensory quality of the doing of work. Yet, for all work, those outside the boundary of the occupation and conventions within it constrain legitimate practice. For the fine arts these limits are flexible, unstated but simultaneously ideologically offensive. The illusion is that there are no limits—that art defines itself. In other occupations, such as assembly-line work, the limits are recognized as a legitimate, if unpleasant, part of the job and are rarely explicitly questioned, even as workers complain and evade these restrictions. Cooks fall somewhere in the midst of this continuum of aesthetic workers, and, as a consequence, focusing on these workers encourages an elaboration of the role of freedom and constraint in the workplace.

Specifically in chapter 6, I examine the forms of this aesthetic constraint. In a restaurant, cooks must be aware of the demands placed on them by standards of customer taste, constraints of time, and the economics of the restaurant industry. These features limit what is possible to create. Each constraint is tied to structural and historical dimensions of the larger world, and the complaints of cooks are a response to the structural conditions of restaurants and public taste. Chapter 7 addresses the development of and limits on an aesthetic discourse in the kitchen. In a language that is not conducive to discussions of culinary issues, how can cooks communicate with each other about taste? How is a culinary poetics developed in practice?

·   ·   ·

I have attempted to write a volume that will be accessible to an audience of nonspecialists. Jargon and technical language has been eliminated wherever possible. Further, while each chapter addresses my theoretical argument, I have attempted in chapter 8, my conclusion, to place my ethnographic conclusions in light of the core sociological concepts of organization, interaction, time, emotion, economics, and aesthetics. Together, these concepts outline an interactionist sociology that takes organizational existence and social structure seriously. While some sociological discussion is necessary in each chapter, hopefully most of this volume will be as lucid to those outside the academy as to those inside. Hopefully this volume will contribute to understanding by cooks and eaters, as well as by researchers and teachers.

This research is based on participant observation and in-depth interviewing in four restaurants of different types, within the Twin Cities. In each restaurant I spent a month observing in the kitchen, during all hours in which the restaurant was open, a total of approximately 50–75 hours in each restaurant. In each restaurant I interviewed all its full-time cooks, a total of thirty interviews, lasting approximately 90 minutes each, with some lasting as long as 3 hours. I describe each of these sites in detail in the appendix, along with a set of methodological issues.

The four restaurants represent a range of professional cooking environments in the Twin Cities. I make no claim that these four restaurants form a representative sample of all eating establishments; clearly they do not. They represent the upper portion of Minnesota restaurants in status; they are not "family," "fast-food," or "ethnic" restaurants:

1.   La Pomme de Terre is an haute cuisine French restaurant, by all accounts one of the best and most innovative in the upper Midwest.

2.   The Owl's Nest is a continental-style restaurant, best known for the quality of its fresh fish. Its primary clientele is businessmen, and the restaurant is a multiyear Holiday Award winner.

3.   Stan's Steakhouse is a family-owned steakhouse. It is particularly well known in its neighborhood, a middle-class area not known for the quality of its restaurants. It has received metropolitan awards for the quality of its beef.

4.   The Twin Cities Blakemore Hotel is part of a chain of hotels that is not esteemed for the quality of its cuisine. The hotel is modern, catering especially to business travelers. The hotel has a banquet service and operates a coffee shop and dining room.

Although the restaurants vary widely in the number of customers served—from 500 on a busy weekend evening at Stan's to about 75 on the same evening at La Pomme de Terre—each hires from five to ten cooks, of whom usually three or four are working in the kitchen simultaneously.

Several issues of legitimate interest to readers are treated only lightly in this volume. While real differences distinguish these restaurants in the skill and aesthetic orientation of the cooks, my goal in this volume is to explore the similarities among them—those commonalities that might be generalized to the occupation as a whole. I downplay the elements that divide them, preferring to generalize from four cases than to use each restaurant with its manifest idiosyncrasies as a representative of its culinary class. Cooks at La Pomme de Terre certainly had a more profound aesthetic orientation than those at Stan's, but what impressed me was how cooks at each establishment attempted to make aesthetic sense of the food that they produced; and for this reason I feel justified in combining discourse from each kitchen in a single argument. Nor do I compare and contrast differences in organization, since I feel that the structural similarities of these establishments overwhelm their categorical differences.

Examining cooks in a second-tier metropolitan area provides a different kind of sample than one based upon elite chefs in a primary cultural center (e.g., New York, San Francisco, New Orleans), where a more self-conscious aesthetic dynamic occurs. These cooks are sociologically interesting because they are not elite artists. Taught in trade school, where cooking was likened to other industrial work, not other arts, leads them within their *habitus* to be inarticulate about taste and to produce imprecise classifications of culinary productions (Bourdieu 1984, pp. 170–73). The fact that, even so, they talk about the aesthetics of food preparation suggests the extent to which aesthetic discourse affects the doing of work. An examination of elite chefs would surely produce different results.

Finally I do not address what customers think of these establishments. I am interested in cooking, not in dining. In this regard, I only address the lives of servers as their lives affect those of cooks. Each of these topics—and many others—should be the concern of other researchers.

In this volume the restaurant industry stands as a surrogate for a wide variety of economic spheres. Obviously every organization is idiosyncratic. Yet, idiosyncrasies and all, restaurants and their kitchens provide a setting in which the demands of the external environment affect the interactional order: where microsociology meets structural analysis.

ONE

Living the Kitchen Life

Heaven sends us good meat, but the devil sends cooks.
                              —*David Garrick*

The day begins slowly. Entering an empty, clean kitchen on a cool summer morning, one has little sense of the blistering tornado of action to come. That the room has no air-conditioning or windows hardly matters when the door to the dining room and the backdoor are left open. Slowly workers arrive to prepare for lunch. Mel, the day cook, enters at about 9:00. The maître d' slightly after. Some busboys arrive early to prepare the dining room. Later a pantry worker, another cook, a potman, half a dozen servers, and a bartender show up. Phil, the owner, and Paul, the head chef, appear shortly before lunch.

Mel begins by checking that the restaurant has sufficient ingredients for lunch. He and Paul have already determined what specials will be offered. Since the special is ivory salmon with a beurre blanc sauce, he checks the fish for freshness. He tastes the beef stock that has been slowly simmering for two days and casually tosses in some vegetable scraps. Denise, the pantry worker, is asked to clean the newly arrived asparagus, peel potatoes and carrots, and boil some eggs. If they fall on the floor, no matter, they will be boiled. Mel and Denise prepare anything that once completed can keep. The goal is to be prepared by 11:30 for the first orders. At 11:10, a supplier brings in tomorrow's walleyed pike, and Paul, dressed casually in chinos and a checkered work shirt, examines the fish and signs for them. He has had problems with this company, which is in conflict with the local Teamsters union, and which had recently delivered tenderloin instead of rib-eye steaks.

But today the pike is fresh and good. Later that afternoon the fish will be filleted for dinner. Slightly before noon, Jon, a second cook, arrives; he has been told to be in later than usual because the restaurant hopes to save on labor costs and does not expect a large number of customers for lunch.

Geri, a veteran server, hands Mel the first ticket at about 11:45. Normally the orders are to be ready in about twenty minutes, but because there is no competition for his attention, Mel begins work quickly, and the order is ready shortly before noon. Paul samples the buerre blanc sauce with his finger and approves. It sits on the counter for a few minutes before Geri's customer is ready for it. Little by little the tempo (and temperature) heats up, and Mel and Jon soon find themselves snowed under—perhaps there is a convention in town, perhaps everyone wants to eat out, but whatever the reason, the kitchen is swamped with orders: a real lunch rush. Some twenty orders are waiting at any given moment. One steak falls on the stove and is wiped off and placed back on the plate. The situation is so desperate that Paul pitches in even though he was planning to work on the books. There is much banging of pans and anger when a server takes the wrong order, and the cooks have to scramble to prepare another. Jon prepares the vegetables, and Mel, the fish. The dish is ready, but not before the server has been abused for her incompetence. The kitchen is sweltering, smoky, and greasy from the large number of salmon and London broil served that day. Paradise has become hell: a communal one. Finally at 1:10 the orders let up, and by 1:30 there are only three orders left to prepare. The cooks survived lunch. The owner strolls in to congratulate and tease Paul. Together the three cooks have served over 120 diners in about ninety minutes. The servers made good tips, which will not be reported to the IRS.

Now the dynamics change. By 2:00, Mel has left to play a round of golf. Two evening cooks, Bruce and Larry, arrive by 4:00. Paul goes to his books and later slices the pike that arrived that morning, and Jon begins to prepare for dinner, readying vegetables, reducing the stock to a beef glaze, and checking the storeroom. Life is easy as Eddie, the bartender, smokes an illegal cigarette in the hall near the cooler; Larry jokes about spiking the drink of Ray, the mildly retarded potman. Those few servers who remain congregate near the door of the kitchen, joking with the kitchen staff about their romantic lives and teasing them about the tips they received.

Not until 5:30 do workers begin thinking about the dinner to come.

Today is Friday, and the restaurant has reservations for several large parties. Paul asks Jon to stay late to prepare for a crowd of nearly one hundred customers. No one expects much business at six o'clock, but at seven the restaurant is still nearly empty, and the cooks stand around chatting. Suddenly Roy, the maître d', enters the kitchen cursing, a party of eight has suddenly canceled, and a party of ten is fifteen minutes late. Kitchen life is pathetic.

At 8:00, things are so slow that Jon is sent home. By nine only thirty customers have arrived, far fewer than expected. Cooks and servers stand outside the backdoor of the restaurant making sarcastic comments about the customers and their own idiocy in becoming involved in such madness. Everyone is frustrated and bored. By ten, the nightly kitchen cleanup is nearly finished. Only one further affront awaits. Minutes before the 11:00 P.M. closing time, a regular arrives and waits to be served. Larry remains, cooking, banging pots, and grumbling about the inconsiderateness of diners. A day that began with hope ends with frustration. Emotions and sauces have been spilled. Friendships have grown and been rended. The community survived. (Abstracted from field notes, Owl's Nest)

· · ·

Consider the life of the cook, who faces enormous challenges, toiling in an environment less pastoral than infernal. Cooks must ready the kitchen several hours before customers arrive, not knowing precisely how many to expect. Preparation must permit flexibility, depending on the walk-in trade and last-minute reservations. They must then be ready to cook numerous dishes, simultaneously and without warning, with sufficient speed that those with whom they must deal—servers and ultimately diners—do not become frustrated. Cooks have several masters. Restaurants are both service and production units, and, so, cooks work simultaneously for customers and management (Gross 1958). While also part of the burgeoning population of service workers (Fuchs 1968), cooks remain part of the diminishing manufacturing segment of the American workforce.

Customers can legitimately return food to the kitchen for additional work and have, as their agents, servers whose economic interests (though not necessarily their social loyalties) are with the customers.[1] Servers do not have authority over cooks, but they can and do make demands to which cooks must respond. Cooks and servers experience different pressures. Cooks hope to have the authority to prepare dishes in an unhurried manner, whereas servers need to maximize the satis-

faction of the customers, who are their immediate source of income.
Since servers do not share tips, cooks have little invested—in the short
term—in insuring that customers are optimally satisfied (Paules 1991,
p. 108).

The second source of control is management. Management wants to
limit costs while maximizing customer satisfaction. As a result, management hopes to employ as few cooks as possible, demanding efficient
performance, and to use inexpensive ingredients and limit waste. In
practice this means that backstage workers will be the cheapest labor
available; the restaurant industry is known for hiring undocumented
aliens and the mentally impaired.   .

As a consequence, cooks operate under heavy constraints and feel a
lack of autonomy, leading to occupational dissatisfaction. This lack is
compounded by the hierarchy within the kitchen. Most restaurants employ a chef, or head cook, one of whose responsibilities is to manage
the other cooks. The distinction between cook and chef is real, and may
provoke friction. Beyond this occupational division, cooks (or chefs)
have different responsibilities and degrees of power and autonomy.

This chapter explores how, despite these forms of social control,
cooks make their lives tolerable, and how they define the satisfactions
and dissatisfactions of their work lives. Specifically I examine the routine grounds of cooking and how personal organization, shortcuts,
tricks of the trade, approximations, dirty work, and a negotiated division of labor among cooks affects the production of food. I further describe those elements that cooks see as characterizing their occupational status, both positively and negatively.

THE ROUTINE GROUNDS OF RESTAURANT COOKING

Like all workers, cooks attempt to "get by." They do not demand paradise but strive for a passably smooth routine. Yet, routine has its dangers. Cooking can be both difficult and boring (Molstad 1986). Cooks
wish to transform a potentially oppressive environment into a regime
in which they can live, and from which they gain a measure of satisfaction. Formal rules and demands are secondary to the practical doing of
food preparation. The classic account of this problem is that of George
Orwell in his memorable, disturbing *Down and Out in Paris and London* (1933, pp. 80–81):

> It is not a figure of speech, it is a mere statement of fact to say that a French
> cook will spit in the soup—that is, if he is not going to drink it himself. He

is an artist, but his art is not cleanliness. To a certain extent he is even dirty because he is an artist, for food, to look smart, needs dirty treatment. When a steak, for instance, is brought up for the head cook's inspection, he does not handle it with a fork. He picks it up with his fingers and slaps it down, runs his thumb round the dish and licks it to taste the gravy, runs it round and licks again, then steps back and contemplates the piece of meat like an artist judging a picture, then presses it lovingly into place with his fat, pink fingers, every one of which he has licked a hundred times that morning. When he is satisfied, he takes a cloth and wipes his fingerprints from the dish, and hands it to the waiter. . . . Whenever one pays more than, say, ten francs for a dish of meat in Paris, one may be certain that it has been fingered in this manner. . . . A customer orders, for example, a piece of toast. Somebody, pressed with work in a cellar deep underground, has to prepare it. How can he stop and say to himself, "This toast is to be eaten—I must make it eatable"? All he knows is that it must look right and must be ready in three minutes. Some large drops of sweat fall from his forehead onto the toast. Why should he worry? Presently the toast falls among the filthy sawdust on the floor. Why trouble to make a new piece? It is much quicker to wipe the sawdust off. On the way upstairs the toast falls again, butter side down. Another wipe is all it needs. And so with everything.

While American restaurants—at least those I observed—are not blessed by the same standards of sanitary "care," Orwell is correct in attributing to cooks the desire to have the food look and taste right without excess concern about the *process* by which it becomes right. Workers do what they must within the reality of the structure of the restaurant.

PERSONAL ORGANIZATION AS COPING

When one asks cooks what is essential to help them get through the day, they frequently point to personal organization—organizing those projects that comprise the arc of work (Strauss 1991, p. 72). Workers with numerous unpredictably arrayed tasks find that it is not the work but the *preparation* for that work that is critical. I asked one cook at the Owl's Nest what he considered the most demanding part of his job: "The job is as easy as you make it. If you get the stuff lined up, it's easy. There's nothing hard once you have a system. You know what you're going to do and when" (Field notes, Owl's Nest). Crucial to culinary success is to segment projects and to know their proper order. Without this ordering, what is doable becomes disastrous. The challenge of cooking (and much work) is less what is done than the *relationship* among acts: "Things seem to fall together really easy for me.

. . . When I have twenty-five different things that I have to prep up, I can usually. I know how to organize things" (Personal interview, Owl's Nest). After my first day in a restaurant kitchen I wrote: "Each action in the kitchen requires but a few seconds. It is almost as though the cooks are working on twenty assembly lines simultaneously—each requires a different action. It also requires remarkable coordination among cooks" (Field notes, Owl's Nest). The skill is to order multiple tasks under intense pressure—even if they are unable to specify the rules for what is to be done when. Each task is relatively unproblematic if provided sufficient time, but the sum is nearly impossible for the inexperienced. The nearly impossible is routine because cooks are experienced enough to adjust their speed and sequencing to meet demands of the arc of work—the totality of tasks. Perhaps the greatest challenge for cooks is when they fall behind or lose track of their tasks. The arc of work assumes detailed behavioral monitoring. The finely tuned system can fall apart, to which anyone who has had their focused concentration disturbed can attest. Cooking under pressure demands attention to an internal agenda. When I asked a cook at the steakhouse about his greatest frustration, he shared concrete instances that confirm the salience of concentration: "Falling behind on your backup supplies like your sour cream and your tartar sauce. Just not having the time or the manpower to recuperate" (Field notes, Stan's). The desire to keep pace means that cooks attempt, whenever possible, to "get ahead," incorporating slack time into the process. Particularly when dealing with cold food (e.g., salads, sandwich fixings, or desserts) that does not spoil, cooks may prepare more than actually ordered (e.g., Whyte 1948, p. 3)—they have the luxury to overproduce for later use.

One means of facilitating this organization of work is to limit the options available to customers and, hence, the degree of organization needed by workers. This is output control of kind, not quantity. To control the work pace, restaurants may provide limited menus or incorporate the same elements in a large selection of dishes (the latter practice is common in Asian establishments). Restaurants with extensive menus have either simple preparations or a large staff. Repeatedly preparing the same items is easier to organize than offering a wide range of choices: flexibility can go too far in an industrial workplace. As a result, large parties are given restricted menus to ease the chores for the cooks: "A party of seventy-five will arrive for dinner at 7:30

P.M. They are given a choice of two items. Charles, the manager, tells me: 'We'll sheet pan the steaks.[2] We'll seer the steak, then bake it. We must be restrictive with them. That's how all restaurants which serve parties do it. . . . It comes out nice.' Charles admits that he can taste the difference" (Field notes, Stan's). A limited range of selections effectively controls the enormity of the task. This limitation, however, may provoke dissatisfaction among clients, who if they do not find choices to their liking may patronize other establishments.

EASING THE WAY

Every occupation has informal, sub-rosa procedures that make work tolerable: techniques labeled "the underside of work." Despite the "official" practices that workers are expected to follow, the practical accomplishment of the job encourages other techniques that lighten the burden of work.

I classify these sub-rosa techniques into three classes: (1) approximations, (2) shortcuts, and (3) tricks of the trade. Approximations are techniques that deny the primacy of formal rules, suggesting that workers have the autonomy to make choices around a zone of acceptable practice. Every cook has the option to make decisions, and, in fact, measuring and timing devices are never so precise that approximation is absent. Professional cooks take these approximations as necessary and natural, whereas some home cooks (and novice professionals) attempt to avoid it, unsure of the effects of their choices. Shortcuts are techniques accessible to all those who know the task: options of which every cook—professional or amateur—is potentially aware. These involve making "improper" choices that bend or break the rules of production, but that save time and effort. Tricks of the trade are primarily known within the occupation, whether in an individual establishment or in the industry as a whole, and are contained within the boundaries of the occupation as subcultural knowledge. Unlike shortcuts, these need not be formally improper but are easier techniques of reaching a desired end.

These techniques differ in the degree to which they do violence to the final product—whether they affect the quality of the finished dishes. Tricks of the trade are generally less noticeable in the final outcome—thus, we label them "tricks"—than shortcuts. Approximations, depending on how approximate they are, may have little or great effect. These terms are used in professional restaurant kitchens with similar meanings although without distinguishing between tricks as knowledge held within the boundary of the occupation and shortcuts as accessible knowledge.

APPROXIMATIONS

Some occupations demand precision. Yet, all produce "slop" with which workers can mess. Few occupations require the microscopic precision of draftsmen or machine-tool operators, but even for these workers there are micromillimeters of choice. To permit approximation is to provide autonomy. Entering through the portals of a commercial kitchen, a home cook may notice a lack of precise measurement. The head chef at the Blakemore emphasized that he stresses conceptual, practical working knowledge:

> The basic recipes are in the book. As a matter of fact, when we were in school we didn't figure this out 'til [final] quarter. In first quarter everyone expected that this is how we make whatever it was. Salisbury steak. This is how we make it. It got to second quarter, they said no, this is how you make it, and they gave you a new recipe. Third quarter they said this is the recipe we're going to use. You thought to yourself, "What kind of education are we getting if they can't even decide how it works?" By fourth quarter we finally figured out that what they were telling us is that if you took all three recipes, the base is going to be there. Hamburgers and vegetables are your base. Whether you put in oregano, basil, tomato juice or tomato paste, that's your option.
>
> (Personal interview, Blakemore Hotel)

Although cooks have recipes, they ignore them, interpret them, and move beyond them to creative autonomy. Recipes are suggestions, not orders, although many home cooks follow them. Restaurant cooks have a different perspective:

BARBARA: I think there's a lot of common sense in knowing how to interpret a recipe.

GAF: What do you mean "interpret a recipe"?

BARBARA: It just seems to me that when I read a recipe and I see certain instructions how to fold something in, but common sense tells me that I have to do that very gently in this specific recipe because of the ingredients that are in it.

GAF: Beyond the recipe?

BARBARA: Yeah. And I've seen people make all the same recipe at the same time, and you have five different results, anywhere from disaster to marvelous. It all was dependent on whether that person was paying attention to what they were doing and whether they were concentrating or whether they had common sense to realize how that should look at a certain stage.

(Personal interview, La Pomme de Terre)

Dishes can be prepared in many ways; the skill is to decide which preparation should be used so the food is consistent and fine. Even here the knowledge is from memory and experience. When Jon asks Mel whether he has a recipe for making crepes, Mel replies: "I just mix things together." No more specific instructions are given, and Jon's crepes turn out well.

Because it is difficult to recall specifically how dishes taste, cooks work "by the seat of their pants." Much cooking involves adding approximate amounts of ingredients. While this might surprise those who imagine the cook must follow a recipe precisely to have the food meet an ideal standard, it reflects practical cooking. Adding ingredients in this way not only saves time but also allows the cook more autonomy.

Perhaps the best example of the use of approximation is the production of stock, the basis of sauces and soups. The stock has been described as the key to haute cuisine. The great chef Escoffier believed: "Stock is everything in cooking. At least in good and well-flavored cooking. Without it, nothing can be done. If one's stock is of good flavor, what remains of the work is easy; if on the other hand, flavor is lacking or merely mediocre, it is quite hopeless to expect anything approaching a satisfactory result" (Crocker 1945, p. 109). Cooks at the Owl's Nest and La Pomme de Terre are proud that they prepare their own stock, avoiding canned broth or powdered stock, but, despite its crucial quality, they do not follow a recipe. What is added to the stockpot is a matter of convenience, rather than planning:

> Paul, the head chef, prepares beef stock for brown gravy. He tells me that he usually lets the stock cook for forty-eight hours, but Mel needs the vat tomorrow, so it will only cook for a day. . . . Later Bruce dumps egg whites and shells into the vat. Larry comments: "Sometimes it's just the garbage can." The stock vat is located right under the water faucet, so excess water falls in the vat.
>
> (Field notes, Owl's Nest)

GAF: What things in the kitchen do you think a layperson would be most shocked by?

DIANE: The stocks, how gross it looks to look in a stockpot. The first time I ever saw them I thought it was just repulsive. I think . . . for a layperson they think, "Oh, my God, don't you just throw that away."

(Personal interview, La Pomme de Terre)

Stocks and soups represent instances in which workers' choices may seem arbitrary if, indeed, they are conscious decisions. We may have confidence that we know our work, and that everything will be fine, and it usually is. The fact that the stock cooked on Monday differs from the stock on Thursday doesn't affect the evaluation of the meal—it tastes close enough for unknowing, mortal tongues, just as cars, surgical operations, and cowboy boots can pass muster despite their microdifferences. As the ingredients are approximations, so is timing (as discussed in chapter 2). When the Owl's Nest prepares gravlax (smoked salmon), they marinate the fish for anywhere between twenty-four and forty-eight hours, depending when it is needed.

Approximations are so integral in the work environment that cooks josh about the significant margin of error in their work: "Mel pours a dash of vinegar into the salad dressing and jokes to me: 'It comes out perfect every time' " (Field notes, Owl's Nest). The nice thing about many foodstuffs is that no matter what one does to them they taste "the same" to most customers. They are "forgiving." This doesn't mean, of course, that they taste identical, but our memories of flavors are not so precise as to distinguish between tastes not dramatically distinct. Although we may be more sensitive to textures, cooks can get away with a world of imprecision that would not be possible if their customers were able to engage in comparative tasting. To be sure, customers make judgments between good and bad dishes (and dishes that are better and worse), but most consumers accept the expertise of the cook and do not have sophisticated or educated palates. The evanescent character of cooking, distinguishing it from most other arts that are either material or can be captured in a written, auditory, or visual record, allows for imprecision that is not possible elsewhere. Memory is a capricious judge.

To the degree that workers use forgiving materials, they have flexibility and opportunity for error denied to others. This, for instance, gives psychiatrists an edge over anesthesiologists in malpractice suits although, as the latter practitioners are aware, bodies can stand a range of gases. One illusion that "professionals"—or those who claim the label—demand for themselves is that they work with unforgiving materials while they hide their secrets. It is trying for workers to per-

form before a knowing and critical audience, but even here the knowing audience may be unaware of the script, and some errors can be re-
scripted into the drama (Goffman 1974).

SHORTCUTS

While preparing meals, home cooks make many decisions outside the
rules of the recipes they follow (Tomlinson 1986): do you fry bacon
for a crumbled topping or just add Bac-O-Bits; should your whipped
cream come from a mixer or a can? Similar culinary trade-offs characterize professional cooks. Any competent food preparer would be
aware of these techniques but might not select them because of their effects on the outcome. Some shortcuts have noticeable consequences as
when instant whipped cream is used instead of cream whipped by
hand; others have minor effects as when a food is defrosted in a mi-
crowave, rather than at room temperature. Of course, what constitutes
a significant change in sensory quality is a matter of personal judgment
and collective construction, rather than objective fact. The representation of a dish is engraved in a customer's mind, but the means by
which a presented dish is judged in light of this representation is complex, affected by cost, the reputation of the house, sophistication of
one's palate, and the spirits consumed. The contextual understanding
of objects is critical to their evaluation (Dickie 1974).

Audience awareness and demands determines what constitutes an
acceptable shortcut. Each occupation has its own audience, but all are
evaluated by someone. The question in each work sphere is not
whether to limit quality, but how to do so. If the client will not notice
the difference, does a difference exist? A difference exists in that the
cook knows that he could do "better," and this affects his occupational self-esteem; yet, other pressures may make this trade-off necessary or desirable. Like all service workers, cooks have at least three audiences for their products: (1) themselves and their peers, who strive
for high subcultural standards as long as they can be reasonably met
with appropriate effort; (2) management, which demands profits by
keeping labor, material, and fixed overhead costs low, and by having
customers return to the establishment; and (3) customers, who insist
on what they define as high quality, but who are possibly unaware of
what quality consists of, and who also demand "good value" (low
profit) in the given market niche.

The culinary challenge is to balance these demands. These are not personal standards but demands built into the structure of the setting and the expertise of those evaluating. How dishes are prepared, while grounded in interaction, is also constrained by a set of external and communal standards.

In order to ease their burdens, workers often cook a large quantity of a food at one time and then reheat the food as needed:

> The mushroom mousse is cooked halfway through. As Diane tells me: "It takes a long time to set. So we do it this way to save time." They also do not cook beef Wellington to order but reheat slices when needed.
>
> (Field notes, La Pomme de Terre)

> The cooks prepare prime rib by putting it in the hot au jus sauce to heat up, after having previously cooked it to certain degrees of doneness. Al comments: "It's not really the best way to do it, but here [he shrugs] it's what we got to do."
>
> (Field notes, Stan's)

Cooks also reuse pans to prepare most dishes, only briefly wiping it out to remove some of the previous flavor. Doors of walk-in coolers remain ajar because they are too much trouble to open dozens of times a day. Likewise, all food is cooked at the same temperature. Kitchens do not have enough stoves to vary temperatures. All food that needs to be floured is dipped in the same flour—whether shrimp, scallops, or onion rings. There is not enough staff or energy for cooks to do differently. These techniques are practiced in home kitchens and do not presuppose extensive knowledge. Anyone is capable of choosing these techniques, even though many customers have idealistic views of backstage life in a kitchen.

Convenience foods.   The most compelling balancing of values and outcomes can be seen in the decision to serve convenience foods. In theory, all who work in, or are served by, a kitchen object to convenience foods. Customers desire food made from scratch, or what is the point of dining out? Likewise, managers do not want the public to know they serve convenience foods, scarring their reputation. Cooks dislike convenience foods, which diminish their role in the kitchen, transforming them from skilled craftsmen to manual laborers—culinary de-skilling. The chef at the Owl's Nest commented that his goal was for the restaurant to be a good "scratch house," preparing food from "scratch." Yet, each restaurant served some convenience foods although "more" convenience foods were served at Stan's and the

Blakemore Hotel than at the Owl's Nest and La Pomme de Terre, and their staffs seemed less defensive. With the exception of La Pomme de Terre, each restaurant served instant mashed potatoes, and La Pomme de Terre used canned tomato products, which could have been made from scratch if the chef desired. The issue is not *whether* to use convenience foods but *when*. Every occupation engages in shortcuts; the question is what kind, and how will their use be justified rhetorically.

Instant mashed potatoes demonstrate the value of convenience foods. Few customers consider "real" mashed potatoes glamorous, and, thus, these spuds have little economic value. Yet preparing them is labor intensive. As a result, cooks admit the utility of instant potatoes: "Some chefs will say, 'Well, only fresh vegetables, we'll stick to that,' and that's good. And others will . . . use boxed vegetables or canned vegetables. There's a quality difference. . . . Stuff like mashed potatoes, it's unrealistic to cook off eight thousand tons of potatoes and then mash them. Instant is so much easier" (Personal interview, Blakemore Hotel). Yet, there are limits to what is legitimate. Cooks who rely too heavily on convenience foods are scorned by others. They have chosen to be de-skilled:

> One cook complains about the current chef: "They shouldn't have any canned, I'm not real big on frozen vegetables. . . . They had a chef [previously] . . . he didn't even like dry garlic powder. He was picky. Denver likes everything in cans. . . . They use too much fake stuff, too much canned stuff. They ought to use real stuff."
>
> (Personal interview, Blakemore Hotel)

> The head chef describes the adjustments that he instituted when he took the job: "Probably the hardest part of the whole thing was retraining, to reestablishing things and getting back, doing things the basic way, cutting out the shortcuts, incorporating as much as possible fresh items as I can. Getting back to a good basic cooking."
>
> (Personal interview, Owl's Nest)

Cooks resent those who use too much convenience food, but they recognize that they themselves indulge. The decision about when and where to use convenience foods is not personal but organizational, with policy set by the head chef or the manager, who responds to imagined customer demands. Rather than operating under rules shared by the industry as a whole, each restaurant has its own cooking traditions, in which the proper use of convenience items has been negotiated and then established.

Shortcuts are inevitable but are troubling reminders of ideal standards and the distance between reality and these standards. They measure what could be achieved given ideal conditions. The time-space limits of the kitchen direct the kinds of dishes that come forth.

TRICKS OF THE TRADE

Like all workers, cooks rely on techniques that make their occupational lives easier but are not widely known to the public. These tricks of the trade are subcultural in character. One cook asserted: "It takes a degree of skill to be a cook, and it takes a greater degree of skill to be a good cook. If a new man were asked to make something . . . he wouldn't even know how to cut. He would use a layman's method to cut something, not a chef's method. Also he wouldn't have the knowledge of the materials—the meat, produce, staples, and other things" (Schroedl 1972, p. 184). The novice cook must be socialized to acquire the "operational knowledge base" of the work (Bishop 1979). Just as some tasks are imagined to be easy and are not—preparing mashed potatoes or consommé—other tasks seem difficult but are easy. Preparing a tomato peel in the shape of a rose ("a tomato rose") looks complicated but with practice can be done in seconds, even by a clumsy sociologist. Omelettes have a frightening reputation but are easy to prepare: "Denny, the day cook, prepares a mushroom omelette by cooking one side, adding the mushrooms on top, and broiling it for thirty seconds, then folding it. He pokes with his fingers to prod it into an 'ideal' omelette shape" (Field notes, La Pomme de Terre). A key skill is knowing those techniques that transform a difficult, time-consuming task into one that is easier, without a loss of quality: "Ron is preparing a dish that requires chopped orange peel. Denver, the head chef, explains that he should grate the oranges rather than chopping the peel. Ron immediately recognizes that this is more efficient. Denver replies: 'That's why I get the extra nickel' " (Field notes, Blakemore Hotel). To melt sticks of butter, cooks casually toss the wrapped stick in the pan. When the butter melts, they remove the paper (Field notes, Blakemore Hotel). At one restaurant, cooks wash parsley in Dreft, a dishwashing liquid. A cook explains that soapy water "perks up" the parsley (Field notes, Stan's). As a potential customer, I was shocked at this cleansing ritual; the cooks were amused at my reaction. The techniques are simple enough, but the boundary of knowledge is real. All occupations have tricks that are unknown to outsiders, and which collectively constitute socialization.

Some tricks of the trade involve misleading customers. A thorny problem is preparing meat to a requested degree of doneness. For buffets, cooks employ impression management skills to encourage the co-operation of customers: "Denver tells Ron that one technique to satisfy buffet customers is to illuminate the roast beef with red light, making the beef appear rarer than it is. If a customer doesn't want rare meat, the chef holds the sliced meat away from the light" (Field notes, Blakemore Hotel). These techniques ease the life of the cook, without, in theory, affecting the taste of the food. Of course, the customer may not receive what he or she expects, but that is the lot of the client in a mass-service organization, particularly when the client has a loose tie to the organization and none to the worker.

Restaurants sometimes sear steaks on the grill to add the distinctive grill marks and then bake them in a conventional oven. From the lack of complaints and the routine use of the technique, it seems that most customers cannot determine that their meat hasn't been grilled.

Tricks of the trade are not only used to make hard things easy but also to correct seemingly uncorrectable errors. To work is to err. Whether a doctor who misses stitches in surgery, a scholar who makes an erroneous citation, or a carpenter who places a screw poorly, every worker requires slack and the means to cope with that slack (Hughes 1971; Bosk 1979). Cooks acquire techniques for coping with inevitable mistakes. It is the ability to deal with errors, not the ability to avoid them, that characterizes the skilled worker. The following incidents are typical:

> Paul is frying eggs for hash, and an egg yolk breaks and begins to run. Paul quickly picks up the pan, holding the point of the broken egg over the flame, sealing the egg. That side of the egg will be served face down.
>
> (Field notes, Owl's Nest)

> Howie tells Barbara, the pastry chef, that he mashed one of her cakes when he pushed a dish into the refrigerator. Barbara isn't upset, saying "That's all right, I can cut it down to a smaller portion."
>
> (Field notes, La Pomme de Terre)

The cracks that appear when cakes and tarts are baked are hidden by covering those areas with topping or whipped cream, with customers blissfully unaware (e.g., McPhee 1979, p. 94)—a technique known to barbers and realtors. Cooks serve the more appealing side of a piece of meat or fish face up—giving them two chances on every dish, just as a photographer has two profiles from which to select. The competent cook can manage the inevitable problems by advantageously using subcultural knowledge of cooking science and customer psychology. To be "professional" is to transform a disaster into a culinary triumph.[3] As Orwell recognized, the final product is judged, not the backstage process that produced it.

DOING DIRT

When backstages become front stages, workers face a challenge of cleanliness. Production leaves little time for amenities. Kitchens, like many production lines, are dirty. We recognize this from our own kitchens, but in such settings it is personal, known dirt, under our control. In restaurant kitchens dirt is anonymous; diners wish to believe that the backstage of restaurants is as spotless as the front stage. Alas, the real kitchens of restaurants are not like the "display" kitchens that some restaurants use to entertain their customers.[4]

Coping with filth is a classic instance of what Everett Hughes (1971, p. 343) speaks of as "dirty work": "Dirty work of some kind is found in all occupations. It is hard to imagine an occupation in which one does not appear, in certain repeated contingencies, to be practically compelled to play a role of which he thinks he ought to be a little ashamed morally." To prepare food in a dirty environment is potentially identity smudging.

I asked all the cooks what in their kitchens would most upset the public. A strong plurality cited the mess and dirt:

> There's times if you don't know the business and you don't have to do [things], you don't know what it's like to get hit. I guess I'd be upset if I walked back into the kitchen, and there was meat sitting on the board and a fish over in the sink, and the cooler door was open, and there was a couple of buckets sitting on the floor. That would upset me.
>
> (Personal interview, Owl's Nest)

DENVER: Fifty percent of the American public, if they saw what goes on inside of the kitchen, they would never eat out again.

GAF: Give me some examples of that.

DENVER: Chicken laying out for a couple of hours while you're panning it up [for a banquet]. When it sits on the table and you're in the middle of doing something else when it came out, and so it's sitting there for a while. . . . As a matter of fact, my brother-in-law was in here the other night and was absolutely appalled that someone was cutting chicken on the cutting board and didn't sanitize the cutting board again, which the health department really would get you for.

(Personal interview, Blakemore Hotel)

These seemingly candid comments echo Hughes's insight that while this dirt is "structurally" necessary, it is undesirable and seen as embarrassing by the workers. In their values workers are not so different from their customers, except they eventually must take dirt for granted. As one cook stated explicitly: "You want it to look nice, but, you know, it's so busy that you can't possibly clean it" (Personal interview, Blakemore Hotel).[5] The demands of the front stage limit sanitation: "[I]f those serving find it difficult to provide quick service and maintain standards of hygiene, it is poor hygiene which can be readily concealed. Many examples arise; for instance, reusing unwashed dishes, using spittle to clean cutlery, wiping china and cutlery with a serving cloth that is dirty through over-use, handling food to test how hot it is, and so on" (Mars and Nicod, 1984, p. 42).[6] George Orwell's observation cited above does not reflect how food is treated in these restaurants. His horrifying "traditions" have been largely erased as governmental control over health and concerns about germs have increased; still, the challenge of cooking efficiently and pleasantly while maintaining standards of hygiene is a trade-off, even if it is not always explicitly recognized.

Observing kitchens, I became inured to sanitation "problems"—from not refrigerating sauces for hours—letting bacteria grow—to using filthy towels to wipe pans to touching food with sweaty hands. Perhaps the most salient problem is what to do when a piece of food gets "dirty." People are fumblers, and food often falls from plates and pans. Food costs money and takes time and energy to prepare. While cooks do not want to waste, they prefer not to serve what they would hesitate to eat.

Among the criteria used by culinary workers in their decision to dispose of "dirty" food is whether it is prepared or "raw" (untransformed). The latter is less problematic—it is believed that heat cures all ills, particularly as the customer will never discover the mishap: "I get Bruce a dish of escargots from the freezer. One of the snails falls on the floor, and I ask Bruce: 'Can we use that one?' Bruce assures me: 'Sure. They won't know' " (Field notes, Owl's Nest). Even when prepared food lands on the floor, the cook must not be overly fastidious—wiping or reheating will solve any problem:

DIANE: Once when I was doing Sunday brunch [at another restaurant], and this was during the French toast day, [another cook] dropped a piece of French toast on the floor, and he picked it up and wiped it off and put it back on the plate. He didn't have time to do another piece.

GAF: Does that ever happen here?

DIANE: If it does, we usually wipe it off. A lot of people have dropped a piece of meat on the floor, and you pick it up and wash it off with hot water from the sink and throw it back in the pan, and it's fine. I really don't think that anything creepy-crawly got into it in that amount of time.

(Personal interview, La Pomme de Terre)

The fact that the customer never learns justifies the worker's doing what is easiest. Workers have too much work to do, and customers can rarely trace a flaw (or illness) to a hidden event. Doctors, for instance, like cooks, know that the iatrogenic illness that they cause cannot be traced.

The emotional tension of accepting sanitation standards below one's professed values is implicit in joking, grounded in a need for role distance, that takes place when food does fall on the floor and others notice:

Al drops a steak on the floor and serves it after quickly putting it back on the grill, warming both sides. He jokes to one of his fellow cooks: "What's that saying, Gene. You'll serve it off the floor, you won't eat it off the floor. That's how we professionals do it. I'd like to meet a germ that could live off that floor."

(Field notes, Stan's)

Bruce drops an order of spaghetti on the floor and mutters: "Son of a bitch." Roy, the maître d', jokes: "Just pick it up and wash it off. Who'll know the difference?" They don't, but the remark suggests staff solidarity.

(Field notes, Owl's Nest)

Dropping food on the floor is a mistake, but one that, on account of work pressures, can hardly be avoided. Cooks must make the best of what they have despite shared values with customers. Customers are partly responsible for being served dirty food because of their desire for reasonably priced food, rapidly prepared. As I describe in chapter 6 when considering the aesthetic structure of food, temporal and economic constraints affect what is served.

Workers are frustrated in responding to those who do not know the "practical accomplishment" of the job—or who pretend not to know—professional outsiders such as journalists or government regulators. In the kitchen this is evident in the attitudes of cooks toward health inspectors, who are a source of annoyance and not taken seriously:

> I ask Jon about the report of the health inspector who had been there a few days before. Jon says that he hadn't read the report, but "he always finds something to write. There's something sitting on the floor, the ceiling's dirty. They'll always find something." Inspectors regularly complain about Mel's ashtray. He smokes in the back alcove of the kitchen, even though regulations require a break room.
>
> (Field notes, Owl's Nest)

DENVER: [The health inspectors] and I have never seen eye to eye. If you did everything their way, you wouldn't be able to run your operation at all. I went to two of their seminars, and I was really appalled by their ideas because they just aren't working. You're taking advice in the kitchen from people who have never been in the kitchen other than to scream at you for doing something wrong.

GAF: For example?

DENVER: Like spaghetti sauce. They want you to put it into a two-inch-deep pan to cool it. If you're making fifty gallons of spaghetti sauce, do you know how many two-inch-deep containers you would have? A lot of them, and you don't have room to put those things.

(Personal interview, Blakemore Hotel)

Fortunately for cooks, but perhaps not for patrons, local governments do not enforce their rules effectively and do not constrain kitchen activity much. A smart restaurant can agree to change and then return to cooking as its culinary staff wishes. The loose structure of government oversight, in which visits are infrequent and often inconsequential, permits the cooks more leeway than would be possible with a government that took its assignment more conscientiously—and funded more inspector positions. Semiannual inspections, with options for corrections and appeals, permit kitchen workers latitude to cook as they wish. Thus, although government inspection could be a major concern, directing behavior, in reality it has little effect. The structure of government oversight permits a range of activity that might not otherwise be tolerated.

For governments as well as cooks, sanitation is a trade-off. In principle, everyone believes that kitchens should be clean, but keeping them clean may cost more than the cleanliness is worth, particularly in the absence of an immediate health threat. Epidemics of food-borne illnesses—such as hepatitis or salmonella—are infrequent. Responses to such threats occur only after rare, major, publicized food-poisoning scares. Routine poisonings, however often they may occur, are ignored by cooks, inspectors, and journalists. They are part of doing business and dining out, and rarely can be traced. Closing down an independent small business is not something that a government that embraces capitalism wishes to do. This oversight is similarly light in hospitals, nuclear plants, chemical refineries, poultry plants, and high schools, suggesting the limits to the intrusions of ideals enforced on dirty work practice by external agencies. Organizations depend on the trust of regulators and clients. This trust is typically well placed; but even when it is not, it is difficult to monitor without increased commitment.

DIVIDING LABOR IN THE KITCHEN

All occupational work is grounded in collective action and a division of labor (Becker 1974; Strauss 1991). Cooks in large kitchens are no exception, even when their work appears chaotic to the untrained eye. The haute cuisine French restaurant in this journalistic account differs only in degree from the restaurants I observed:

> The pressures mount to a peak. The orders are like a barrage of machine-gun fire. One has the vague feeling of a crew of white coated seamen trying to keep their ship afloat in a hurricane. The blare of noise, the figures rushing hither and thither, the irresistible chaos of enticing smells, the heat and spitting of the frying, the clang of pots, the bloomp-bloomp of chopping knives all beat down with enveloping force until one feels dizzy. Yet, in reality, everything is proceeding normally, everyone is efficiently absorbed. A boy is quickly shelling a bowl of beautiful, pink crayfish. Michel is adding a shower of bright-green sorrel to a brilliantly yellow sauce. Andre is making patterns with peach halves on a tart shell. Pierre [the head chef] watches everything and misses nothing. He could take over any job, from anyone, at any moment, and do it better. Everyone knows this and the effect is both disciplinary and exhilarating.
>
> (De Groot, 1972, p. 246)

The same system operates in modified form at the Owl's Nest as the head chef explains: "Everyone knows what everyone is doing. Because you work together, you begin to think alike. Three people become one person. The only time I go around the kitchen is if there's a problem or somebody calls for help. Otherwise, I work at the kitchen" (Field notes, Owl's Nest). This chaos consists of "the fitting together of lines of action" (Blumer 1969), particularly when cooks collaborate on the same plate (e.g., one preparing the meat, a second, the accompaniments, and a third, the garnish).

An ideal-typical instance of the division of labor is the preparation for a banquet, which because of the number of customers to be served simultaneously requires fine-tuned organization, overseen by authority. The head chef at the Blakemore Hotel described the banquet setup at a large hotel at which he had once worked:

> I was in the banquet kitchen. It was a fantastic setup. . . . The people who worked in the evening would come in, and they would set up the entire breakfast and the entire lunch for the next day. And put their meals out for that evening. You came in the morning, your eggs were cracked, your bacon was set out, everything was ready to slide in the oven, to put on the plates. And then you would set up the dinner for them in the evening. So when they came in, their vegetables were ready to be warmed up, they may even be half-cooked. It was just a matter of putting them in the steamer for six minutes and get[ting] them back to temperature and out they'd go. The steaks would all be scored off and on a tray.[7] Another example of banquet cooking: When you cook up a banquet with steaks, you go to your broiler which you have for à la carte, but instead of cooking it, you just score it, put the lines on it. You put them back on a sheet pan and put them back in the refrigerator. Then fifteen minutes before they're to be served, you slide them in the oven to finish cooking to get them back to the temperature.
> (Personal interview, Blakemore Hotel)

Even though some might see cooking as a solitary activity only mediated by the food itself, professional cooking, like many occupations embedded within organizations, demands teamwork and coordination, particularly in restaurants that attempt complex presentations. The work team is as much the unit of analysis as is the individual worker.

The division of labor is not a given but must be negotiated with more or less strain. Flexibility is, of course, desirable, but when interests diverge or when communication is ineffective, tension results as workers have different ideas of what is expected of them and their colleagues.

FLEXIBILITY IN A COMMUNITY OF INTEREST

One means by which a division of labor becomes flexible is through explicit or implicit expectations of direct and reciprocal cooperation. Even though a division of labor exists in midsize restaurant kitchens, this is negotiable in practice. As noted in numerous descriptions of the informal organization of occupations, workers perform each other's jobs and cover for each other. They do so willingly because they assume that later this cooperation will be reciprocated. The articulated structure of the kitchen need not be repeatedly negotiated, because of an unstated assumption that others will be available for future aid. Flexibility is built into institutional relations of co-workers. Cooperation is required, and when it is not easily given, there is surprise and tension. A lack of cooperation demands an account. For an occupation to operate efficiently, a community of interest is assumed, which makes patterns of aid flow through a network without a specific debt and obligation incurred.

In smoothly functioning organizations, workers are socialized to believe that asking for help is both expected and desired. In kitchens this is explicit in occupational rhetoric, but elsewhere mutual aid may be more sub rosa. As the head chef at the Owl's Nest comments to his workers, "Don't be afraid to ask for help." A fellow cook chimes in, "It's always easier to ask for help before you get in the shits" (Field notes, Owl's Nest). When describing the kitchen as a work community, I note that this instrumental cooperation is tethered to expressive friendships and perquisites—cooks getting drinks from the bar, dishwashers being served steaks, and servers eating fancy desserts. A "favor bank" operates in most occupational worlds.

Perhaps cooperation in the kitchen is most dramatically evident in the surprising reality that cooks regularly work unpaid overtime to help peers. Day cooks often choose to finish tasks that they have not completed during their paid hours to prevent inconvenience to the evening staff. Evening workers routinely remain until everyone has finished cleaning up, even though only one of them—or none—is paid for that time. A breakfast cook at the Blakemore Hotel regularly arrived an hour early to complete his assigned work. A norm of community lightens the establishment's labor costs, but this norm can disintegrate if workers believe that management is consciously manipulating their fellowship for profit.

THE TENSION OF DIVISION

Although cooperation is far more frequent than the lack of it (Gross 1958, p. 387), anyone who has worked in kitchens can attest that they are not settings of eternal harmony. Yet, in my observation, emotional displays are rare, not the rule. As a result, whereas emotional outbursts in kitchens are notable when they occur, they typify the scene for outsiders.

In one tense restaurant a kitchen staff meeting diffused much interpersonal annoyance through negotiation and clarification:

> The structural positions of the cooks were clarified by the chef in response to the complaint of Larry, a cook, who claimed that "we used to know what was expected. . . . I got upset. I walked off the line. I was upset about what was happening. . . . People don't know what they should do." The problem was a function of role ambiguity: the role of the "middleman" (aka the "slouch cook," or "swing cook")—a "backup" for the other cooks. After Paul, the head chef, detailed how the middleman should collaborate with the broiler cook and the stove cook, the tension lessened. That evening every cook made a special effort to demonstrate publicly that [he or she] could cooperate. Each man pointedly commented to me privately on how effective the meeting was. As Larry explained, by the end of that evening: "I felt a lot more relaxed and a lot more free. Jon [the cook with whom he had been annoyed] understood. . . . It's funny that's all it takes, fifteen minutes of talking and everything's different. It's the way it should be every night."
>
> (Field notes, Owl's Nest)

The point is not that cooks always work harmoniously, but that—in American kitchens (and much of American culture [Stearns 1987])—an ideology of harmony prevails.[8] Americans believe that cooks should be able to get along with each other, and that if anger is evident and full cooperation absent, the organization is "dysfunctional" and needs help. A therapeutic model applies to organizations as well as persons. Cooperation is a central ideological tenet of the lived experience of work.

BEING A COOK

To understand the experienced reality of cooking as a practical activity, we need to address how cooks and chefs see their work, how they perceive public attitudes, and how they were recruited to kitchen work. Occupational identity is tied to the pleasures and pain of work, and the imagined responses of the "other," the consuming public.

Cooking is demanding work; it is experienced as hard labor. Like athletes, cooks must "play" in pain; like a policeman, a cook only rarely has the luxury to call in sick. Those cooks employed by small organizations find their presence is required daily. One cook described his severe back pains, necessitating physical therapy, but continued cooking (Field notes, Owl's Nest). I was often told that cooks must work no matter what:

> I ask Mel if Paul will be in today. He seems surprised by the question and tells me that as far as he knows Paul will be here, adding "In this business, you don't get sick. You're either drunk or shacked up. You gotta drink or shack, so you better decide which. When I was young and working at the Lexington, I called in sick one day, and the next day the manager called me in and said that to me. Cooks don't often get sick."
>
> (Field notes, Owl's Nest)
>
> Paul, Jon, and Mel joke about one of Jon's absences. Mel is cracking eggs, and Paul tells him: "You should let Jon do it. He was the best breakfast cook we had [at the hotel at which they both worked]—when he would come in." This is a reference to one occasion on which Jon didn't show up; Paul jokingly accused him of shacking up with someone. The cooks then talk about the excuses that cooks use, including one who said that he was late because his mother tripped over the cord of his alarm clock. This joking colloquy has a strong element of social control.
>
> (Field notes, Owl's Nest)

This reality would surely be disconcerting to customers, who might be horrified to realize that all too often the cooks are sniffling, sneezing, exhausted, hungover, distracted, or bleeding.

THE DOWNSIDE

In addition to being required to be "iron men," other structural drawbacks mark cooks. They face challenges of time, pressure, working conditions, and a lack of personal satisfaction. Food preparation, although currently a trendy job for children of upper-middle-class baby boomers, will never have wide appeal.

Hours.   Those in some occupations labor while their clients play— restaurant workers are among them. As the head chef at the Owl's Nest notes sarcastically, "What an exciting way to spend a Saturday evening!" (Field notes, Owl's Nest). Some cooks like least "the long hours, weekends, holidays. . . . Everybody else is out having fun, and you have to work" (Personal interview, Owl's Nest). Others most dislike "having to be here when you'd like a little time off to do some of your own things. Take time to be with your family. Things you should be doing, but you can't be. Being involved more with community things, home things, PTA meetings, kids' baseball games, and stuff like that. You have to forfeit a lot" (Personal interview, Owl's Nest).

Pressure.   Even at its best, cooking is not known for its calm placidity. It can be a draining, pressured occupation—low paid, poorly regarded, and hard (see chapter 2). As one cook explained: "It wears you. Try to cook the way I [do] now, and I'd be dead by the time I was forty" (Personal interview, La Pomme de Terre). Another emphasized he wouldn't be a cook for the rest of his life because "I don't want to be forty years old and grouchy" (Personal interview, Owl's Nest). Cooking is a young man's game.

Working Conditions.   A kitchen is a hot, dirty, close place—no expansive office with flowers and big picture windows. Over time this reality affects cooks. For some the prime frustration is the ill-fitting uniforms or hair nets; for others, the odors. One told me that cooking "gets into your pores. When I go home, my kids can smell me. I'm told by a lot of people that 'you smell like vegetable soup' " (Field notes, Blakemore Hotel). Leaving the steak house, I was perfumed by cooking oil. Other cooks mentioned the stifling heat from standing over stoves and burners, and the pervasive dirt and grease. Although restaurant work is cleaner than some outdoor blue-collar jobs, it is far from the white-collar life that some desire.

Personal Dissatisfaction.   Cooks feel unappreciated, which translates into a general sense of despair. One cook at the Blakemore reported a motto on a button that she found symbolically relevant to her situation: "The Torture Never Stops." She joked that being fired might be the best thing that could happen to her. Another cook commented that "my job is worthless. There's so many incompetent people there. It's like a big joke" (Personal interview, Blakemore Hotel). Although her view is not universal, it is a feeling many cooks have experienced.

Public Suspicion.   However cooks may judge their own work, they must cope with a widely shared belief that the public does not respect them. They are, of course, not alone in this concern. Even such a high-paid professional as a lawyer, or a credentialed one as a doctor, must cope with what may seem a tide of public scorn. Most, if not all, occupations are challenged by outsiders. Every occupation develops strategies to cope with public attitudes. If one asks cooks, one will hear that the public, often ambivalent, does not give them the respect that they desire. The images of the drunken, ignorant chef and the artistic chef may be superficially contradictory, but they can coexist. Genius and deviance are, despite their distinct images, compatible.[9]

The public frequently sees restaurant kitchens as brutal places. One cook felt this lack of respect especially deeply:

> AL: I think people should know how cooks feel. They're human beings and some people treat them like they're robots, and they have to do this and that. They should have more respect than what we get.
>
> GAF: Do you think that if you had more respect, you might continue to be a cook?
>
> AL: Probably. I don't know. . . . Working at a place like this, a lot of people say you do a good job, but you just don't get the respect that you want.
>
> (Personal interview, Stan's)

Many cooks felt that their contacts just didn't see their career as suitable for someone who could get a "professional job," or who could be a success:

> GAF: What do you like least about being a cook?
>
> LARRY: Right now the feeling of not being respected as much as being a doctor. Right away when you hear someone say, "Well, he's a doctor," you think, "Well, he's got money; he's got a nice house, and a nice car, and a really nice family, and an airplane and a cabin." I'm a chef. "I bet he's got a dumpy apartment, and he's not married. His plants die on him. He's a loser. He's a high school graduate. He's just a dummy." . . . "Well, what do you do?" "I'm a cook." "What are you going to do when you get out of school." "I'm going to keep doing it." "Really? Is that all you're going to do. You're not going to go [to college]?" There are times when I feel that when people ask me what I do, I'm not going to tell them. I just say, "Well, I don't know. I'm just doing it for now, so I can get through school." I think it's a respectable job, and I'll stand up to anybody and say that I enjoy what I do.
>
> (Personal interview, Owl's Nest)

This cook reveals the ambivalence within the occupation—the beginnings of an embarrassment bordering on self-loathing, revealing pride mixed with defensiveness. Cooks are unsure of how they appear in others' eyes—the stigmatized others are too polite to insult, like African Americans in a society that does not tolerate public racism. Cooks wonder about the thoughts beneath the veneer of toleration.

THE BRIGHT SIDE

Balancing the problems, satisfactions are an integral part of kitchen work. While one's reaction to work is a function of individual needs and what we label "personality," several components of cooking are frequently mentioned as benefits, including employment options, self-satisfaction, and the potential for pleasing others.

Employment Options.   Throughout the 1980s, the restaurant and hospitality industry expanded rapidly. Americans increasingly ate outside the home, particularly as the upper-middle-class had more disposable income and more women were in the paid workforce. Since entry-level positions didn't require extensive training and positions were opening rapidly, opportunities to work where they wished arose for cooks. One cook explained that "you can always change [jobs]. It's so easy to find another job if you're good; if you have the skills" (Field notes, Owl's Nest). Several mentioned that kitchen work satisfied their desire to travel. They could relocate and search for a comparable position with the confidence that one would be readily available. One cook remarked that job security was no problem, even though restaurants frequently closed: "In my job hunting I wasn't that worried about finding one. I knew I would eventually, and now that I'm here in Minneapolis, and I do have a job, I think that even if La Pomme closed, I would be absorbed into another place real fast. Once you get attached to an area, established, I think it's pretty secure. One of the few jobs left that there's a need for, you always have to eat" (Personal interview, La Pomme de Terre). Job mobility permitted cooks to decide where they wanted to be. By changing restaurants, they could climb the industry status ladder.

Self-Satisfaction.   Cooks are producers. They create products that can be beautiful and appealing to the senses. Anyone who can produce such things has the "right to feel proud"—to recognize his or her accomplishments. Skill is associated with an occupational identity (Grzyb 1990, p. 176). Cooks gain a sense of identity from their work, and from this they learn to identify with their occupation (Hughes 1971). These workers produce within an organization, and these organizations attempt to generate assumptions about the *proper* identity of workers—why they should feel satisfied despite limitations on autonomy, wages, and benefits (Leidner 1993). Many cooks commented that their prime satisfaction derived from pleasing customers. In the words of one cook: "That gives me a real feeling of satisfaction that I know that I've pleased someone" (Personal interview, Blakemore Hotel). For others, it is the ability to cook up to one's "internal standard" (Personal interview, La Pomme de Terre). For still others, it is the ability to know what one can do with food, and that one can control a situation that would be impossible for those outside the occupation: "It's interesting that guys come home, and there's nothing to eat in the house, and I come home, and I look around and throw all this stuff together, and I can make a really nice dinner. They don't even realize that it's possible to do that. . . . It's really an accomplishment thing. You feel like you've accomplished something when you're a cook. Like working at the [display kitchen]. Ron, when he has 160 people in there, he might be really tired out, but he can handle it. He was in control of the situation, and he could feel the accomplishment" (Personal interview, Blakemore Hotel). Through these skills and their public display, cooks persuade themselves that they matter in an institutional order that sometimes disregards them; they are worthy of self-respect and honor, achieving things of which others only dream.

Public Acknowledgement. Although cooks typically do not have *direct* contact with customers, they do on occasion; often these relations are mediated by servers who routinely inform cooks of a significant compliment. Many cooks are young men without much training or education, and it is understandable that they marvel that "it's amazing people are eating what you cook. It's really self-satisfying, but it's also amazing that people will pay eighty, ninety dollars a meal" (Field notes, Owl's Nest). When this is combined with stroking—public recognition—one's satisfaction is complete. Seeing the smile is important, but having the smile verbalized can be equally significant: "The reason that chefs don't make good food and beverage directors is that being a technician [i.e., a chef], you need stroking. You need a pat on the back. You need somebody to say, 'Hey, this is a really good meat loaf.' You need that stroking. . . . You make something, and 'That was a wonderful table,' somebody would say. 'You really outdid yourself. That was a wonderful meal. That was great.' That's what you're here for. You're not here for the money. You need the money, you want the money, but there's more to it" (Personal interview, Blakemore Hotel). Workers judge their satisfaction both internally and externally, and they need both internal and external positive feedback to be satisfied.

When workers gain this satisfaction, they feel that they are making a difference, and that they are competent. This feeling increases the likelihood that they will remain in the kitchen.

RECRUITMENT AND SOCIALIZATION

All cooks were at one time outsiders to their trade; they were members of the general public. As is true for many occupations whose practitioners are youthful, first entrance occurs early, often in one's teens.[10] One either stays, transforming work into a career, or exits. With the growth of fast-food restaurants and informal family dining outside the home, the hospitality industry has become a major employer of adolescents. This easy entry emphasizes the lack of "professionalism" evident in many corners of the occupation.

ENTERING THE KITCHEN

Several paths lead to the kitchen, but, in my sample, few admitted to a childhood yearning to become a chef, as some youngsters dream of being scientists, political leaders, or doctors. While some believed that they had a knack for cooking or enjoyed working with food, often recruitment was mundane. Some informants were helped by older chefs, but in no case did a formal apprenticeship occur, which used to be common in the grand European restaurants. Recruitment to kitchen work in my sample is through family connections, social networks, promotion from related occupations, and chance connections.

Family Connections. Family connections are important for many European chefs—often fathers or grandparents had owned an inn or were otherwise involved in the "hospitality industry" (Wechsberg 1980, p. 36; Wechsberg 1975, p. 36; De Groot 1972, p. 244; Kimball 1985). While family involvement was not as prevalent in my American sample—here children are not encouraged to follow in their father's footsteps, and personal connections for occupational involvement are not as prominent—in some instances parents set children on the road to the kitchen. Typically this meant that a child acquired a love of cooking from his or her parents:

DIANE: My father was an excellent cook.

GAF: Did he teach you how to cook?

DIANE: I guess so, just from watching him. Also we had maids. It was very
          customary in the South, black ones. They did all the cooking. I
          watched them, and that's how I think I learned how to bake pies
          and make collard greens, fried chicken. My father was also a
          butcher. He'd get some game and bring it home and put it in the
          backyard and slice it open and let the blood drain out, and I was
          just totally fascinated. It just intrigued me. I was exposed at a very
          young age.

                                    (Personal interview, La Pomme de Terre)

Only in one instance did a cook enter the occupation because of a family member. Doug's grandmother cooked at Stan's for twenty years, and while in high school, he was hired as a busboy through this connection and later promoted to dishwasher and cook. After leaving to attend the University of Minnesota, he discovered that he preferred cooking. He has worked at Stan's for over a decade, finally becoming in charge of the kitchen (Personal interview, Stan's). While relatives may influence one's interest in cooking, within American society this linkage is attenuated.

Social Networks.   Friends are much more likely than family to help the future cook actually land a job. As Mark Granovetter (1974; see Prus and Irini 1980) suggests, acquaintances or weak ties are important in one's job search. These connections were most prominent at the three freestanding restaurants, perhaps because the personnel office at the hotel made personal ties less significant. The networks of chef-teachers at the trade school proved valuable for some workers in that these men could vouch for their students' ability: "After I started school, I didn't work for a while . . . but then the instructors were real good about [making connections]. Employers would call in and say we're looking for a cook. Just about like that you could get a job if you're in the vocational system" (Personal interview, Owl's Nest). This cook eventually wound up working for one of his former instructors, and this led to meeting his current boss.

Relatives play a role in hiring through their networks, more than providing direct motivation: "I ask Barbara, the pastry chef, how she got her job at La Pomme de Terre. She answers that her husband had known Brandon, the owner, when he worked [for his previous company]. Brandon suggested that she might try cooking, and she attended trade school. He then offered her a part-time job at the restaurant, which eventually became a full-time position" (Field notes, La Pomme de Terre). Acquaintances are probably the major source of recruit-ment, particularly if these friends recommend the new employee:

> I had an old roommate who worked at La Pomme de Terre as a waiter, and he said he'd get me an interview with Tim [the head chef].
>
> (Personal interview, La Pomme de Terre)

> One lady was a waitress at Primos. . . . She was getting new furniture, and I was moving at the time, and she said, "Do you want some chairs?" and I said, "Sure." I went over and picked up the chairs, and she said, "Well, what are you going to do for a living now," and I said, "I don't know. I haven't decided yet. I think I'll take a little vacation." She said, "Well, I know somebody who's looking for a cook," and so she called up the guy, and he came over with a twelve-pack of beer, and we sat there and got drunk, and he said he'd hire me.
>
> (Personal interview, Blakemore Hotel)

These network connections occur at each stage of the career and are as valuable for head chefs as for those entering the occupation.

Promotions within Restaurants.   Restaurants differ in the likelihood of internal job mobility. In all kitchens employees are promoted within their occupation line, but at better restaurants little opportunity exists for promotion across work lines—for instance, for dishwashers to be-come cooks.[11] This promotion was most common at Stan's and other lower-status restaurants:

JON: I started when I was thirteen at Country Kitchen right across the street. I was a dishwasher and busboy. Then started to be fry cook.

GAF: How did you move from being a dishwasher to a fry cook?

JON: Promoted and some people quit. I was always there, and I was always watching, and I showed interest, so I knew I could move up. I didn't want to stay a dishwasher all my life. I also knew that if I showed in-terest, I would move up the ladder. It is better pay.

> (Personal interview, Owl's Nest)

> I never really decided to become [a cook], I don't think. I think that deci-sion came as simply as I was washing dishes one night, and [my boss] came up to me, and he said, "Tim, you're pretty responsible. How would you like to become a cook? I'll give you a twenty-cent raise."
>
> (Personal interview, La Pomme de Terre)

> I started as a dishwasher [at Stan's]. Then I became a swing cook, and now I'm up to a cook. . . . I didn't really decide to be a cook. I was just looking for a job, and he had an opening for a dishwasher, and he gave me that job, and a couple of cooks quit, so I got pushed up.
>
> (Personal interview, Stan's)

If workers are perceived as interchangeable and training derives from observing kitchen happenings, job transfer is readily arranged. Frequently financial concerns motivate the switch although those who remain in the kitchen must find the work somewhat appealing.

Chance Connections.   It is rare for adolescents to make definite choices early; often they fall into their work by chance and through unplanned opportunity. Book publishing is a good example of such an "accidental profession" (Coser, Kadushin, and Powell 1982, pp. 99–101). Few publishing careers are planned; so it is with kitchen work. Editors and cooks who see their work as relatively permanent are "hooked" by the work and have set aside plans to leave.

Some cooks who enter the occupation through trade school made their program selection by happenstance without careful consideration:

> GAF: Why did you decide on the cooking program [at trade school]?
> DENVER: I didn't cook that much at home, but when I did I enjoyed it. When we were down there, they were really working doing wedding cakes, and I was really impressed by that. It was just kind of a whim. I thought that would be fun, and so I just went into it.
> (Personal interview, Blakemore Hotel)

> When I figured out I was wasting my time [in college], I went to vocational school and took the test to see what field I should be in, hoping that they'd tell me, and they said I could do anything I wanted to with the aptitudes that I had. The first three choices that I picked they vetoed. One because I didn't like to read, one because I didn't have any art classes, and one because I couldn't spell. We had an interview session, and I told them I had some interest in cooking but thought I was only [interested in cooking] because my best friend had gone through the program a year prior. They told me to try it, and I liked it.
> (Personal interview, Blakemore Hotel)

Some cooks find themselves in the right place at the right time, even though they lack culinary background: "It was an accident. It was completely by accident. I didn't choose it. I was working for Macalester College at the time, and I was a custodian, and I was going to train and get my boiler's license, and I was working on a Saturday morning, and a couple of cooks didn't show up, and since I got along well with the manager of the kitchen, and they asked me if I could fry up some french fries and some other things, and I said, 'I don't know nothing about that.' He said, 'That's OK. We just need the help.' That's how it started" (Personal interview, Blakemore Hotel). This cook entered the occupation because he was a warm body. When the pay, conditions, and satisfactions proved adequate, he continued and made the work his career.

Cooking lacks a routine career trajectory; the career depends on unpredictable contingencies. To have contacts, to move up from low-status jobs, or to be where one is needed opens the door. Whether one will enter and stay is a personal choice, hard to predict in advance. Work choices depend on the satisfactions that emerge from one's personal experiences and one's incorporation into the community. In a long-term career a series of contingencies and opportunities affects one's ultimate position in the occupation and one's decision to leave, resign, or retire. Some depend on conscious choices and hiring decisions—how jobs are supposed to be allocated—while others occur by chance.

SOCIALIZATION TO THE KITCHEN

A key indicator that a novice has become a competent cook is the development of a professional stance: a set of public behaviors and attitudes that validates that one shares the abilities and values of one's fellows. The techniques by which one presents oneself as a professional reveals the presence of socialization. Professionalism is a strategy for the display of self, and socialization involves proper display (Manning and Hearn 1969), even if that display blinds one to the economic-instrumental aspects of the occupation (Dickinson and Erben 1984). One cook explained: "There are only four things that are important in this industry to be professional, and that's determination, drive, and common sense, and attitudes and heart. Your heart's your work" (Personal interview, Blakemore Hotel). These concepts are symbolic representations of what must be revealed in practice. When individuals do not demonstrate these components of community and competence, they must be separated from their position, preferably by being "cooled out." Just as careers are constructed, so are terminations (Faulkner 1974). For example, the cook fired during my observation was defined as lacking "professionalism." She explained: "The way that Tim explained it, he thought that my work was good, and I was really meticulous. [Food was] very pretty when I got done with it, but that I never did pick up the speed. . . . They really didn't give me any feeling that this was coming, but I understood it, and I know that that's his way too. I had never been in this kind of position in that kind of restaurant, and I was afraid of disturbing him by asking too many questions. . . . Tim told me he thought I was really cut out to be a hobby cook, not a professional" (Personal interview, La Pomme de Terre). Even though this young cook had talent, she was unable to convince others (or herself) that she was a professional, and so she had to be terminated. She had not learned subcultural techniques through the three standard methods: watching, formal education, or being trained on the job.

Learning by Watching.   Entering a kitchen, one encounters a booming, buzzing confusion. Everything happens simultaneously; nothing makes sense. If one has attended a cooking school or has a mentor, entrance is easier, but even with these advantages one must imitate others' actions. One is expected to acquire rapidly the unstated rules in the kitchen. It becomes painfully obvious when these rules are broken (Schroedl 1972, p. 184). One watches and learns to cook "by feel." The novice observes, errs, and learns from those mistakes so as to avoid them: "Practice makes perfect." A dishwasher, eventually promoted to cook, explained: "As a dishwasher, you sit and watch what the cooks do, and what the shrimp should look like, what color it is, and when it's done and stuff like that. When you're cooking, you try it out, and you get to know it" (Personal interview, Stan's; see Herman 1978, p. 33). This technique, prominent at low-status restaurants, is also evident in higher-status establishments, where the ability to watch trained professionals offsets modest salaries (Waldemar 1985). A cook at the Owl's Nest explained: "I've only been there for a couple of months, [but] I'm really learning. . . . I would like to come in on a slow night with just [the chef] and I, and let me work the sauté station, and he can work the broiler" (Personal interview, Owl's Nest). The circulation of cooks and chefs spreads techniques throughout the industry. Cooks learn informally from each another and share their techniques with new colleagues:

> Tomorrow we do a salad which we haven't served here since I've been here, which I stole from the other hotel. . . . That's why chefs move around so much. I mean, I can sit here for two years and get everything I know. While I'm here, I can pick up a couple of new things—just from other people who have worked here. I'll leave here just because I'm drained out, and I've got nothing new to offer. I'll then go to another establishment and give them what I already learned, plus what I've just learned here, and things that they

have never seen before, and they're happy, and I'm happy because I get to
show off what I know. I learned a few things that they were doing differently. Take all that to the next place. In the meantime, you're just expanding and growing.

(Personal interview, Blakemore Hotel)

The informal side of socialization is crucial in any occupation but
seems particularly salient in locales, such as kitchens, in which formal
models of education are weak, and where some assume that the job
can be mastered by anyone with sufficient motivation. If socialization
is assumed routine and painless, little provision is made for acquiring
knowledge, even though the cost for not learning properly is high.
Cooks have, in the words of Wilbert Moore, "a fellowship of suffer-
ing," in which all are attempting to master difficult and unpleasant
tasks through role modeling, coaching, and peer support (Bucher and
Stelling 1977, p. 268).

Formal Training.   Increasingly, cooks learn their craft in institutes
such as trade schools (Fine 1985)—some state run, and others private
or proprietary, such as the famed Culinary Institute of America. Of the
thirty cooks interviewed, eighteen (60 percent) were trained in public
trade schools; none of my sample were trained in private schools. Programs in Minnesota required students to attend classes daily for either
eleven or twenty-two months. Students learned basic cooking techniques, quantity cooking, restaurant cooking (line cooking) and service, and specialty techniques, including bakery and some ethnic cuisine. These skills are acquired in the artificial environment of the trade
school, where students are rarely pressured, overworked, or sharply
criticized. While they acquire technical skills, some claim they graduate
ignorant of the culinary "real world."[12]

Because of this artificial training environment, some chefs fret over
hiring trade-school graduates, in absence of information that they
know how to prepare food in restaurant kitchens:

I ask Tim, the head chef at La Pomme de Terre and a trade-school graduate,
if he likes to hire students with a TVI [Technical Vocational Institute] background. He tells me: "Not really. If they have common sense, I can teach
them how we cook. I look for their ambition."

(Field notes, La Pomme de Terre)

Denver explains to me that "TVI is a great little institution, but there's
more to industry than they can teach you. I don't want to belittle the

school, but it's a rude awakening when you come out of school. The industry doesn't work like that. There's no way that they can teach you to improvise. There's no way they can tell you to get along with waitresses."

(Field notes, Blakemore Hotel)

Trade school builds expectations for which the real world is a "rude
awakening." Some consider trade school to be a "dream world."
Cooks agree that while trade-school training is not worthless, it is not
an adequate introduction to the skills that they need when hired by a
restaurant. Industry lacks a safety net.

Being Taught.   American industry does not rely—at least in this century—on apprenticeship. This applies to virtually every occupation, including cooking. Contrasted to European, particularly French, culinary
traditions, American cooks either learn by observation or formal
schooling (Fine 1985). Even though American restaurants do not rely
on apprenticeship, a fortunate cook may gain a mentor, an older cook
or chef who takes the young worker under his or her wing and teaches
culinary techniques. The respected cook-teacher Anne Willan writes:

> I think it is almost impossible to learn to cook completely on the job. Sure,
> if you have the quite extraordinary luck to find an outstanding chef who's
> willing to take the time to teach you, then perhaps in that exceptional case,
> you can get really good training on the job. . . . very few chefs have the abil-
> ity, the time, and the willingness to pass on everything they know to young
> people who are working in the kitchen. It just isn't practical. You're under
> pressure; you want to go and do the orders for tomorrow's food; you've got
> someone on the telephone; you can't spend time saying to somebody,
> "Don't chop like that, chop like this." . . . Chefs, quite simply, don't want
> nice boys who are totally inexperienced messing around as unknown quan-
> tities when they have to pay them a sort of basic wage. It's becoming more
> and more an idealistic thing to pass on skills to the next generation, rather
> than an economically reasonable one. . . . So some structured instruction is
> almost indispensable.
>
> ("Cook's Interview: Anne Willan" 1985, pp. 18–19)

While in some sites, those to be socialized are resistant to or ambivalent about the staff's goals (Becker et al. 1961), novices are often en-
thusiastically supportive of these goals, more than willing to conform
(Garnier 1973). Whereas much research on occupational socialization
describes schools, the same process occurs on the job, with less opportunity for resistance. If one chooses to resist, the easiest option is to
exit and move to a more congenial location.

Novices are typically delighted to learn at the knee of their superiors as a means of self-fulfillment and advancement: "Lured by its reputation as a standout on the local culinary scene, he landed a lowly post at the New French Cafe. 'It was like a breath of fresh air,' he recalls. 'Before you went there, you knew you weren't going to get paid [much], but it's like going to graduate school'—with lessons in beautiful food handling. . . . He started at the bottom. . . . 'I'd work like crazy so I could get up and watch the chef. He'd show me certain things, then let me do them' " (Waldemar 1985, p. 154). Cooks in my sample had similar role models in their early work—men whose concern and teaching transformed them into sophisticated cooks:

> You take that guy like that Frenchman. He took me right underneath his wing, and I'd do anything for him. He liked you, so he'd take you back in the corner and explain to you what you were doing wrong. One of his instructions to me is that I'm going to show you once and tell you once, and that's all. So I've got a little blue address book that I used to carry in my back pocket, and the minute he'd tell me to do something, and I didn't think I could remember it, I'd write it right in that book.
>
> (Personal interview, Owl's Nest)

GAF: What do you like most about being a chef?

PAUL: Being able to take in people and work with them. People who are really anxious to learn. Jon's a real good example. He's a hardworking young kid that wants to learn. He's so excited to learn something new. Teach him how to do this or how to do that. I reflect back and see my own excitement about the first time that I was able to do this or that. It was fun; it was an adventure.

(Personal interview, Owl's Nest)

The chef who chooses to mentor adopts that role in addition to his other duties as an act of altruism, which may be dangerous because some managers replace high-paid workers with low-paid ones. Although mentoring relationships are ideal and produce dedicated and well-trained cooks, they are serendipitous: a chance encounter that makes a life.

TWO

Cooks' Time

Temporal Demands
and the Experience of Work

The chargings to and fro in the narrow passages, the colli-
sions, the yells, the struggling with crates and trays and
blocks of ice, the heat, the darkness, the furious festering
quarrels which there was no time to fight out—they pass
description. . . . It was only later, when I understood the
working of a hotel that I saw order in all this chaos.
    —*George Orwell,* Down and Out in Paris and London

As a principle of social life, temporality affects the life of an organization as much as physical space or hierarchical organization (Maines
1987).[1] Indeed, organization and time are intimately connected. For an
organization to run efficiently, schedules must be meshed (Cottrell
1939; Zerubavel 1979), and work products must be generated at a regular or intermittent rate that permits the organization to prosper (Baldamus 1961).

The way that people experience the passage of time is a central, yet
frequently ignored, feature of organizational life. Industrial capitalism
depends upon temporal structure and synchronization (Thompson
1967); time is a resource like material and personnel. Much research—
notably those studies inspired by the tradition of Taylorism—attempts
to improve the efficiency of work. Time is a cost that must be minimized, but how time is experienced by workers is not considered.

Observing work life reminds us that features external to the doing
of work constrain the use of time, and temporal constraints influence
how work is experienced. Time can be transformed into a mechanism
of social control, as is dramatically evident to those who labor on assembly lines but also is true for those who work in medical clinics or

restaurant kitchens. Workers develop techniques to cope with demands on their time and, as a consequence, gain a measure of *temporal autonomy* (Lyman and Scott 1970, p. 191; Hodson 1991, p. 63), carving out *temporal niches*.[2] Time operates on several levels: from lengthy periods of work (seasons, weeks, days) to smaller chunks of time (portions of days, or the time taken to achieve particular work tasks).

Time passes whether or not a worker or sleeper experiences that passage, and both "objective" and "experienced" components of time affect organizational life (Flaherty 1987). The philosopher Henri Bergson emphasized that effects of time cannot be fully separated from how it is felt (1910, pp. 236–37). Time, like organization itself (Strauss 1978; Pettigrew 1979), can be negotiated or used symbolically, and is treated as if it were concrete. The experience of time is created by workers, given the constraints on their actions (Roy 1952, 1959–1960; Roethlisberger and Dickson 1939).

Five dimensions are critical to temporal organization: periodicity, tempo, timing, duration, and sequence (Lauer 1981, pp. 28ff; see Hawley 1950 and Engel-Frisch 1943). Periodicity refers to the rhythm of the activity; tempo, to its rate or speed; timing, to the synchronization or mutual adjustment of activities (Moore 1963, pp. 45–47); duration, to the length of an activity; and sequence, to the ordering of events.

Each dimension connects to the demands of the workplace. Although they are "objective" features of time, their effects depend on how they are experienced. The workers' negotiation of these dimensions is particularly likely when temporal organization ("too much" or "not enough" time) is felt as unpleasant or dysfunctional; as a result, workers adjust their routines to increase their satisfaction while accepting organizational demands. Workers create temporal niches—to do their jobs in a satisfactory and satisfying way while "creating" personal time (Ditton 1979; Bernstein 1972). They synchronize their activities to create an efficient routine in the face of uncontrollable and unpredictable durations and tempos. Workers strive for autonomy from management's and clients' temporal demands. The structure of time is a critical means of social control.

Successful restaurants are those that use time effectively. Anyone observing a moderate-size kitchen could not miss the central position of temporal organization in defining workers' reality. Time is as important to cooking as any herb. For food to be cooked properly, the cook must be simultaneously aware of the timing of multiple tasks. Awareness of duration is essential, distinguishing a rare steak from one that is charred, crunchy vegetables from mush, and sour milk from fresh. Sequence, too, is integral to the temporal organization of cooking, as is obvious to anyone who has ever used a recipe (Tomlinson 1986). Synchronization of tasks is more complex but equally essential for preparing a plate on time. Starch, meat, and vegetables must be ready simultaneously; on the counter a product rapidly loses sensory appeal. Periodicity and tempo are linked to the pace of orders, not to the individual order.

Because of the relevance of each temporal dimension to professional cooking, restaurant kitchens are an auspicious site to investigate how temporality is tied to organizational life. Every occupation must deal with these dimensions, if not always as directly or obviously.

THE EXTERNAL ENVIRONMENT AND RESTAURANT TIME

All organizations have a temporal structure—times when they are "peopled," when they are "operating at full capacity," and when they are preparing and recovering from peaks of activity. How an organization fits into the temporal life of a community provides the basis for how the organization structures the time of employees (Engel-Frisch 1943, p. 46), which, in turn, affects their emotions and attitudes.

PROCESSING THE CUSTOMER

Organizations must make products available to those who are likely to be interested; they must maintain and staff an "output boundary" (Hirsch 1972, p. 643). In the service sector an operation must be open when clients are likely to be present—when organizational "output" can be provided to clients. Clients, in turn, expect different classes of organizations to maintain different hours (e.g., banks, supermarkets, or taverns); further, they have different temporal expectations based on the location (bars in SoHo as opposed to Salinas, or bookstores in Berkeley and Bexley). To maximize profit, the establishment needs to be closed when it is not profitable to be open (although some establishments may use long hours as *temporal loss leaders,* so that customers believe they are "always open"). An efficient service establishment should have no more employees on duty than necessary to cope with customer traffic (Leidner 1993, p. 63) although, again, some establishments may employ more workers than needed to insure that customers will expect that they will be served quickly. Indeed, lines are often longer in "off-peak" times than at relatively busy times because fewer workers are on duty to handle the customer flow.

Operating in a highly competitive environment, restaurants must respond to the timing of customer demand, at least as perceived by management. Although regularities exist, the temporal organization of business changes from season to season, month to month, week to week, and day to day. Management's concern is to select when the restaurant will be open, a decision that may lead to organizational failure (Miller 1978). In the United States restaurants have no widely accepted times of operation, reflecting the diversity in American schedules (Melbin 1987). Few industries have regular hours—the formal "banker's hours" of a previous generation are no more, as organizations compete with each other for temporal access. Each restaurant I observed had a different schedule of operation:

Blakemore Hotel: Main Restaurant: Lunch: 11:00–2:00, Monday–Saturday; Dinner: 5:30–10:30, Monday–Saturday; closed Sunday. Coffee Shop: Breakfast and Lunch: 7:00–3:00, daily.

La Pomme de Terre: Lunch: 11:30–2:00, Monday–Friday; Dinner: 6:00–10:00, Monday–Saturday; Brunch: 11:00–2:30, Sunday.

Owl's Nest: Lunch and Dinner: 11:00–1:00, Monday–Friday; Dinner: 4:00–1:00, Saturday; closed Sunday.

Stan's: Lunch: 11:00–2:30, Monday–Friday; Dinner: 5:00–12:00, Monday–Saturday; 3:00–10:00, Sunday.

We often classify restaurants by hours of operation: luncheonettes, all-night diners, tearooms, supper clubs. Restaurants that cater to breakfast eaters often announce that in their name: the Egg and I, International House of Pancakes, or Al's Breakfast. In addition, location influences hours of operation. We do not expect restaurants in the suburbs, central business districts, inner cities, and bohemian neighborhoods to keep the same hours (Hawley 1950). Some restaurants are closed on Sunday; some, on Monday. Some serve breakfast; many don't. Some serve lunch every day; some, only on weekdays. Some are always open; others are open only for lunch and dinner; some cater to late-night crowds.

The hours of a restaurant depend on the market niche to which the owners aspire. Hotels whose guests are potential hotel-restaurant clients typically have food service throughout the day and evening, and room service at night. Gourmet restaurants such as La Pomme de Terre have shorter hours because walk-in customers are rare, and because they can afford to have customers come to them for a unique service. Neighborhood restaurants such as Stan's are open on Sunday afternoons when a traditional "family dinner" is served. While Stan's has customers at that time, if La Pomme de Terre were open then, it would be empty. La Pomme de Terre, with a clientele from a different social class, serves Sunday brunch.

To a degree, restaurant hours determine the times that the cooks work, but the two sets of hours are not identical. Cooks arrive several hours prior to the opening and generally work until after the restaurant closes. Unlike more tightly structured organizations, managers and head chefs are flexible in scheduling cooks, and schedules change weekly with cooks having some say. Schedules respond to "external" forces, such as the number of reservations and special parties. Head chefs occasionally tell cooks to take the day off, leave early, or appear on short notice. While cooks are not on call, the head chef and the manager are aware of who is willing to work extra hours.

The irregular and unpredictable need for workers gives the chef or manager power within the workplace. In coordinating schedules, he must keep his staff happy and treat them in ways they consider fair—both in the number of hours they work and the sequence of those hours (see Zerubavel 1979, pp. 21–22). The chef has an interest in allowing his most competent cooks to work more frequently than those less conscientious, but this choice may create friction. Unlike fast-food restaurants (Leidner 1993, p. 62), in only one restaurant that I observed were hours assigned for social control: a head chef decided to discipline a dishwasher by cutting his hours to teach him to show more deference to the cooks.

The extreme case is when workers are laid off to cut labor costs. This not only causes strain by having fewer people to do the same work but also sends a signal about management's intentions and makes all workers feel less secure. The decision of the Blakemore Hotel to terminate the popular assistant chef caused considerable dissatisfaction, in part because workers felt overburdened, and in part because they felt that management didn't care. From the standpoint of the hotel it was a necessary decision in that labor costs were too high when compared to income (Field notes, Blakemore Hotel).

Employers in all industrial segments have similar problems although these problems take different forms. How does one synchronize the staffing of an organization? In pure production units (e.g., factories) machines may run at any time, and electricity may be cheaper at off-peak hours; but it may be difficult to find workers willing to adapt to off-peak schedules.

FOOD PROCESSING

While the temporal structure of a restaurant is greatly affected by its desire to attract customers, other external influences affect internal decisions. Every organization must maintain an "input boundary," as well as the "output boundary" discussed above. Simply put, a restaurant requires ingredients (foodstuffs) for its internal production. Most restaurants contract with middlemen or brokers for food to be delivered at set, albeit negotiable, times. These deliveries are arranged to occur before the restaurant needs the food, when the restaurant is not busy, and when cooks or other kitchens workers are present to check or sign for the goods. The restaurant and the vendor select a mutually agreeable time, and cooks need sufficient time to store the food and to prepare whatever portion of the delivery is expected to meet the demands of the day's customers.

Food itself has a temporal dynamic. Most food spoils the longer it is kept—beef and wine that "age" are, to a point, notable exceptions. As a consequence, high turnover is crucial not only for revenue but also to avoid losses from spoilage. Restaurant management sometimes attempts to manipulate customer choice through specials or by having servers "push" a dish. The clients' decisions, in turn, affect cooks by forcing them to spend their time cooking some dishes and not others. To the extent that some dishes are easier or more pleasant to prepare or are prepared by special workers (e.g., main-course salads or broiled dishes), culinary life is influenced by the "life" of the food.

While food has its own dynamic because of spoilage, other objects deteriorate over time or go out of fashion, and this puts pressure on workers to "move" them. Medicines and film have expiration dates, which customers may check. Fabrics become mildewed, and toys, dresses, and automobiles are subject to changes in fashion and technological innovation. Some clothes—swimsuits and overcoats—have their seasons and styles. Although food may be a particularly dramatic instance of how the timing of material objects push workers, it is not unique.

LIVING THE DAY

Kitchen work has both rhythm (periodicity) and tempo that stems from customer demand. Restaurants have slow times and times of incredible demand; each influences how cooks respond to their environment. Some cooks use a theatrical metaphor with its images of preparation for a performance, the emotional "high" of the performance and release after the curtain descends:

> It's very much like an actor preparing to go onstage and go into work and start in a quiet place and figure out what you're going to be doing. You get your equipment ready, sharpen knives, cut meats, trim your fish and make your vegetables and make your sauces and get everything set up, and it gets a little bit hotter, people start talking more, and the waiters start coming in, and this is going on over here, and by the time everything starts coming together, it's like you're ready to go onstage. It's there. . . . Once the curtain goes up, everyone knows exactly what they're supposed to do.
>
> (Personal interview, La Pomme de Terre)
>
> A pantry worker tells me: "I like the atmosphere in kitchens, the speed. It always reminds me of a play. I understand how actors feel. It starts out slow and then it speeds up."
>
> (Field notes, Blakemore Hotel)

Life in a restaurant is not structured by the clock per se, but by events such as lunch, dinner, or banquets, indirectly set by the clock (Marshall 1986, p. 40). Cooks rarely look at the clock and may profess surprise when, after a busy evening, they learn how late it is.

SYNCHRONIZATION

Professional cooks face the problem of synchronization in that they are not merely cooking "dishes" but for "tables" or "parties," and must prepare several dishes at once, each timed differently (e.g., steak and fillet of sole). Cooking to order is an occupational challenge to be overcome by skills of synchronization: the recognition of a temporally grounded division of labor. This skill determines their competence in the eyes of others, distinguishing the professional cook from the home cook:

Part of the job is knowing how to take a piece of fish and a piece of chicken up to the window at the same time. If the chicken will take fifteen minutes and the fish two, how do you get them up there at the same time?

(Personal interview, Owl's Nest)

I like to read the orders and time everything. It moves, you think and cook, and everything has to be just right. It's a real test of your dexterity and your ability to concentrate.

(Personal interview, La Pomme de Terre)

How is synchronization achieved? What organizational procedures promote this competence? Each restaurant had a slightly different system for achieving the orderly production of food, but each relies on the presentation of tickets by servers to cooks—the temporal linkage or sequencing of occupations sedimented into a structure. From the presentation of the ticket, cooks know that they have a set amount of time until the dishes need to be ready, until servers and their customers will complain.[3] As they know approximately how long each dish will take to prepare, taking these constraints into consideration they can organize their work and gain some temporal autonomy.

The point at which the main course is needed is an approximation based upon the length of time that customers are expected to spend eating appetizers or are willing to wait. While cooks would like to know the exact times that dishes are needed, servers and customers desire food to be ready when it is wanted—different for fast and slow tables. The preparation of food involves a delicate negotiation among cooks, servers, and customers, with each having demands, constraints, rights, and privileges. For example, servers frequently inform cooks that they need dishes sooner or later than expected. To some extent this is modified by flexibility built into the structure:

Tim explains to me how the wheel operates. The wheel is a metal turntable with clips on which servers place their tickets when customers have ordered. Cooks examine the orders on the wheel and assume twenty minutes until the dish is to be served. When it is about seven or eight minutes from when the customers will want their food, the server places the ticket on the counter (generally when the customer is half finished with the soup or appetizer). When the ticket is placed on the counter, cooks "go full blast." Some dishes such as lamb en croûte are started immediately when the ticket is placed on the wheel, because it takes twenty minutes to prepare. This structure means that no dish can be served by this restaurant that cooks for longer than twenty minutes.

Sometimes the system breaks down. When servers see many tickets on the counter, they put theirs down early, even though it doesn't need to be ready in seven minutes. They believe that the cooks will be running behind, and they want to insure that their customers (and their tips) are protected. As a result, food is ready ahead of time.

(Field notes, La Pomme de Terre)

The chef at La Pomme de Terre describes himself as an air-traffic controller, suggesting that dishes have the potential for "stacking up" and, if processed in the wrong sequence, they can create disaster. A chef, like any worker with multiple responsibilities, must manage the demands of the kitchen. Another cook at a different restaurant used a similar image of flow control in describing his difficulties: "You have to be really thinking about timing. It's really kinda like a science. You can control the flow. You can control if they [the servers] are running [i.e., if there are a lot of orders]" (Field notes, Owl's Nest). Still, the temporal ordering of dishes is so imprecise that cooks sometimes joke about occasions when they do well in the face of expectations of failure, as when Howie, the sous chef, comments to Mickey, a server, about a slow order:

> HOWIE: Those people must have been waiting a long time.
> MICKEY: .Nope. They just got finished with their salad.
> HOWIE, joking: Great. What finesse.

(Field notes, La Pomme de Terre)

Timing food reflects a concern with synchronization—a division of labor among cooks and servers. The cook must internalize the ordering and timing of dishes to permit the production of fifteen different dishes, each at the peak of quality, and must believe that other cooks are acting similarly. Cooking decisions are not analyzed at leisure but are split-second decisions, barely permitting a comment between co-workers.

DISTRACTIONS

Ideally cooks as crafts artisans would be autonomous, leading to satisfaction with the temporal organization of work (Baldamus 1961; Ditton 1979). Such a world is impossible in restaurants and most industrial workplaces. Cooks are challenged when they cannot set their own schedule: "Where it's busy enough that it requires somebody to help me, I really have to concentrate. People, waitresses come up and ask questions. It's really hard. When we're busy enough, I can't break my stride or break my train of thought. Sometimes I just tell them to be quiet and go away" (Personal interview, Blakemore Hotel). Like all focused workers, cooks must "bracket" the extraneous events that swirl around them while establishing a rapid rhythm and coping with organizational demands. When the tasks have been completed, they can luxuriate in those events that they had previously bracketed, sometimes not "really working" for an hour or more (Marshall 1986, p. 40), creating a temporal niche: "The previous night the Owl's Nest had 116 customers, a heavy Friday evening. This included a party of 25. Fortunately there were no tickets behind that order [i.e., they didn't have to cook for other customers]. Larry tells me: 'It can be hard when you have other tickets up. We were lucky last night. It's hard when you have four tickets right behind it. You just want to sit down and rest after it' " (Field notes, Owl's Nest).

EXPECTATIONS

Workers have expectations about when their work begins and ends; sometimes to their frustration these expectations are dashed. Workdays should have *temporal cues,* of which the factory whistle or school bell are models. Unfortunately breaking the serenity of work, customers arrive late, important clients want special meetings, or the boss demands overtime. Once routine and legitimate tasks become an imposition: "At 11:30 P.M. the cooks are almost finished cleaning the kitchen, when a new order comes in from a 'regular' who often arrives late without a reservation. Larry is so annoyed that he throws a lamb chop bone and later throws a sharpened knife across the counter, fuming 'That's what's really frustrating. You're ready to close and another order comes in. You get kinda cranky sometimes' " (Field notes, Owl's Nest). Frustration with the violation of temporal boundaries applies to an extension of the opening boundary as well as the closing boundary. Although the Owl's Nest is open for lunch at 11:00 A.M., cooks are disoriented if customers arrive before 11:45 A.M. They're not ready for lunch to begin, and they resent it. Within their rights, customers arriving when the restaurant is open in practice disrupt the rhythm of the cooks' work. Cooks typify when their "real work" should occur, even though this expectation may be shattered by a client's exercise of his or her rights. As at colleges, where early morning meetings are taboo, "real" hours differ from the "official" hours of the organization.

THE RUSH

The effects of an organization's environment on its temporal structure is dramatically evident when the system is loaded to capacity. In the kitchen this is the rush, but it has equivalents in many organizations: emergency rooms, fire stations, theater aisles, airline counters, and toll booths. Seen collectively, clients do not use services at regularly spaced intervals. For some workers (ushers) the rush will be predictable; for others (emergency medics), much less so.[4] Every restaurant, especially those that are successful, has a rush—a period in which the demands of customers threaten to overwhelm the capacity of the kitchen employees to cope—a time at which the restaurant is "slammed" (Kleinfield 1991, p. C24). Customers, unaware of the "backstage" problems, expect their food when they are ready for it. Food should be served after what "feels" like the proper interval, neither rushed nor delayed—comprising the mysterious variable of "good service." In an attempt to control labor costs, managers hire just enough staff so that the kitchen is on the edge of chaos but not so few that customers are dissatisfied with the service.

From these demands derives the experience of the rush. External demands produce a pattern of action by workers, and this use of time produces the lived experience of the rush (Denzin 1984). Its felt emotion—what Henri Bergson (1910) refers to as *durée*—differs from other "times" (Flaherty 1987).

The rush represents a distinct behavioral characteristic of restaurant life, which is noted for its demanding tempo (and associated rhythm) and intense pressure (Schroedl 1972, p. 187). The journalist John McPhee (1979, p. 78) describes the temporal life of a master chef: "As his usual day accelerates toward dinner-time, the chef's working rhythms become increasingly intense, increasingly kinetic, and finally all but automatic. His experience becomes his action. He just cruises, functioning by conditioned response. 'You cook unconsciously,' he says. 'You know what you're going to do and you do it. When problems come along, your brain spits out the answer.' " Those I observed relied on similar metaphors. "You're fighting a battle of chaos," one cook explained. Another emphasized that coping with a rush involved "keeping calm. Lining up the station. Getting ready. The setups. Getting organized before the rush" (Field notes, Owl's Nest).

The rush feels similar at each restaurant, even though vastly different numbers are served. A rush is characterized by rapid movements (proper sequencing) and little talk, except for brief, subcultural exchanges ("an ivory downtown," "nine tops, three shrimp, all baked, all medium")[5] or curses and insults. Because of the clattering of pans and plates, the kitchen is noisy, making the rhythms of work seem discordant or nonexistent to an observer (e.g., Kleinfield 1991, p. C24). The number of cooks present is barely sufficient to handle the expected number of customers. When more customers than expected arrive or when mistakes happen, the kitchen extends the duration of preparation; the customers do not get their food "on time," and the servers may receive smaller tips. The food may be of lower quality than when the restaurant is not so busy.[6] The success of the restaurant during the rush rests on a thin line.

Although cooks operate similarly during the rush, they experience it differently. Some cooks claim to enjoy the rush and relish the pace. Others find it unpleasant. The experience differs from person to person and from day to day. One cook remarked: "You can't keep up with your orders. It feels like you have to do everything in a second. Back and forth and back and forth. I don't like the feeling. It's not good. . . . You just feel like you're gonna cave in and collapse" (Personal interview, Stan's). In contrast, others noted:

> It's a high. You have to get yourself up there. You have to get your adrenaline pumping. It feels good really if everything's going smooth. You're just cranking. It feels good. I enjoy it.
> (Personal interview, Blakemore Hotel)

> I'm pumped up till you wouldn't believe. I just want to go, go, go.
> (Personal interview, Blakemore Hotel)

These cooks are like "trauma junkies" among emergency medical technicians, who enjoy those calls that demand their skills (e.g., heart attacks), as opposed to "pukes," which are boring calls, not requiring training (Palmer 1983). They are like detectives challenged by the game of matching wits with criminal suspects (Stenross and Kleinman 1989).

Although personality, age, ethnicity, and gender affect how workers experience their busiest periods, most cooks whom I observed indicated that their reactions depend on the "quality" of the day. The rush has a situated quality, determined by what has occurred before and during. This is evident when a cook notes that his "high" occurs when work is "smooth." Cooks (and other workers) may use a drug metaphor to explain feelings of mental transformation: "It can be a downer or an upper. When you're all set and you're ready for it, it can be great. When things are happening that aren't supposed to, it can be a nightmare. It's a good night when you look at the clock and it's already ten-thirty" (Field notes, Owl's Nest). As with drugs, the emotion is not merely chemical but also social. Cooks distinguish between days in which things go well and other days in which things have not been prepared or external forces break their expectations: "I ask Ralph whether he enjoys the breakfast rush. 'Some days I do; some days I absolutely hate it.' [Then I ask him] what does it depend on? 'How smoothly things are going. It can be very stressful. Mr. Businessman has to get to his meeting, so you have to get his eggs on the table quickly. . . . You've got to perform' " (Field notes, Blakemore Hotel). Despite the situated character of the rush, several cooks remarked that their reactions are "automatic" in that they do not consciously plan or control their emotions or behavior resulting from the demands made of them. They have incorporated the response to the rush into their behavioral repertoire. This image of the rush is similar to "flow" in leisure (Csikszentmihalyi 1975). Cooks can be so caught up in the tempo and rhythm of their work that all else is transfixed. Just because these experiences respond to external forces—an interaction between self, other, and context—doesn't mean that they are consciously willed. Cooks remarked:

> [A rush is] like a beat to music where you get a beat and start working with it, and bang, bang, food's being done automatically. I get a song in my head, and if work's going great, I can hear that song in my mind and work with it.
>
> (Personal interview, Owl's Nest)

> I concentrate totally, so I don't know how I feel. I'm not even conscious of it. It's like a third sense just takes over.
>
> (Personal interview, La Pomme de Terre)

> It's kind of like walking on air. You don't really know what's going on, and for some reason you're in a good mood. Things get done.
>
> (Personal interview, Stan's)

Of course, emotions can be manipulated by the self—commodifying one's feelings (Hochschild 1983; Gordon 1981). People can make themselves angry; happiness can be encouraged as when one is admonished to smile in order to get in a good mood, as service workers know well. While the public presentation of emotion is not as relevant in the kitchen backstage, something similar happens when cooks "pump themselves up" and experience an adrenaline rush. They brace themselves for the "flow" experience.

CONSTRUCTING WORKDAYS

Through the interplay of external forces, behavioral demands, and emotional responses, elements typical of the rush may characterize a day as a whole. Most days have a temporal routine that workers expect. Yet, circumstances can give a day a distinct character (e.g., a crash near a trauma center, an art gallery opening, a community festival, or a blizzard). Cooks are dissatisfied with days that are either too pressured and disorganized or too slow and routine. This distinction speaks to the degree to which workers can step back from their work and gain control over time: what Erving Goffman (1961b) speaks of as the distinction between underdistancing and overdistancing. Too much pressure (a too demanding tempo) does not permit cooks enough role distance from their tasks; mistakes take on exaggerated importance because time does not permit the cooks to step back and regroup, and because they find it difficult to claim that the error does not mirror their true ability. Continuing a rhythm, operating in a rapid tempo, cannot be easily altered if customers are to be satisfied. Other days prevent cooks from demonstrating their professional competence by not allowing for a rhythm and tempo of work. Little is demanded, and consequently the cook's attention is not firmly tethered to the job—cooks are overdistanced. They search for the entertainment that a slow pace cannot provide (Sutton and Rafaeli 1988). Too many side involvements compete for attention, coupled with insufficient organizational demands.

PRESSURED DAYS

To appreciate how demands exhaust and frustrate cooks, consider a day destined to be remembered without fondness at Stan's Steakhouse:

> Stan's had recently been featured on a local television show, which publicized their high-quality steaks and reasonable prices, and announced a discount on steaks for customers who mentioned the offer. The restaurant was overrun with customers. On previous Saturday nights they had served about 400 customers, now they had over 600. The rush lasted all evening (from 6:30 P.M. to 10:30 P.M.). Al was the head cook that evening, and Evan was a fellow cook on duty.

AL, grumbling: Bad night, tonight.

GAF: What's the matter?

AL: Can't get it together.

AL (to Evan):   Do you know what time it is, Evan?

EVAN, joking that the
evening has just
started: Half past six. (Actually it's 7:45.)

AL (to Evan):   That's all the steaks I'm putting on tonight.

AL (to another cook):   Ready to push the panic button, Gene.

AL (to everyone):   This is unholy. There is no God. . . . This is the pits.
           . . . This is a losing battle, man.

Throughout the evening the cooks and the servers are upset and become
more upset whenever steaks are returned. For much of the evening there is a
thirty-five-minute delay on orders.

I ask Lew, the fourth cook, about the evening. He says: "It's terrible.
None of us are prepared. Everything's coming in at the wrong time."

(Field notes, Stan's)

Anger and tension fill the kitchen. Cooks are sarcastic to servers, and
servers bother cooks for their dishes. No one has the time to do things
right or be polite. The customers received an odd bargain: inexpensive
steaks, sloppily prepared. When one cannot maintain control, reestab-
lishing it is difficult until a lull allows the staff to regroup. That night,
the lull never came. One cook claimed frustrating nights like that are
what he dislikes about cooking: "Being so busy you can't put the food
out [well]. . . . You've got to put the food out so fast, you don't care
what it might taste like. You put it out for what it looks like. Maybe
sometimes you might forget something, put it in there late. You might
have to cook it fast, like under a broiler [not in a stove]" (Personal interview, Stan's). On these nights cooks do not think of themselves as
professionals—as *cooks*—although they must continue to cook. Errors
in timing, such as problems of synchronization or judging duration,
tend to cause this loss of momentum and consequent frustration (Adler
1978), particularly when problems are serious or repeated:

A waitress gives a duck to the wrong person. Apparently two people had
ordered duck, and she had apparently not properly informed the cooks, so
their timing was thrown off. The cooks are angry and insult her after she
leaves the kitchen.

(Field notes, Owl's Nest)

The cooks have had a difficult evening with several mistakes. For instance,
an order of lamb *en croûte* is burned but is still served—something that
would normally not be tolerated. The problem was that cooks had to pre-

pare food for a reception for seventy, a wedding rehearsal party for thirty-four, and fifty customers. The chef tells me that they could not give individual attention to each dish, adding "Haute cuisine and large parties don't mix."

(Field notes, La Pomme de Terre)

Cooks make external attributions for bad nights, keeping their sense of competence intact (Nisbet et al. 1973). They provide accounts for their "misuse" of time. Sometimes, however, a discrete problem cannot be easily identified, and the frustrations of a bad night and poor timing are expressed through generalized anger, a stereotype of culinary life (Orwell 1933, p. 109).[7] The temporal strains provide justification for anger, a justification used after the fact with which all sympathize. Temporal strain is not only a cause but also an account. This strain leads to a work environment in which emotions are fueled and then legitimated.

Emotion in the kitchen or other work spaces need not be defined as negative. The idea of catharsis readily justifies anger. One cook, who routinely rages, argued anger is valuable: "To let your emotions out, but not on somebody. . . . If something happens where you burn your hand or you forgot to put something on, that irritates you. 'Damn!' It's good to get that first emotion out, to get that out of the way, so that you can go on to the rest of the night. If you don't let it out and you let it bother you, it's going to build up, and all of a sudden you're going to burst and it's going to be worse" (Personal interview, Owl's Nest). Anger permits time to be controlled: permitting workers to "go on to the rest of the night." By expressing anger, one closes a frustrating event and reestablishes rhythm. Whether this catharsis is effective is less significant than that it is believed to be. Anger is seen as a means of achieving temporal stability and coping with the behavioral reality of the kitchen. Of course, while anger may have therapeutic benefits for individuals, it also raises collective tension and may be contagious. What may preserve the temporal order for one may undermine it for others.

SLOW DAYS

Just as days that are too stressful are disliked, so are those when "nothing" happens. Boredom is an affront to workers and a misuse of time (Molstad 1986). The Owl's Nest, which expects about 100 for a busy lunch, may have as few as 30 customers. Some evenings La

Pomme de Terre draws only 20 diners, whereas on a good night they serve 75. At first, slow days are pleasant in that stress is not palpable. Yet, on these days the restaurant underutilizes cooks and does not permit them to feel that they have earned their wages. Cooks dislike "standing around, waiting for something to happen" (Field notes, Owl's Nest) and joke about the absence of customers, as in this exchange between Paul, the head chef, and Eddie, the maître d':

PAUL: Are we up to forty [reservations] yet?
EDDIE: Maybe if you pray real hard. . . . Does anyone have any cards?
                                                        (Field notes, Owl's Nest)

The inability to fill one's time with a productive activity is frustrating. This is different from break times, which are inherently satisfying. In slow periods, there is no work to which to return; the pleasure of leisure is its contrast with work (De Grazia 1964): "When you're standing around for an hour and a half with nothing to do, you really feel useless. 'What can I do, Paul [the head chef]?' 'Oh, gosh, nothing.' That's what I don't like, the standing around. I have better things to do" (Personal interview, Owl's Nest). At these times no external demands impinge. Slow days are not only boring, but cooks also claim that their cooking suffers. One might imagine that on a slow day, cooks would devote time to insure that each dish is perfect. A slow day might be seen as a luxury to a cook who is often so overworked that dishes are sent out without the care necessary for competent performance.

Yet, cooks do not experience slow nights this way. On these occasions the cook stops "thinking" and may make foolish mistakes, given the disparity between the time available and the small amount of work to be done: "Now that I'm working the day [shift] I enjoy an occasional slow day, but if it's slow too much, I find I get bored. No tension, no overloading. It's like all your circuits go out. You don't know which way to turn. You can't think. You become angry, that clouds over. You're in a bad mood, and how can you be an efficient worker then?" (Personal interview, Blakemore Hotel). On slow days cooks are unprepared for the required work. Each order starts a new rhythm; cooks are not in sync and do not have a satisfying emotional relationship to the task. Shifts that either are too pressured or have too few occupational challenges are equally disliked. Workers do find work satisfying—when they help set the pace and when the pace is suitable (Hodson 1991).

OPTIMAL DAYS

Like all workers, cooks strive for pleasant employment. Organizational demands and time should mesh to create satisfying working conditions. As cooks describe it, the key is for a day to be "smooth"—with a steady rhythm, permitting them to stay ahead of orders, without errors of judgment or miscommunication (Whyte 1948, p. 3). When I questioned cooks as to what made a day "good," they invariably cited temporal considerations, exemplified by *smoothness*, part of the felt character of "goodness":

> No problems. Everything goes *smoothly*. Preferably moderate to busy. If you're happy with each plate, each dish that goes out.
>
> (Personal interview, La Pomme de Terre)

> If it's a good, even flowing. You don't get hit at once, and the food you put out you're satisfied with. That makes a good day. The other Monday is a perfect example. I was working, and we got ninety people. That was totally unexpected. When I came in, there were twenty-some in the book. I thought it was going to be a slow night, and we ended up [with] almost one hundred people. Everything went really *smooth* and really nice. We were never behind. I felt really good.
>
> (Personal interview, Owl's Nest)

> Easy. Don't make any mistakes. . . . You get everything done. You still feel good after. You've got all your preparations done. Then as all the food [orders] come in, you just put it out. Everything just goes nice and *smooth*.
>
> (Personal interview, Stan's)

> When things don't go wrong. When things go *smooth*. I like to be busy. It's too boring when it's slow.
>
> (Personal interview, Blakemore Hotel)

Pace and "flow" are central to satisfaction. Cooks prefer evenings when they discover that time has passed; *unexpectedly* to find that it is time to leave is desirable. When work is too slow, one is continually reminded of clock time; "flow" is absent (Csikszentmihalyi 1975). One is reminded of the challenging physical and social conditions of the kitchen and of the lack of autonomy and freedom. Time is transfixed when work goes well but has an omnipresent, oppressive character when there are too many or too few external demands.

The idea of "too much" or "too little" to do is a social construction, depending on the cook's mood, preparation, and attention. One cook contrasted two days when he was cooking: each night was busy, but one went well and the other poorly:

LARRY: During the whole night I really felt good. I felt I was doing a good job. Things were really going well. It was really funny because right after the rush I was cleaning up and Phil [the owner] came back and said, "Larry, everything really looked good tonight." The products really looked good. Everything I did that night was really sharp. I guess everything was the way I want it, the way I was satisfied, the way I would like to see it. The things that were fried were golden, had a really nice color to it. The sauces were reduced down real nice, a good product. You're at your best, you're at your peak. I felt really good about it when he came back and said everything really looked nice tonight. Bingo. That's my paycheck. I went home and I felt really good.

GAF: What about last night?

LARRY: I had other things on my mind. . . . I wasn't concentrating on work. I had a lack of ambition. We got hit really hard. That was the hardest I ever got hit since working here. Tickets at once. There were a lot of orders where you're not ready for. Sweetbreads frozen that you have to thaw out and cook, and cut all these garnishes. You can't prep up for them because you don't use so many of them. You get a couple orders like that, and you have to stop and take time for that and things go awry.

(Personal interview, Owl's Nest)

This extract suggests the relationship between the external features of work life—here, timing of orders—and the psychological and emotional character of the worker (mood, personality, sense of self-worth). The quality of a day depends both on temporal demands and the situated self.

THE TEMPORAL ORDER OF THE DISH

Up to this point, I have ignored the production of specific dishes, but production work is primarily concerned with creating objects *on demand*. Timing in restaurant kitchens depends not only on the need to control the flow of orders but also on the production of individual dishes. As any home cook can attest, preparing food is a challenge. This is difficult enough when cooking one thing; but the problem of synchronicity may seem overwhelming when preparing a meat, a vegetable, and a starch.

DONENESS

When home cooks use a recipe, time is simple. The recipe specifies the period and temperature that food requires (Tomlinson 1986). One sets the heat and the timer, and the food "takes care" of itself. If one wishes to check on a dish, one can take a bite, knowing that the informality of the serving occasion does not risk complaint. In restaurants what is done to the food is less important than what *appears* to have been done (Orwell 1933, p. 79). Restaurant cooking demands impression management. Whatever happens in the kitchen, the customers must be none the wiser if they are to enjoy their food and the restaurant is to retain their allegiance.

Yet, despite the emphasis on appearance, a parallel belief in perfection exists. Cooks claimed that each dish has a peak of perfection, and it is their responsibility, as much as the structure allows, to reach that peak: "When you're working with seafood, there's a time where if it's in too long, it's overcooked. If it's not in long enough, it's undercooked. There's that time right in the middle where you have to have it, in order to have it taste really good. Especially with fresh fish. You can get a piece of fresh fish right off the boat and still flip it in your hand and run it all the way to the restaurant, and if that person overcooks it, it's wrecked. It's not a fresh piece of fish. In a sense, it has to do with perfection" (Personal interview, Owl's Nest). Even though cooks believe that there exists a moment that food is at its best, they also recognize that there is a *temporal window* in which food is of acceptable quality, which, depending on the dish and the pressures of the kitchen, may be relatively wide or narrow.[8] Most events have a temporal window, but few have a single moment of acceptability. Otherwise, few patients would survive anesthesia or astronauts would survive liftoff.

No one technique can determine whether a dish is properly cooked, overdone, or underdone. Several strategies serve for judging the proper duration of preparation, depending on cooking skills, restaurant traditions, the amount of work pressing, and the dish. In determining whether dishes are ready, cooks rely on timing (internal and external clocks), taste, smell, sight, touch, and, occasionally, sound. Together these senses suggest how temporal demands are cued.

Timing.   Even when busiest, cooks never use timers and rarely depend on clocks or watches. Trade-school students are often warned about relying too heavily on external clocks (Fine 1985). The illusion is that cooks just "know" when food is ready: an internal clock ticks with practice. The journalist A. J. Liebling (1986, p. 111) speaks of the "thermotactic gift" and asserts that "the good cook, like the good

jockey, must have 'a clock in his head.' " The cooks I observed also
cooked on automatic pilot:

> Once you learn your equipment, it's almost like a sixth sense. All you have
> to do is look at it, and you know if it's done or not . . . by subconsciously
> timing it. You know roughly how long something's been put in, and it's
> done. There's very seldom I ever check.
>
> (Personal interview, Owl's Nest)
>
> It's just something that clicks in you. It's been so long, you better look, and
> you open up the oven and check it out.
>
> (Personal interview, Blakemore Hotel)

Inexperienced cooks prepare food by the clock because they lack experience and confidence, marking them as novices. Too great a depen-
dence on reading a clock provides the *illusion* of control. Since equipment may be variable, constantly checking a clock, while ignoring
what is happening in the stove, is ineffective and may lead to failure.

For many occupations microtiming is not as crucial, but rarely is
timing ignored. Just as jockeys have a mental clock, so must air-traffic
controllers, assembly-line workers, and emergency medical technicians.
Seconds may make a difference. Professors, comedians, hawkers, and
other paid talkers must know how to space their words to be effective.
They need "timing." These talkers must have a sense of when their
time is up and how to get to the end of their allotted time having covered (or having *appeared* to cover) all that they wished. These acts of
timing are rarely based on formal clock time but on a sense of what
constitutes the "proper" length of time for the activity.

Occupations use different approaches in coping with clock time. For
instance, bakers and cooks do not view time similarly. Cooking is
more like an art, in which the ingredients are forgiving. Baking, in contrast, is closer to an exact science where precise amounts and times can
produce dramatically different results—the rise or fall of a cake depends on its time in the oven, even though bakers have some leeway, as
noted by a pastry cook: "Most of the things that I do are dictated by
recipes, and so they have their own time. . . . Some things are visual, as
far as cake goes, and every recipe gives you a range, but with those gas
ovens being the way they are, you still have to have the capability of
looking at it and checking it with a toothpick" (Field notes, La Pomme
de Terre). Although culturally similar, the two occupations—cook and
baker—contrast in their attitudes toward and use of time.

Taste and Smell.   As I noted in chapter 1 when I discussed the tricks of the trade, often what seems the most obvious technique of testing the doneness of food is not used. On its surface, knowing how food tastes should be critical to judging whether it is ready to be served; many home cooks operate on this principle. Yet, in commercial kitchens other cues must stand for taste. One cannot cut pieces of steak or pie to judge its progress: maintaining the customer's impression of the dish is critical. Other senses must substitute for the one that appears most relevant. Cooks do, in practice, taste some foods, particularly liquids such as soups, sauces, and dressings or dishes made in large batches, such as stews and vegetables. These foods can be tasted without the final display altered. As in Orwell's descriptions of Parisian kitchens, cooks use a finger as a tasting tool although they may also use a spoon—often without wiping it.

Some foods are judged by aroma although smell tends to be a secondary sense, supporting other judgments. Yet, on occasion smell may suffice: "I can tell a lot of what's in the ovens by the smell. You can smell when scallops are done. You can smell when you initially bake off the ribs. You can smell when that's done" (Personal interview, Stan's). Since the flavor of a food depends largely on its smell from inside the mouth (more than on the simpler sense of taste), external sniffing can provide usable cues, even if these smells are not as robust as those present when one consumes food. Anyone who has burned a batch of cookies realizes that at times smell can predict doneness, often too late.

Looks.   How food looks while being heated is an obvious and convenient clue, notably for those foods that dramatically change shape (e.g., souffles, noodles) or color (e.g., shrimp, eggs)—a technique that is also found at steel mills and pottery kilns. The material is its own thermometer. Fish is perhaps the foodstuff where visual change is most obvious. Raw fish is translucent; cooked fish is opaque. When sautéing thinly sliced fish fillets, one hopes to heat them until just opaque, not overcooked and mushy. Food to be "browned" is also visually inspected to insure the "brown" is "golden."

Not all foods change form when prepared; vision reveals knowledge only about a surface. Through experience cooks correlate their perception of the outside of the dish with the inside. Cooks value the consistency of this correlation.

Touch.   An outsider might be surprised at the importance of touch for working cooks. Touch seems an odd surrogate for time or taste, but just as some foods change color as they cook, others change texture. Cooks suggest, that like pianists, masseurs, and palpating specialists in internal medicine, they need "sensitive fingers" (Field notes, Owl's Nest). The role of touching food can hardly be overestimated:

> People would be appalled . . . if they saw touching of food. You're constantly touching; that's the only way you can tell if something is cooked. . . . You put it in [the pan] and you know the color on certain things, not everything. You have to touch and you have to feel. Texture. . . . How it bounces. It tells you a great deal. You can also tell if it's good or bad. If it's old or real fresh. . . . You just learn certain feels. Your nose may not pick it up, but just by touching you feel something different. . . . It may look just beautiful, a little bit of juice, and you may touch it, rub your fingers just to see how it is, and if it feels sticky, then it might be a little low or it may have cooled down or warmed up.
>
> (Personal interview, La Pomme de Terre)

Touch is particularly important in preparing steak. Customers have the right to request that their steaks, unlike most other dishes, be cooked as they choose without overstepping the boundaries of their role as client. Doneness is measured by the customer by the color of the meat in the center of the steak and its flavor and tenderness when chewed. How can a cook visualize the inside? Although timing is a clue, this is a challenge when many steaks are prepared simultaneously. In fact, cooks judge the doneness of meat by poking it, believing "you can feel tenderness" (Personal interview, Blakemore Hotel):

GAF: What do you look for in firmness?

DOUG: OK, [like they taught us] in cooking school, this is how they describe it when you want to know when a steak is done. This [the webbed area between thumb and index finger] is real soft, it's rare. If the middle of your arm, it's firm and that's medium, and if it's hard, it's well done.

(Personal interview, Stan's)

Touch more than any other technique of timing distinguishes commercial cooks from home cooks. Food has much to communicate to those who, through occupational socialization, can understand its messages.

Sound.   In culinary work, in contrast to automotive mechanics, plumbing, or piano tuning, the auditory dimension is of minor significance. Although a deaf cook might face challenges communicating with co-workers, the preparation of food itself would not be a major problem. Still, the head chef at the Blakemore Hotel told me that his kitchen "talks," and he meant this in more than a poetic way: "An instructor [in trade school] once told me, 'Let your kitchen talk to you.' If water is in the french fryer, you can hear it. Listen to what your kitchen is saying to you. . . . Is the fryer sizzling? Is something happening there?" (Personal interview, Blakemore Hotel). Another cook reported that he knows that veal *cordon bleu* is done when the cheese sauce bubbles (Personal interview, Owl's Nest). While sound plays a relatively minor role, cooks use whatever sensory information they can to control their work.

The dimensions of occupational skill reflect adjustments to the specific circumstances of the tasks. In fact, all work is "embodied" and requires adjustment to the physical reality of its environment. While cooking is partially cognitive, a worker would not be competent if the sensory messages were ignored. Whether we consider the auditory feedback of an audience, the sound of a drill, a bouquet's aroma, the touch of fabric, or the taste of cognac, the senses are key to all productive activities.

ORGANIZATIONAL TIME

Worlds of work are temporally ordered, and their order depends upon the reality of duration, the experience of time, the situated quality of tempo, coupled with demands from outside the occupational boundaries. Connections exist among external temporal demands, the performance of work, and the experience of that work. Felt emotion results from temporal demands—too much to accomplish in too short a time can provoke anger; not enough can bore; a fit between time and attention characterizes "flow."

As organizations control the linkage between time and task, they channel behavior and experience. The kitchen "rush" demonstrates how structure, emotion, and time interact. Although the kitchen rush is notable for its drama, all organizations create and channel temporal dramas, producing emotional reactions mediated by workers' moods. Workers' reactions result from how the sponsoring organization and the individual worker structure time.[9]

Throughout the chapter, like symphonic themes, I drew on Lauer's dimensions of periodicity (or rhythm), tempo, timing (or synchronicity), duration, and sequence. These are the building blocks of the temporal organization of work. We rely on a mix and a variation of these themes to create routine activity. No single tempo, for example, characterizes an occupation, but each occupation is characterized by tempo ranges and sets, and these patterns are channeled by external demands that produce emotion.

Occupations in which periodicity (rhythm) is stable—and, hence, central to the temporal analysis of that occupation—are those with routine tasks. Factory-line workers are the stereotypical example although breaks and breakdowns intrude even in their work. In most occupations workers are required ·to perform a variety of tasks and so, like cooks, have opportunity to construct their own periodicity. Craft work implies temporal control as well as decision-making autonomy. In contrast to rhythm, tempo refers to the speed at which tasks must be completed. The factory worker does not set the tempo, lacking temporal autonomy (but see Roy 1959–1960; Ditton 1979).

Synchronization demands a division of labor and connections among those divisions. Workers depend on co-workers; cooks depend on other cooks, pantry workers, and servers (Paules 1991; Whyte 1948). For dishes to be served, cooks need temporal coordination. The work is relational. For occupations that depend on group activity (e.g., surgical teams, theater troupes, bomber crews) synchronization is crucial, and the organization must structure work to reinforce such cooperation.

Sequence coordinates larger chunks of time: which tasks have priority? When faced with an array of tasks, which are selected for attention? Again, occupations differ on the autonomy of workers in making these choices against management demands. Still, the task constrains: cooks must prepare a dish before servers can present it; cooks must receive the order from the server first. This division of labor is sequential, rather than simultaneous. Yet, for some tasks, sequence hardly matters: who cares if the cabbage or carrots is shredded first for coleslaw, so long as they are mixed before the dressing is added. Sequence, like the other dimensions, depends on both the situated character of work and on the reality of the task.

Duration is often controlled by the external demands that impinge on the organization. Lectures end at someone else's bell; a soft-boiled egg waits for no one. Still, doctors can control the length of their examinations to some degree by withholding or adding small talk (Yoels and Clair 1994). Railroad men must make their trains leave and move at particular times and speed if the schedules of others are not to be endangered (Cottrell 1939). Duration can be squeezed if the tempo needs to be speeded, or it may be stretched if boredom is the alternative, the workers' recognizing limits to this stretching or squeezing.

Evidence from restaurants suggests that the organizational environment influences the temporal structure of work. The temporal structure of work is, in turn, tied to the emotional responses of workers and, through this, to the production of workers. While these linkages are mediated by the character of the work task and environment, these ties among structural demands, patterning of time, and lived experience are central to the understanding of occupations.

THREE

The Kitchen
as Place and Space

It is rush hour in the kitchen. Imagine a large room, and in it twenty or so cooks all busily at work, hastily coming and going in this gulf of heat. . . . to heighten our sufferings, all doors and windows are closed for about half-an-hour to prevent the food from getting cold. This is the way we spend the best years of our lives. But when duty commands one must obey even when physical strength fails. Our greatest enemy is coal.

—*Carème*

In the previous chapters I analyzed the doing of food preparation; here I focus on the organizational work that surrounds culinary activity. In all occupations work is surrounded by activities that belong *to* the workplace but are not *of* the work task itself. An occupational scene comprises more than its essential activity; it also includes that which surrounds this activity. The label of an activity is only part of what those in that job category are supposed to accomplish. When coupled with an organizational division of labor, with workers with other titles, relations among activities can become complex. The arc of work requires an array of secondary projects and personnel to support occupational accomplishment. Of course, what is primary for one occupation (e.g., cooking) is a secondary concern for another (e.g., serving). First, I ask how the equipment in the kitchen affects what cooks do, how cooks deal with occupational danger, and how the physical environment of the kitchen affects their behavior and attitudes. I then explore the relationships among the occupations that share the kitchen: chefs, cooks, waiters, waitresses, busboys, dishwashers, and potmen. How are the division of labor and differences in status negotiated in light of conflicting work projects? These practices are part of the structural arrangements that constitute an organization (Blau 1984, p. 11).

ENVIRONMENT AND EQUIPMENT

SPACE

Every activity is set within a physical space that constrains, channels, and encourages it (Fine 1991). The shape, size, ambiance, and equipment of a workplace affect which products will be manufactured, and how that production will be organized. Factories are built or renovated to provide for the spatial needs of a certain type of production, as are classrooms and operating theaters.

Restaurant kitchens are known for being small, nasty, cramped places in which a wrong move spells disaster. Because of the tight spaces, cooks need considerable discipline: "You move in one direction and time your moves to avoid physical conflict with those who work around and beside you. You anticipate such moves reflexively and a timing, co-ordination, and precision are achieved equal to that of a fine Swiss watch movement. If you are casual in your motions as a chef or cook or maître d'hotel or waiter, you're going to wind up with an awful lot of soup on the floor" (Claiborne 1982, p. 95). Close quarters provoke interpersonal tensions, just as the luxury of space permits easy impression management. Zones of comfort between co-workers are sacrificed in cramped spaces.

The kitchens that I observed differed considerably in size and shape. The kitchens of the Owl's Nest and Stan's were, like the stereotypical restaurant kitchen, small and inconvenient. The pantry area of Stan's was not visible from the stoves, cramping communication. At the Owl's Nest the tight quarters prevented servers from retreating to the kitchen, a circumstance acceptable to the cooks. Kitchen workers frequently bumped into each other, a cause of friction (Field notes, Owl's Nest). The kitchen of La Pomme de Terre was, in contrast, spatially luxurious—communication was easy, and waiters could lounge in the kitchen. The cavernous kitchen of the Blakemore Hotel was too large for efficient work, making communication difficult. Perhaps this was because the hotel was not doing as well as expected, and a larger staff might have made the space seem more reasonable. As at Stan's, cooks and pantry workers could not see each other at work, complicating co-operation.

Cooks, like other workers, accommodate themselves to spatial constraints, marking territories in which other workers should not intrude without permission unless absolutely necessary. Stoves are assigned to particular workers, and when this is ignored, as sometimes happened at the Owl's Nest, bitterness results. One's workplace becomes an extension of one's identity.

The spatial layout of the kitchen also influences the relations between cooks and servers. Servers were ordinarily not permitted into the kitchen of the Owl's Nest. Movement was difficult, and there was no standing room. Servers picked up dishes from a window between the kitchen and the dining room. At Stan's, the other crowded kitchen, servers entered the kitchen, but a large metal table divided the room. Servers stayed on the side of the table near the dining room door while cooks worked the stoves, grills, and fryers opposite. In La Pomme de Terre the kitchen was structured similarly with a long metal table dividing the cooks' working area from the area where servers picked up dishes. At the Blakemore both the stove and pantry areas had shelves on which the cooks and pantry workers placed dishes to be picked up by servers. Servers moved and congregated in a large central area.

In each restaurant the built environment separated cooks and servers. In each, additional areas were set aside for potmen and dishwashers. Space contributes to the division of labor, and, in some instances, distance precludes cooperation and increases friction. Every occupation is spatially situated, and the spatial arrangements channel the possibilities of emotional displays and limits the audience.

AMBIENCE

Victor Hugo once likened a restaurant kitchen to the devil's forge; others call kitchens "foundries." Such an extreme analogy would have been confirmed by many cooks I studied. Heat is oppressively part of kitchen life, particularly in the summer months, where, according to one chef, the ambient temperature reaches 120 degrees. The Blakemore chef remarked sarcastically: "That's what they say, if you can't stand the heat, stay out of the kitchen. It goes with the territory" (Field notes, Blakemore Hotel). One cook explained that he sometimes feels that he may pass out and always keeps a large pitcher of cold water near the stove (Field notes, Blakemore Hotel). He adds: "I sweat like a stuck pig. It just drains you and your temper gets shorter" (Personal interview, Blakemore Hotel). The heat not only is believed to have physical effects but also shapes behavior and emotion.

Along with heat come smoke and grease: a infernal trinity. Observing at Stan's I returned home reeking of grease. Grease fires regularly occur in restaurant kitchens. When food drops in ovens or on grills, the kitchen may fill with smoke, causing coughing fits. The kitchen shares with many factories a decidedly unpleasant atmosphere.

EQUIPMENT

Although humans are the agents of work, given credit for outcomes, we could not act as we do without tools, furnishings, and machines— the equipment of an occupation. These inanimate objects permit the worker to transform raw ingredients into a finished, processed product. Changes in technology alter the social structure and interaction patterns of the work (Finlay 1988). A cook in a barren kitchen cannot cook; he or she is helpless. Cooking reputations depend on equipment: knives, stoves, refrigerators, tables, pots, and pans.[1]

Of all the equipment in the kitchen most important and symbolic are knives. This centrality is exemplified in an account of a Japanese chef: "Oiled and stored in wooden sheaths, the long knives are forged at a high temperature, kept razor-sharp and cost around $100 each. The knives, he says, mean life to a cook. Another person is never allowed to use them" (Winegar 1982, p. 172). Most cooks preferred to use their own knives:[2] "If people buy their own tools, then they're going to take care of them better. I enjoy having my own set of tools. . . . I know how my knife operates. It has a different balance" (Personal interview, Blakemore Hotel). Cooks discuss the relative merit of their knives, analyzing whether stainless steel is better than carbon, whether it matters if knives are stained, and whether the balance of a knife is more important than the quality of the metal. For instance, the head chef at the Owl's Nest commented to a cook: "You want them to balance right, and they have to be good steel. They've got to feel comfortable in your hand." Cooks routinely oil and sharpen their knives. While there may be *relatively* little difference between types of knives, the quality of the knife and the cook's ability in using it typifies the cook and is a status marker. The only kitchen workers at the Owl's Nest who regularly used knives provided by the restaurant were pantry workers, the lowest status food preparers. Cooks were criticized for borrowing others' knives with or without permission. This emphasis on the quality of equipment reflects a hierarchy similar to that of film school (Mukerji 1978, p. 132), where "real" film makers use the best equipment, but student film makers do not. One's equipment is a mark of identity.

Although cooks have a special, personal regard for knives, other kitchen equipment, provided by management, is important as well. Cooks become frustrated when management forces them to work with poor-quality equipment, complicating their job, limiting what they can prepare, and lowering the esteem that others have of them. At each restaurant cooks complained about the equipment, notably at the Owl's Nest, an older restaurant with pretensions to high quality:

> The knobs on the stove burners do not turn properly; the only way to light a burner is to toss a match at it. Bruce comments: "I wonder what it's like to work over a good stove. One you don't have to use a match for." He adds sarcastically: "Sunday, Paul and I went over to a church to deliver a cake, and it scared me not to have to light a match to turn [the stove] on." Larry tells me: "It's terrible. We have the worst equipment. All of our equipment is twenty-five years old. That's some of the worst stuff I've ever worked on. The stove never lights. You have to light them by yourself. When you're busy and you have to turn a burner on and stop and get a match. When you're busy, every few seconds is valuable. In two seconds I can be in the cooler and half way out with something. But the burner didn't light, so the pan's not hot, so I can't cook. I have to stop and light the fire." When Paul comments about the excessive heat from the poor stove: "You think Phil [the owner] would get the hint," Bruce adds cynically: "He doesn't care. It's not close to his house."
>
> (Field notes and personal interview, Owl's Nest)

Cooks at other establishments have their own complaints. La Pomme de Terre lacked a double convection oven for making souffles; Stan's steam table was considered of poor quality, and the leaking steam pipes were a source of complaint at the Blakemore. Cooks are never satisfied, because better equipment can always make their lives easier. Yet, acquiring the most technologically sophisticated equipment can produce anxiety, as anyone who has attempted to master a computer can attest. Further, too much equipment threatens to de-skill the occupation, either in the view of management or in the psychological perspective of workers. At the minimum, new technology alters the basis of competence (Finlay 1988). I once asked a cook if the restaurant had a food processor; he held out his hands, scorning a need for such

"toys" (Field notes, Owl's Nest). A cook who can chop rapidly, efficiently, and without injury is esteemed. Some can even chop with a
knife in each hand. Thus, while one might imagine that cooks welcome
electric choppers, which can lighten their workload and prevent injury,
these machines are a decidedly mixed blessing. Cooks do not wish
equipment that looks nice (some reject copper pans, for instance) but
that facilitates their professionalism. The meaning of equipment depends on the needs of work tasks and status politics.

A DANGEROUS WORLD

Just as equipment can ease a worker's life, it can threaten it. Cooking
can be dangerous work—a danger not set by the choices of cooks but
by the structure and content of the tasks that they must perform. One
nineteenth-century physician claimed that there were more injuries in
the Parisian kitchens than in the mines (Herbodeau and Thalamas
1955, p. 71). Although few cooks claim that their work is among the
most dangerous, all recognized the real dangers in food preparation:
notably cuts and burns.[3] According to 1991 Occupational Safety and
Health Administration (OSHA) statistics, of one hundred workers in
eating and drinking places, 7.4 percent suffered on-the-job injuries,
with 2.9 percent involving lost workdays. One cook responded when I
asked about the hardest aspect of his job: "Probably the hardest thing
is putting up with cuts on your hands and burns on your hands and
being covered with food" (Field notes, La Pomme de Terre).

Yet, like many other workers, they are fatalistic about a reality that
they believe is unchangeable and part of the essence of their work: "A
lot of things you have to learn how to put up with. Burns, cuts, injuries. Those are the things that nobody likes, but those are the sacri-
fices that you have to make. You're going to get burned and you're
going to get cut" (Personal interview, Owl's Nest). This fatalism derives from working within an organization (e.g., Rubinstein 1973;
Haas 1974); yet, it is a fatalism tinged with pride—they can stand the
"heat" and do not have to leave the kitchen. Concentration can inocu-
late cooks although such focused attention is difficult to maintain con-
sistently. If injured, cooks must live with it; it is common to see cooks
bleed and work with open sores.

Fortunately serious injuries are rare. Only twice did kitchen workers
require medical attention during my four months of observation.

Humor was used to distance the workers from unpleasant realities, and these injuries were transformed into jokes: "Denver, the chef, tells me that 'we just sent Melissa to the hospital. She cut herself [with a dull knife]. Nothing too serious, at most a few stitches. [Then he jokes.] She won't be able to play piano again, but I don't know if she could before. Hardy-Har-Har.' No one in the kitchen seems upset by her cut, although they want to know how it happened. When Melissa returns the next day, her co-workers joke about it" (Field notes, Blakemore Hotel). Cooks recall and repeat "horror stories" of grisly injuries that have occurred in the kitchen—reminding us how narrative structures occupational memory. Such stories warn fellow cooks about the need for care and concentration. Many stories deal with cuts:

> Denver and Ron are talking about injuries fellow cooks have sustained. Ron describes one cook whose knife fell through his foot, but he had to continue to work because the restaurant was so busy: "When he took off his shoe at the end of the evening, his sock was just soaked in blood." Denver tells Ron about a cook whose knife slipped and split his stomach open.
>
> (Field notes, Blakemore Hotel)

> I worked with a kid who put his thumb in a cuber, and it took his whole thumb off. To me that would be one of the worst things that could happen. I could be standing here daydreaming like I would and move this knife up and down, and forget to move that finger back and lose the tip of that finger.
>
> (Personal interview, Owl's Nest)

A similar set of stories revolve around getting burned:

> The only thing that would scare me is if I'm carrying a bucket of real hot grease, and you happen to slip. The only reason I say that is because it happened to a friend of mine. We were going to [vocational] school, and he was carrying a hot bucket of grease, and somebody went out the door in front of him and let the door go, and it hit the pot enough just to get things sloshed, and it sloshed all over his arms from here down, and what could he do? He was holding a bucket of 350-degree grease.
>
> (Personal interview, Owl's Nest)

> The worst thing that happened to me was that steamer back there. It blew up on me one day. The worst thing about it, I knew that there was something wrong with it for months. Every day I told them there was something wrong. They never believed me. Finally one day, it was Sunday, I had dressing heating up, and I went to open it up, and this time it had filled completely with scalding hot water, and this was like a waterfall. I had hot burns. And finally it was like "now do you believe." They didn't get it fixed right away. I came back to work, and it still wasn't working.
>
> (Personal interview, Blakemore Hotel)

The combination of poor equipment, blamed on organizational apathy, and lack of concentration, sometimes blamed on anomie, leads to injuries—linking organizational decisions and individual traits. The potential for danger is omnipresent, and we forget about it in practice until something happens suddenly and dramatically that forces our attention to it, creating an organizational problem—and, occasionally, in some dangerous occupations, a social problem. Most workers have little control over the equipment they must use although they attempt, as best they can, to alter the equipment for their own ends. They must make do and must trust their co-workers to do them no harm (Haas 1974).

THE MESH OF KITCHEN WORKERS

One cannot understand an occupation without recognizing the circle of surrounding colleagues. Scott (1992, p. 10) defines organizations as "social structures created by individuals to support the collaborative pursuit of specific goals." Cooks work within a kitchen mesh in which collaboration is essential. How do restaurant occupations fit together—chefs, cooks, pantry workers, servers, potmen and dishwashers?[4] I postpone discussion of the relationship between cooks and managers until chapter 5.

The well-run kitchen is an improbable triumph of a rough division of labor in which workers collaborate to satisfy customers, alleviate tension in each other's jobs, and make a profit. The negotiated order in the kitchen demands that co-workers be cordial, or at least civil. Without such pleasantness, interpersonal sabotage can undermine the work for all:

> The waitresses have to be nice to the bartenders because we need our drinks fast. The bartender has to be nice to us [waitresses], because if our customers complain and it's his fault, [the manager] may blame him too. The bartender cannot serve his own customers if the busboy ignores his pleas for more ice. The busboy relies on the dishwasher for fresh supplies for the waitresses. The waitress cannot serve her customers efficiently if the cook is slow or forgets part of her order. The cooks are the least dependent on others, but they have to be nice to the waitresses to get the secret drinks we bring them from the bar. The waitresses have to be nice to the busboy to get our dishes and glasses and silverware on time. We need each other too much to get on top of each other. We all know that if one section doesn't come through the whole system will fall apart like a house of cards.
>
> (Howe 1977, p. 100)

To be sure, this is not unique to restaurants. Hughes (1971, pp. 294, 306–9) emphasizes that even highly "professional" occupations (e.g., a doctor) rely on alliances with lowly workers. Occupations are inevitably part of webs of interaction, ties that are not only technical but also social.

COOKS AND CHEFS

From one perspective, a chef is merely a more experienced cook.[5] No one starts their culinary life as a chef. Cooks receive entry-level positions and then, if competent and loyal, may be promoted. Eventually the cook may manage other cooks. Yet, despite the seamless connection between cook and chef, the two "occupations" have quite dissimilar characteristics.[6] The chef is the organizer, the manager of the kitchen, and the restaurant's creative force. With this comes higher status and salary. The restaurateur Vincent Sardi (Sardi and Gehman 1953) labeled chefs "the aristocracy of the business." The cook, in contrast, is the line worker who prepares food on a routine, quotidian basis—a manual laborer.

A common cliché in trade school and restaurant kitchens is that "a chef is many things." The chef must be a generalist while the lower-status cook may be a specialist. The cook may specialize in frying food, broiling steaks, or making salads; the chef should be able to do everything: keep a food budget, repair stoves, hire personnel, provide counseling, and know about food (Schroedl 1972, p. 185). One cook explained: "A chef is someone who knows all or most aspects of the kitchen. If the baker's ill, the chef can go over and bake some desserts or bake some bread. If the prep person is ill, the chef won't feel it's beneath him to prep vegetables or make potatoes. Sort of fill in the whole line. A cook is someone who would cook the soup, cook the bread, cook the vegetables. The chef should know one end from the other" (Personal interview, La Pomme de Terre). Although the cook is paid more than his staff (during the mid-1980s, at good restaurants in the Twin Cities, chefs earned about $30,000), he also has less job security. As in baseball, it is easy for the owner to fire his chef if his restaurant is suffering and blame the chef for organizational failures. The chef's job is always on the line. One chef contrasted cooks and chefs: "Chefs are a dime a dozen. Cooks have pretty good security. A cook could always work. [He says to a cook standing nearby:] You could walk out of here and find a job cooking tomorrow. A chef is a different story. Your security is thirty seconds. Every month they look at food costs. Your job is on the line every month" (Field notes, Blakemore Hotel). Because of management experience, the chef may be seen as overqualified for many jobs that cooks could fill. Finding a *position* as a head chef is harder than simply finding *work* as a cook. I met only one cook who had ever been a chef; he "demoted" himself because of the pressure and hours of being a chef.

The most important skills that distinguish chefs from cooks include creativity, personnel management, and organizational abilities. Together they constitute the chef's role.

Creativity. One cook modestly suggested that the fundamental difference between a cook and a chef is that "chefs can make something out of nothing, and a cook can't" (Personal interview, Owl's Nest). Another added, "I think a chef has more of a feel for cooking, and is more creative and artistic with food" (Personal interview, Stan's). A third elaborated that creativity is not necessary for a cook: "It depends what you want to be. If you want to be a chef, creativity is very important. If you want to be a cook and work in a kitchen and do labor, you don't need to be creative; you need to do what you're told to do" (Personal interview, La Pomme de Terre). Cooks are creative in some measure, but if they create outside a narrow range, they must clear their vision with the chef. This varies in each restaurant: for example, relatively little creativity is expected at Stan's, much more at La Pomme de Terre. The creation of new dishes, tastes, and flavors is required of chefs whereas novel placement of food is often left to cooks—with the chef glancing quickly at what is served. Culinary creativity contributes to "the authority to know" (Mukerji 1977)—the granting of decision-making autonomy. Chefs achieve this through their office while cooks must negotiate for this right, and only certain cooks are granted this privilege.

Personnel. In most restaurants the chef has the day-to-day responsibility for managing the kitchen staff, including pantry workers, potmen, and dishwashers, and typically a house manager or maître d' is in change of servers and bartenders. As described above, an effective kitchen is characterized by cooperative workers, but pressure makes this climate hard to achieve. Chefs believe that a significant part of their managerial responsibility is to keep their employees happy:

These people [cooks] need stroking. You can't constantly put them down. That hurts them worse than a punch in the nose. You need a blend [of praise and criticism].

(Field notes, Blakemore Hotel)

GAF: What is the most difficult thing about your job?

PAUL: The people, the employees. Having to know each one of them inside and out. That's where psychology can come in. How to handle every person which has a different personal makeup.

(Personal interview, Owl's Nest)

The cook's focus is the food, but becoming chef involves new demands and requires new skills, in which he or she has little training. From the line they become management and face problems akin to those foremen who are promoted from within the ranks.

Organization.   A chef organizes the kitchen. While the cook focuses on limited tasks, the chef is responsible for a wide range of activities. Chefs "orchestrate," much as symphony conductors do; within the kitchen they are the decision makers and negotiators:

A cook cooks and a chef chefs. The chef is the synchronization of the transformation of the kitchen. He blends all the cooks together, all the different departments. The pantry and the lines and the banquets. Making sure that the assembly line comes together, the proper timing and all.

(Personal interview, Blakemore Hotel)

There is a lot of difference between a cook and a chef. The cook has the responsibility of this is what I must do today. The chef says today the first thing I do is go and look into my cooler. I see what condition it's in. Do I need any supplies there? Does it need to be cleaned? I go in and check the line. I ask the cook how everything is today? Have you any problems? Ask everybody down the line what they need. I set my schedules up for the day, my buying for the day. Special party is coming up for this weekend, is there anything I need? Special things to do. Anything special I want to create today. Is there a special customer coming in today? . . . The chef is the overseer, creator, supervisor.

(Personal interview, Owl's Nest)

Not having responsibility for cooking, the outcome of that work remains the chef's responsibility. Although controlling the staff, like any manager, the chef is at their mercy. Their doings determine others' judgments of his or her competence. Like all supervisors and foremen his or her reputation depends on underlings. Despite being a hired worker, he or she is expected to be entrepreneurial in dealing with organizational challenges (Smith 1991).

Working with Food.   In contrast to chefs, cooks are food handlers. One chef reported that "ideally a chef shouldn't really have to handle a knife very much." Cooks realize that the preparation of orders is their responsibility. Cooks expect the chef to be present when needed. They became discouraged at the Blakemore, in part because of the perceived unwillingness of the head chef to prepare food in a period of staff cutbacks. This chef defined himself as an executive chef, rather than a working chef, and preferred to avoid routine cooking, generating resentment among his staff. The cooks watched him arrive late and felt that his "visible absences" indicated that he didn't care about his job. Mere presence is a prime symbolic indicator of commitment. One cook complained:

> Denver came in late as usual. We started to do these deli platters. They had [a noncook] do these platters, and he had never done them before, and they looked like garbage. [The mayor and a local foundation] were having lunch there. [The mayor] said, "I'll start my speech early because the food is so terrible." He was joking, but really! Today is one of the busiest days of the year; [Denver] came in at 11:15, and said how far are we behind. It's like he doesn't want his job anymore. He's going out of his way to screw up. . . . He's got to realize he's got to work, but he doesn't. . . . How did he know that things would be OK. He didn't call. How did he know that the restaurant didn't blow off the face of the earth. That would be the best that could happen. Where is he now? I can't stand it. . . . It makes us look like fools.
> (Field notes, Blakemore Hotel)

While the chef's absence might not have mattered much if the cooks felt an attachment to the hotel and were not stressed because of staff cutbacks, without this emotional support it was a major complaint. This cook reminds us that despite complaints, not looking "like fools" is important to workers. A sense of personal satisfaction comes from doing the job well, even if the organization and conditions of work are despised.

Even when this chef was present, cooks did not perceive him as willing to help. He explained to me while cleaning mushrooms: "I'm an administrative chef, but I do work a $3.35 an hour pantry cook could do" (Field notes, Blakemore Hotel). With that attitude he was loath to share this work, an attitude justified in terms of his formal responsibilities. The organizational chart meant more to him than a sense of community. Rather than being another cook with more authority and knowledge, this chef was a hotel executive who happened to oversee the kitchen: "I don't think our chef applies himself as good as he could. He doesn't like to cook at all. . . . One day I think he even put it that he likes brains over brawn, which means he would rather sit and do his paperwork than sit and get his fingers dirty. [He'd] rather sit in his office. There are times when a chef can put on a white shirt [their uniform] and help out because of pure necessity" (Personal interview, Blakemore Hotel). This chef magnifies the strain between cooks and chefs—one between management (foremen) and labor when both come from the same labor pool. Cooks and chefs can be seen as members of the same occupation or as members of distinctively different ones. They can belong to the same community or to different ones. The problem at the Blakemore was that, in the context of organizational strain and financial hardship, the chef was not perceived as on "the same side" as the cooks: cooks felt that he had "sold out." He confronted the problems that factory foremen face when job categories shift (e.g., Gouldner 1954). Cooks' requests for help didn't have sufficient negotiating force to change his definition of their relationship. He was embittered toward the organization and not committed to his work—a perspective he shared with his cooks. Perhaps a chef more committed to his occupation and his employer, or cooks similarly committed, might have adjusted more easily. In less than three years that hotel had had four chefs. Shortly after the completion of the research, they had another.

THE STATUS STRUCTURE OF COOKS

A restaurant is a small organization and must be analyzed as such: through the lenses of organizational theory and small group dynamics. In the restaurants studied, no more than five cooks were at work at one time and often only two or three. As is true in any organization, cooks have distinct roles, in part due to experience, formal title, and the qualities of the individual cook.

In larger restaurants, such as hotel kitchens, one's tasks defines one's status (Willan 1977, p. 185). William Foote Whyte (1948, pp. 34–38) writes:

> Other things being equal, the employee who prepared the finished products tended to have a higher standing than one who worked at earlier stages of preparation. . . . [T]here is another factor powerful enough to overrule all these considerations—the prestige value of the materials used. . . . We found first that the stations themselves were socially ranked. At the top, of

course, stood the range where all the cooking took place. Here were the positions that were most highly paid and considered more skilled. . . . Toward the bottom were the chicken-cooking and vegetable-preparation stations. Vegetable preparation was under the supervision of the vegetable cooks, who worked at the range. . . . [T]he higher status workers worked on the higher status vegetables, whenever there were more than one being handled at a time. When they were all working on the same vegetable, the higher status workers handled later stages in the preparation process.

Whyte does not present sufficient ethnographic detail to examine how such fine status distinctions made sense to kitchen staff. One's materials apparently ennobled or contaminated one's public identity, in the classic model of "dirty work" (Hughes 1971). In my restaurants there were too few cooks for any meaningful divisions although some distinctions were evident.[7] At La Pomme de Terre preparation of side dishes (e.g., vegetables) and cold dishes (e.g., salad) was the domain of the most junior, lowest-ranked cook. In contrast, cutting large slabs of raw meat was regularly done by the head chef, symbolic work, to be sure. At Stan's Steakhouse the cook who grilled the steaks had more status than the fry cook, who had more status than the cook who worked the broiler, preparing fish and scallops. As one cook explained when I asked whether the fry cook or the broiler cook had more status: "The fry cook has higher status than the [broiler] cook on the other side. . . . He's got more control over the orders, and he works a lot more with the other [stove] cook rather than the broiler cook" (Personal interview, Stan's). The most senior cook had the right to choose where he wished to work; he always chose the stove. The second cook usually—but not always—chose the fry station. Tasks in the kitchen are apportioned on status although cooperation is common because of the small number of cooks and their friendliness.

Personal status differences are also evident. A new cook, like workers elsewhere (Van Maanen and Schien 1979; Haas 1972), is tested by colleagues. Novices must demonstrate that they are sufficiently trustworthy to be co-workers:

DIANE: I think I had to prove myself when Tim hired me.

GAF: Even though you had a lot of experience?

DIANE: It was listed experience that didn't mean shit when you were behind the stove. People want to see you work out. They don't care what you say, they want to see it.

GAF: What convinced them?

DIANE: That I just kept it up. I was fast. I just came right in, and no one had
           to show me how to do things; they knew I had experience because I
           could take the meat and portion it fast.
                                        (Personal interview, La Pomme de Terre)

This harmonious acceptance is not invariable. At the Blakemore certain cooks didn't trust others and would patronize them, as one said to
a foreign-born cook searching for some supplies: "Are you looking
after those eggs out there? Please go cook them. Don't let them burn"
(Field notes). This cook meekly returned to his station although the
criticizer misunderstood his legitimate purpose. A worker with collegial status is allowed more errors than one without such status—they
have sufficient idiosyncracy credits (Hollander, 1958) to deflect blame:
"Howie burns a plate of pine nuts he is cooking and jokes to Tim: 'I
think these nuts got a little overdone.' Tim doesn't seem upset. This
contrasts to Tim's anger when Lesley, whom he eventually fires, burns
a pan of cheese puffs" (Field notes, La Pomme de Terre). I do not suggest that Howie and Lesley were equally competent; they were not.
Yet, as in all things, one's social position has behavioral consequences,
even among those who are theoretically equals.

THE PLACE OF PANTRY WORKERS

Functionally cooks and pantry workers have similar work. Both are
paid to transform raw ingredients into finished products for which customers will gladly pay to eat. Both are under the authority of the chef,
but their status and training differences are enormous. Pantry workers
prepare cold foods, notably salads and desserts, whereas hot food, except toast and hard-boiled eggs, are prepared by cooks. Only two of
the four restaurants employed pantry workers: the Blakemore Hotel
and the Owl's Nest. At La Pomme de Terre a pastry chef created
desserts, which waiters "dished out"—a mundane way to describe
such glorious creations. Salads were prepared by the junior cook working the *garde manger* (cold food) station. At Stan's lettuce and
coleslaw was prechopped and desserts were purchased from outside.
Both were served by waitresses. At the Owl's Nest and the Blakemore
pantry workers prepared salads and apportioned prepurchased desserts.
In sharp contrast to the largely male cooking staff, seven of the eight
pantry workers at these two restaurants were female.

These workers were not extensively trained. One pantry worker was
a high school student; a second was marginally retarded. Only one had

any post-secondary training. These women would not have been hired
as cooks had there been openings, and none of the cooks had previously worked in the pantry. As the head chef at the Blakemore explained: "[At] some places the pantry will handle everything that is
cold. Here they will not prepare anything for banquets or cheese plat-
ters. They don't have the training. They will not [cook] anything [to be
served] cold, except eggs. They are not doing the canapés, but, of
course, they have their own work" (Field notes, Blakemore Hotel). His
perspective was underlined by comments by several pantry workers
who explained that I didn't really want to study them because they
knew nothing about cooking. They performed their jobs but felt that
these were quite different than cooking—their work was manual labor,
a blue-collar, feminine occupation in contrast to more "professional"
male work. Pantry work rarely connected to the work of cooks. If
everything was proceeding normally, the cooks would ignore the
pantry (see Whyte 1948, pp. 57, 61). Cooks and pantry workers had
segmented their occupational domains and divided status accordingly
(Abbott 1988).[8]

Although cooks and pantry workers shared the kitchen and both
prepared food, no one would claim that, by any definition, they were
doing "the same thing." Each occupation had its own "career," and
each had distinct occupational ideologies.

DOING THE DISHES

As Everett Hughes notes, virtually every high-status occupation has
low-status occupations surrounding it. Although cooking cannot make
the status claims of law or medicine, cooks, like lawyers and doctors,
require an "alliance . . . with the lowliest and most despised of human
occupations" (Hughes 1971, p. 306). In restaurants this means dishwashers and potmen, who clean half-consumed meals and burned,
caked-on food from dishes and pots. As one cook explained, in the tradition of Hughes: "At hotels there is a very definite class structure.
Dishwashers are the bottom of the ladder. They're the backbone of the
kitchen" (Field notes, Blakemore Hotel).

These secondary occupations provide employment for those who
are not easily employable elsewhere: newly landed immigrants (often
undocumented Latin Americans and Asians), the mentally handi-
capped, the mildly mentally ill, and the physically challenged. It is part
of the dual labor market. While some of the dishwashers are "nor-

mal," or not defined as other than normal, many are in protected categories.[9] The restaurant industry provides a service for the American economy: providing what some consider human "refuse" the opportunity to deal with culinary refuse. These workers receive modest wages for their onerous and unattractive work.

When two groups of workers are mutually dependent, have different statuses associated with their work, and are from divergent social backgrounds, accommodations are needed. These permit cooks to engage in friendly patronization toward these lower-status "dirty workers": just as culinary workers may themselves be dirty workers in the houses of princes and the cafeterias of schools.[10] Further, dirty work may have its own division: staff distinguish between potmen and dishwashers at the Blakemore Hotel and the Owl's Nest. Although both groups had low status, the potmen had less status because they had to clean off more food by hand: they dealt directly with pollution (Douglas 1966).

In their flexible and informal kitchen organization, cooks had leeway to order the potmen and dishwashers, and these lower-status workers obeyed, even though taking such orders was outside their job description. These "status claims," beyond the formal chain of command, are expected and need no extended negotiation, reminding us that status work translates into physical labor:

> Diane asks Gus, the dishwasher-potman, to scrape asparagus for her, which he does.
>
> (Field notes, La Pomme de Terre)

> Mel, the day cook: "Ray [the potman], why don't you peel a couple dozen more potatoes, so we can cut them up for french fries tomorrow." Ray does as he is asked.
>
> (Field notes, Owl's Nest)

This differs from a simple request for cooperation—although it involves that as well—in that the requests always flow from cook to washer. The dishwashers and potmen never requested help of the cooks. Whereas cooks enjoy free time and carve "temporal niches," they become upset when they see the washers take breaks and often request that these workers do *something*, even if unrelated to their jobs. Professionals have temporal discretion not allowed to manual laborers. Their status gives them the right to interfere with the work lives of others in ways that would offend them if they were on the receiving end:

Tim, the chef, says to Gus, the washer: "Gus, I'm gonna find you something to do. You're making me nervous. Why don't you take out some of the bottles."

(Field notes, La Pomme de Terre)

Jon, a cook, says to Ray, the potman, after having him bring a towel: "Just trying to keep you busy, Ray." Ray jokes: "I'll throw the towel at you." He doesn't.

(Field notes, Owl's Nest)

Dishwashers tend to be pretty flaky individuals just because people don't consider it a very pleasant profession. People wash dishes who can't do anything else. . . . You do have to see that they have something to do.

(Personal interview, Minneapolis chef)

The right to make demands of these washers also permits cooks to be nasty in ways that are unlikely between cooks who regard each other as status equals. Admittedly, washers and cooks often were friendly, and cooks would occasionally make steaks and other food for the washers; however, certain forms of joking would not have been possible if the status differences were not solidified:[11] "The bell on the stove rings, indicating that the rolls are ready. Bruce, a cook, tells Dean, a potman, that he should get the rolls out of the oven. Dean responds jovially: 'It's time to leave. Punch me out, Bruce.' Bruce jokes somewhat nastily: 'I'll punch you out if you leave.' On another occasion Bruce snaps a towel at Dean's buttocks" (Field notes, Owl's Nest). A similar status claim is evident in criticism of these potmen:

Gordon is angry because he cannot find his bread hook and yells at Cal, a potman, who he thinks has misplaced it. Cal responds in some way, to which Gordon says: "I don't want to hear any more smart-ass." Cal: "I'm just telling you." Gordon (angry): "This is a restaurant. I'm not going to play games." Later another worker finds the hook, although it is never clear who, if anyone, misplaced it. Gordon restates: "I don't like people being a smart-ass."

(Field notes, Blakemore Hotel)

Dean, the pot washer, accidentally closes the cooler door on Jay, a pantry worker. Dean apologizes to Jay, who remains annoyed: "I didn't know you were in there." Jay snarls: "Next time I won't notice your face is in there."

(Field notes, Owl's Nest)

Such talk would be unlikely among those who considered themselves to reside in the same status universe (cooks, pantry workers, and servers). The washers had a different status in the kitchen, and they were thought of as fully expendable and replaceable, even though responsible cleaners may be harder to find than responsible cooks. These are quintessential dirty workers, necessary for operating the establishment but functionally nonpersons.

SERVING FOR A LIVING

The activity most associated with a restaurant is, with the exception of cooking, serving. Virtually all restaurants—with the exception of some cafeterias and automats—have a staff whose job is to serve food to waiting customers.[12] Typically, at least in the more elaborate restaurants, food preparers are not servers. Yet, because cooks and servers are so interdependent, they must negotiate an effective working relationship (Paules 1991, p. 86). The two sets of workers have a different *occupational focus* despite their propinquity. Cooks work on food; servers work with customers. Cooks are product oriented; servers are people oriented. This specialized division of labor with two groups of experts in an establishment is rare organizationally—it would be as if one never met one's surgeon or always tipped one's tailor.

Those in the restaurant industry believe that cooks have higher public status than servers (Whyte 1948; Marshall 1986). Yet, servers—at least in popular establishments—earn more than cooks. Tips count. Few restaurants require servers and cooks to share tips. The claims of customers complicate power relations further. Customers demand prompt service, forcing servers to pressure cooks. Cooks resent these demands in that they do not benefit from this pressure; servers do—shaping their distinct monetary perspectives. Cooks are asked to give up their temporal autonomy so that others can benefit.

The stereotype is that cooks and servers hate each other and fight like cats and dogs. One writer describes them as "natural enemies," picturing a cook and waitress "punctuating their conversation with flying plates" (Koenig 1980, p. 46). Frances Donovan (1920) in her classic sociological study of waitresses witnessed a cook throw a plate of stew at a waitress. The current chef at the Owl's Nest told me that the former chef "would do anything he could to make it more miserable for [servers]" (Field notes, Owl's Nest).

Yet, at these four restaurants, this stereotype didn't fit well although the staff recognized tensions:

> Tom, a house captain, describes a French chef: "He was compelled to be the meanest s.o.b. in the world. He was compelled to be a tyrant. . . . He

yells at waiters, 'All you do is take the tip, you don't do shit.' . . . He had a
real condescending attitude."

(Field notes, La Pomme de Terre)

One cook generalizes: "The bulk of [waitresses] have no common sense and
make more money than they deserve."

(Field notes, Blakemore Hotel)

In turn, servers believe that cooks don't understand their problems, the
pressures under which they work, and that they are always "onstage."
Each occupation holds to its perspective, sparking anger when they
clash.[13]

While all occupational disputes are grounded in the conditions of
contact, examining the conflicts between cooks and servers can be generalized to other turf battles. Neighboring occupations create accommodations to provide perks. The underlying issue is autonomy—the access
to control of work domains and resources (Abbott 1988). As Coser,
Kadushin, and Powell (1982, p. 296) depict the publishing industry:

> Hostility and conflict are likely to emerge when there is intense interaction
> between people who occupy different positions and have different power
> resources, yet who are engaged in what each perceives to be similar tasks
> about which each claims equal competence. . . . [T]he power differences be-
> tween editors and agents lead to conflict, as both are engaged in serving au-
> thors. Editors have the power to accept or reject a manuscript, but agents
> can retaliate by insisting on strict definitions of terms. What is more, just as
> physicians complain about the "rule-bound" and "compulsive" behavior of
> nurses, complaints about the "bookkeeper mentality" of agents and their
> "fidgeting over commas and semantics" can be explained by resentment on
> the part of the powerful [editors] toward people whom they perceive to be
> of inferior status, yet who exercise control over their own activities.

Like editors with regard to agents, cooks are frustrated by the behavior
of servers—attitudes compounded by the reality that most servers earn
more. Both constrained by external clients, their occupational domains
abut, with each group viewing the other with annoyance. Cooks have
status while servers get the cash.

PLEASING THE CUSTOMER

The fundamental desire of the server is to please the customer (Prus
1987). Although servers have techniques of control, the customer controls the server through the power of the tip. Further, in the long run,
the customer has an equally potent weapon: patronage. Even those

servers who claim not to think about tips must satisfy their customers to have them return and recommend the restaurant to others. Given the distinct perspectives of cooks and customers, how can the server gain autonomy?

Studies of waiters and waitresses indicate that servers manipulate customers (see Mars and Nicod 1984; Butler and Snizek 1976; Butler and Skipper 1980; Donovan 1920; Whyte 1946; Paules 1991), even if this manipulation has limited effects (Davis 1959; Karen 1962). This need for manipulation derives from the authority of cooks, as well as from the demands of customers. Servers are at the "mercy" of cooks: "A waitress is held hostage by the cook. She is visible, the cook is not; she suffers the customer's ill will directly, the cook does not. Her very livelihood depends on the quality of food coming out of the kitchen, because the customer is yet to be born who feels obliged to tip gener-ously for a bad meal. A waitress can be efficient, courteous and atten-tive, but she cannot, for instance, make a stale roll fresh" (Smith 1984, p. 13). Cooks, in contrast, emphasize that no matter how well they cook, they receive no additional recompense and precious few compli-ments. Why should it matter to them? Why should they be altruistic for their co-workers, other than to support their own self-identity? Servers must ask, beseech, and occasionally insist that cooks redo dishes to meet the standards of their customers, requests that cooks usually accede to but sometimes without grace. Servers encourage cooks to recook food, especially when it means only additional cook-ing, rather than making the dish from scratch; whereas, cooks resist these demands. These requests are most likely when servers value their customers. Thus, customers perceived as unlikely to tip well, notably women and minorities, may receive poorer service.

Servers ask cooks to please their valued customers, even though this request creates tension:

JON, the cook, who calls out orders written by servers:	Ordering a liver medium.
PAUL, annoyed:	What?! Did [the server] ask if we had any?
MEL:	He's probably got the wrong flyer on his menu. That was on yesterday's.
PAUL, to Jon:	Why don't you ask him what's going on?
MEL, who speaks to the server:	The guy [customer] said, "I know I can get it if I ask for it."

The cooks make the liver, grumbling.

(Field notes, Owl's Nest)

Steffi, a waitress, to Al about baked potatoes she thinks are cold: "Are you going to heat these up?" Al responds, annoyed: "Are you serious?" Steffi answers: "I'm dead serious." Evan replaces the potatoes.

(Field notes, Stan's)

Ultimately, cooks do what the servers request, in part because they value interpersonal smoothness, in part because they recognize that the request is the customer's, and in part because servers can always complain to management.

In pleasing the customer servers not only demand special treatment but additional food. Food costs are a shared concern of chefs and management, not of servers. If more food increases one's tip, servers desire that larger plate as long as they avoid hassle from cooks or management. The question is how much one can reasonably "get away with." This involves negotiation, grounded in the time and place of the request.[14]

Some servers "protect" their customers by warning them not to order certain dishes, because they do not think the customer will enjoy it, because they don't wish to ask if the kitchen has run out, or because they think the dish is of poor quality. The first two justifications are understandable given the constraints of serving; yet, they annoy cooks in that the servers are seen as lazy. In contrast, criticizing food is seen as intolerable. Customers feel that this displays considerable trust and may increase tips (Prus 1987); for cooks and managers this represents a serious breakdown of "dramaturgical loyalty": if the servers do not think that the food their "team" produces is edible, what does this say of their teammates. These servers place their relations with their customers above the standing of the restaurant:

The cheesecake that the pastry chef made didn't set properly and had a runny middle. One of the captains explains this to Tim, the chef, at 9:30 P.M. (The servers had not been offering it on their dessert cart that evening but hadn't mentioned it to the chef.) Tim is really annoyed and says to me: "It kinda makes you wonder what they're doing out there. Sometimes it's intimidation; they're afraid to tell me that something's not servable." I ask Tim if the servers ever tell customers not to order something. He responds: "If someone recommends that [a customer not order a dish because it] wasn't very good, they wouldn't be here for five minutes. That's the worst thing in a restaurant. If they don't like it, they should come to me."

(Field notes, La Pomme de Terre)

As long as there are different reward structures for these two occupations, servers will be oriented toward satisfying the customer while cooks will attempt to maximize their own satisfactions. This is a general problem of organizations that double as production and service establishment: servers look outward, producers inward.

THE TIP

Few things so vex cooks as do tips, reminding cooks of the divisions between them as salaried workers and servers whose income depends on their interpersonal and entrepreneurial skills (Paules 1991). Cooks earn tips but do not receive them. Servers see themselves at the mercy of cooks, but cooks feel unappreciated, only cooking for their own satisfaction. Restaurant industry traditions are such that cooks never receive tips. Cooks are tripped by their "professional" claims: would one tip one's doctor? Some cooks were outspoken about this "injustice":[15]

> I think it would be a very good thing if the cooking staff did get their portion. Not necessarily in equal portion, but a fair portion of the tips. If you look at it in this respect, the dining room can blow up with all the waiters in it, and people can still come through the kitchen to pick up their food and eat it on the back steps. Without the kitchen, they'd all be eating bananas.
>
> (Personal interview, La Pomme de Terre)

> I think tipping should be abolished in the first place. Tipping is a very, very sore subject with me. . . . What I've seen for so many years, the cooks that were trained professionals have gone through an educational process to become good at what they're doing, worked hard, sweated, dripping, greasy, slimy for eight hours over a hot stove listening to a waitress bitch at them for $22.50 a night, when a waitress is walking home with $80 of tax-free cash that they're ripping off from the government.
>
> (Personal interview, Blakemore Hotel)

Not all cooks felt so strongly, and few demanded a full fifty-fifty split, but the tension derived from differential modes of payment touches the heart of this occupational friction. Servers emphasize that they work for less than minimum wage and that on a given night, week, or month, their tips may be minuscule.[16] They risk their security while cooks can count on a regular income. Only once was a tip shared: the cooks were asked to make a large order "to go" for a customer, outside their usual responsibility. The customer left a $15.00 tip which the waitress split with them—even though the work was all theirs. In fact, the cooks appreciated her gesture (Field notes, Owl's Nest).

Servers rarely refer to tips to negotiate with cooks; too many cooks would be offended by the underlining of their separate organizational roles. Such a blatant reference to the server's self-interest only occurs as a last resort of frustrated staff: "Doug apparently didn't see a side order on one ticket. When Amy, the server, tells him, he responds: 'Tell him I can't do it,' although he could if he wanted to. Amy snaps: 'Doug, you know, it's my tip.' Doug answers: 'If he wants to wait for another one [I'll make it]' " (Field notes, Stan's). More often, the discussion of tipping is framed as humor, allowing co-workers to speak in ways that otherwise would be considered illegitimate. Still, the discourse is sensitive, cutting close to the bone:

> Doni, a new waitress, is supposed to observe in the kitchen tonight so she can learn the portion sizes and see how cooks work. She comments that she will make minimum wage tonight with no tips. Paul, the chef, sarcastically responds: "That's all *we* get." Doni laughs nervously, unsure how to respond.
>
> (Field notes, Owl's Nest)

> Howie, a cook, jokes to Tim, the chef, that he should take them all out to the local bar that they frequent, because the night was so busy, and it was judged to go smoothly. Tim jokes: "I think the waiters should be taking us all out." He informs me that tonight the waiters will each make about $80 in addition to their hourly wage of $2.80.
>
> (Field notes, La Pomme de Terre)

These remarks, ostensibly humor, reflect interoccupational tension. Cooking is literally a thankless occupation in that satisfied clients cannot directly communicate their satisfaction. Backstage performers feel underappreciated, in contrast to those who receive thanks through applause and cash. Cooks, like upholsterers and dry cleaners, have only their salaries, occasional complimentary comments by management, and the esteem of their colleagues to provide satisfaction. Aside from being vexing in its own right, the pay differential symbolizes a lack of appreciation.

THE BATTLE FOR TEMPORAL CONTROL

In chapter 2, I emphasized how time and timing affect the occupational lives of cooks, but timing is also critical to the negotiations between cooks and servers. The server must supply food at its peak of readiness, the cook's goal as well. Contrary to the interest of the cook, who focuses on the food, the server must supply the food at just the moment that the customer is ready to consume it. As customers, we recognize how frustrated we become when rushed by a server, or when we must "wait" for food. We imagine ourselves to be the only persons in the restaurant and implicitly assume that cooks are preparing food for us alone. Management and servers wish us to embrace this illusion of organizational focus in that it makes us feel *special,* increasing the tip and the likelihood of repeated patronage (see Prus 1987). This illusion, however, increases the pressure on cooks and the strain between cooks and servers.

Ideally, cooks and servers are in continual communication with each other. Servers judge the progress of their customers in completing the previous course and then tell the cooks when to start preparing the next. This is easier when the course can be quickly prepared: salad or dessert. A main course that requires twenty minutes involves more guesswork: one must start preparing it while customers are sipping their soup. In rush periods other servers are demanding that their customers be served. How then is this problem—a problem of queuing—handled (Schwartz 1975)?

In three restaurants the structure of timing is simple: the server presents the ticket and then—approximately twenty minutes later—picks up the dish, in theory leaving the speed at which customers eat their food out of the process. At La Pomme de Terre life is more complicated. The server places the ticket on the counter when received; approximately seven minutes before the customer needs the main course the ticket is placed on the wheel by the server, and cooks prepare it. This builds flexibility into the system. Yet, this doesn't entirely solve the problem, because of different speeds at which customers are ready for their meals. Inevitably, the servers attempt to influence the cooks to have their meals at just the moment that they need it: even though they are uncertain of this moment in advance.

A strategy of servers is to ask when their food will be ready. The question brings that order to the cook's attention, hopefully speeding up their work. If the answer is not what the server wishes to hear, they can plead for the speedy preparation of their food: a technique, grounded in the belief in collegiality, common in organizations that depend on a linked division of labor. Alternately, servers can "work" the customer through disclaimers and accounts. This can be done by explaining in advance that the dinner will take longer than expected (i.e., providing a disclaimer [Hewitt and Stokes 1975]) or by excusing or justifying the delay (Scott and Lyman 1968). Alternately, servers can slowly clear the table, apparently decreasing the wait between courses, or they can simply avoid visual contact with those customers. Servers learn how to look in precisely the wrong direction when in their interest. If the food is to be ready soon and cannot be kept warm, the servers may attempt to bus the used plates of their customers early.

In addition, servers use impression-management techniques to speed their orders. A server might simply ask cooks to rush his or her order. When, at the Owl's Nest, a server asks for an order "downtown," the order is needed as soon as possible. At the least, servers want to know when the dish will be ready so they can work their customers. This demand can lead to friction: "Maggie asks Al about one of her orders on a busy night: 'Can you give me a rough estimate?' Al answers, somewhat nastily: 'When it's done.' Maggie, clearly annoyed, waits for a further response, but doesn't get one. When Maggie leaves the kitchen, Evan, a fellow cook, says sarcastically: 'Pretty rough.' When Maggie returns, Al says to Evan: 'Pretty rough estimate, huh, Evan.' Maggie looks angry but doesn't respond" (Field notes, Stan's). One cook comments in humorous frustration: "I swear sometimes if we had a gun, we'd turn around and just shoot them" (Personal interview, Blakemore Hotel), while some servers, no doubt, have the reverse desire. Aware of the potential resistance of cooks to requests, servers manipulate the tickets to get their food "early." When an order is received, cooks know that they have a certain amount of time to prepare the order. At the Owl's Nest servers were expected to write the time they submitted their orders, so that cooks would know when food was needed. Some servers systematically indicated that the ticket was submitted a few minutes earlier than when actually submitted. This meant that the food will be ready earlier than it "should" have been, and cooks had less time to cook that order. The server gained at the expense of the cook. Cooks were well aware of this practice and usually did their best to accommodate it, grumbling as they did so. Consequently, cooks didn't treat the time written on the ticket seriously, and if a dish was "late," they did not worry.

Servers, as mediators, need their food when their customers demand it: sometimes this is before the food is ready; at other times after. If servers demand food too early, cooks are stressed; but if they don't pick up the food on time, the food is poor and the cook seems incompetent. Just as the server is at the mercy of the cook, the cook is at the mercy of the server. One cook described the friction between cooks and servers: "The biggest objection is letting the food get up there so it gets cold and [the customers] think it's the cook's fault when actually it's the waitresses who sat at the bar and bullshitted with the bartender and just let the food sit there. [The food] comes back, and we have to cook it twice, reheat it or something" (Personal interview, Stan's). This is particularly salient when the restaurant is busy: for example, on weekend evenings at Stan's:

> Evan says to me: "You see what happens when [waitresses] don't pick up their orders. Al is putting steaks back on because there is no room to put them up" (i.e., the counter is entirely filled with plates).
>
> (Field notes, Stan's)

AL and EVAN, in unison when Lauren enters the kitchen:	Yeah, Lauren.
LAUREN:	I know I'm late again.
EVAN:	We just put [your order] up.
AL, joking:	After it was reheated.
LAUREN:	Those french fries look awful.
AL, sarcastic:	They looked nice ten minutes ago.
LAUREN:	I'll go against my better judgment and take them out.

> (Field notes, Stan's)

Negotiation and social control are implicated in the relationship between cooks and servers. Each occupation has its agenda and domain of expertise; both are dependent on client demands that cannot easily be predicted in advance, but with which only the servers must deal. One cook explained the dilemma in terms of emotional management— the backstage of the smiling front described well by Hochschild (1983) among airline attendants:

> A customer only has thirty minutes, and they want their food; [the waitress] would then bring that hostility back to the cooks. She cannot display that in the restaurant; she has to smile. She comes through the doors, she lets it all hang out. Now you've got anywhere from two to seven waitresses, and the waitresses feel that they have the only tables in the entire restaurant. They want their food and they want it now, and it better be good. At that particular time they don't acknowledge or care about the other six servers, and they hassle the cook enough so they get their food.
>
> (Personal interview, Blakemore Hotel)

Emotional management by the servers and sympathetic identification by the cooks are critical to organizational harmony.

INFORMATION PRESERVES

A routine complaint by cooks is that servers do not understand kitchen life. The problem is the general one of communication and the establishment of a common information preserve between two occupational worlds. It is often more the exception than the rule that *everything* on the menu is available. Further, each restaurant had nightly specials, so some items *not* on the menu are available. How do servers know? Since these restaurants do not schedule daily meetings at which the specials and unavailable dishes are described, miscommunication is likely. Confusion is compounded because once the rush begins the cooks dislike being questioned by servers. One cook retorted when "badgered" by a server: "What are you talking about. We got fifty things going on. You're driving me out of my mind" (Field notes, La Pomme de Terre).

Adding to the difficulties of communication, the availability of foods may change throughout the evening. The restaurant may run out of a special dish, and the cooks will discontinue it or add another. Servers need to be aware of when a dish is *almost* sold out, so that two servers do not sell the same "last" item, a delicate process of negotiating responsibilities.

In each restaurant cooks complained that servers didn't listen when they explained what was available:

> Tim, the head chef, is annoyed when he learns that only one of the servers has been selling the mousse. He comments to me: "It's easier not to offer it than to keep checking to see how many they have. It really rattles me. They don't like to have to go back and tell the customer they're out of it."
>
> (Field notes, La Pomme de Terre)

> A server requests an order of short ribs. Mel tells him: "We've been out of short ribs for an hour." Paul, the head chef, says to me: "See how well they listen. What a life!"
>
> (Field notes, Owl's Nest)

> Bernice, a pantry worker, says to Diana, a waitress: "No more specials." Diana comments: "How many times do I have to hear that." Bernice jokes, seemingly a little annoyed: "How many times have I told you that and you've come back and given me an order."
>
> (Field notes, Blakemore Hotel)

> Doris comes back to the kitchen with an order for scampi, not realizing that the kitchen had been out of scampi for thirty minutes although there was a sign posted to that effect. She says: "Back to the drawing board." Doug, the head cook, says: "I thought I told her." Evan says: "I told her first." Later

Maggie comes into the kitchen and asks for "three orders of scampi." Doug tells her: "We're out of scampi." Maggie jokes: "Just wanted to see if you guys were listening."

(Field notes, Stan's)

When two occupations abut each other, confusion about the content of a shared information preserve is common. It is not only servers who ignore or misinterpret; cooks also sometimes misread or misunderstand the tickets written by servers. They believe that the server has requested something other than what was actually requested. Cooks, like some nurses, are likely to blame these errors on handwriting, no matter the true cause: "Jon tells me that cooks can't read the writing of some servers: 'Some of them write instructions in the corner [of the ticket]. Sometimes we just give [the tickets] back to them' " (Field notes, Owl's Nest). Workers collectively create a system of communication in organizations (Boden 1994)—creating structure through talk. When it breaks down, the involved workers must apportion blame and justification among themselves while still maintaining the illusion for the customer that "everything is normal."

SEPARATION OF WORK DOMAINS

Cooks have their work sphere and expertise just as servers have theirs. Although there is cooperation in the doing of some tasks, this is relatively rare. More often a sharp boundary separates the doings of cooks and servers. This distinction—one of occupational domain and community—is evident in the following dialogue between Mickey, a server, and Denny, the day cook:

MICKEY: We make the best pâtés around.
DENNY, joking: We?
MICKEY: You do.

(Field notes, La Pomme de Terre)

In jest, cooks sometimes ask the servers to cook (never the reverse): "At about 9:20 P.M. Tom, one of the house captains, jokes with Howie that 'we're all in except that 10:30 deuce [table for two] that's gonna have six courses.' The unstated implication is that the cooks will work late. Howie responds: 'You always wanted to cook. Now you get your chance' " (Field notes, La Pomme de Terre). Occupations have their own task domains and guard these areas jealously (Abbott 1988) although an outsider might wonder precisely what is being preserved. An answer, of course, is occupational autonomy and political control of one's work environment as symbolically reflected in the division of labor. Noncooperation may be as strategic as cooperation: one reason for the inflexibility built into union contracts.

Much of the separation between cooks and servers deals with spatial rights. The kitchen is the domain of the cook; the "front" or dining room belongs to the server. Cooks complain when servers intrude into their area, particularly to do a cook's task—even though in theory this intrusion might relieve the work of the cook.

Cooks, especially those who work in tight spaces, routinely warn servers to remain out of "their" areas:

> Paul, the head chef, tells his fellow cooks: "I don't want to see the waitresses in the cooler or the freezer. That's what we get paid for. Some of them are really notorious for that."
>
> (Field notes, Owl's Nest)

> Several waitresses are standing in the cook's area. Doug, the head cook, is annoyed, commenting sarcastically: "Who's working here?" One waitress apologizes, saying "Sorry, Doug." Doug backs down: "Don't let it happen again."
>
> (Field notes, Stan's)

Cooks demand autonomy over their kitchen. Although cooks heed management and a status structure operates in the kitchen, servers have no right to judge the organization of the cook's space. The division of labor is a spatial, as well as a behavioral, reality.

ACCOMMODATIONS AND PERKS

Cooks and servers are not routinely hostile to each other. Indeed, all occupations that maintain regular contact develop techniques to foster pleasant relations. As restaurants trade in food and drink, these items typically are the medium of exchange. In each restaurant cooks provided food for servers, above and beyond the mediocre staff meals provided. In turn, in three restaurants cooks would receive soft drinks and beers from servers and bartenders. These perks improve the conditions of employment. Although this is minor occupational deviance, it is expected. John Simmons, owner of the New York restaurant Gage & Tollner, reflected: "If someone works in an ice cream parlour, he's going to make himself a sundae. You'd have to be crazy if you worked in a good restaurant and didn't sneak a shrimp cocktail once in a while" (Koenig 1980, p. 46). Mars and Nicod (1984, p. 112) note in their study of hotel waiters, "Everyone fiddles a little"; anyone who doesn't would be considered odd or dangerous.

Sharing food was common in the restaurants I observed:

> Kate tells me that she will use some of the steaks left over from the banquet to feed the waitresses for their employees' meal, despite the fact that hotel management wants leftover steaks used for other dishes.
>
> (Field notes, Blakemore Hotel)

Amy, a waitress, asks Doug, the head cook, about the chicken breast specials:

AMY: How many of them do you have left?

DOUG: How many of them do you need?

AMY: I want one for myself.

DOUG, joking: How much are you willing to pay me?

Doug makes chicken breasts for the waitresses.

> (Field notes, Stan's)

Servers cannot assume that the cooks will be willing to give them the food that they ask for, trading favors or pleading may be needed as the cooks are responsible for minimizing food costs; servers become supplicants for the moment. Giving servers perks costs the cooks, and so cooks may refuse to provide food: "Ron, a cook, says to Laurie, a server: 'Special today is rockfish. . . . Tastes like red snapper.' Laurie asks: 'Will you cook one so we can taste it.' Ron responds pleasantly: 'No way.' When Laurie points out that they might sell more fish if they taste it, he relents' " (Field notes, Blakemore). Laurie's argument justifies the provision of perks to the servers. As the head chef of the Owl's Nest reported when he told me that he regularly made specials for his servers to taste: "If they like it, they'll sell it" (Field notes, Owl's Nest). One is unlikely to find a stable relationship among workers in which one occupation continually provided benefits for the other without some measure of symbolic recompense. Servers can make cooks' lives easier by manipulating customers to order certain dishes and by keeping customer complaints away from the kitchen and management; cooks, in turn, reward servers through comestibles. As long as these rewards stay within bounds of fiscal propriety, the relationship will be smooth.

CONCLUSION

Occupations are both bound together and separated from each other. As the poet Robert Frost wrote, walls can make good neighbors—so long as we agree on the boundaries. Gates and the height of the walls surely count. In this chapter I emphasize the nonculinary, occupational structure of life in the kitchen, focusing on how occupations interpenetrate, share information preserves, and guard their domains. Every occupation operates under constraints grounded in their work relations. Workers strive to make their days go smoothly and the work tasks pleasant. To achieve this end they must gain some measure of control over their materials and their colleagues, both inside and outside their world. The kitchen is situated within an organization, between management and customers, and within an economy, and all affect how kitchen work is organized. Merely manipulating foodstuffs is insufficient, however graceful that manipulation might be. Interaction with colleagues, while essential, cannot blind workers to the others who affect choices within an occupation; the place and personnel must be manipulated as well. This manipulation of place and colleagues is an ongoing characteristic of all occupations.

The way that an organization has been structured with its set of occupations, the way that an organization connects with clients and suppliers, and the way that an occupation organizes itself in its domain of expertise affects the specific behaviors and cultures in the workplace. With the desire for control and autonomy, coupled with the hope for smoothness and pleasure, workers shape their actions, not freely, but "realistically," accounting for the macrorealities of the organizational field.

FOUR

The Commonwealth of Cuisine

If, as I believe, restaurants are communities—each with its
own culture—then Chez Panisse began as a hunter-gatherer
culture and, to a lesser extent, still is.

—*Alice Waters*

Workplaces are sites of fellowship, of culture. In a sense, an organization is a minisociety: a world with social structure and culture. The organization is a place where people care about each other; they may not
like one another and may scorn or resent their colleagues, but they do
care. Activities of co-workers matter, directly or indirectly.

Restaurants as small organizations are communities, often consciously. With the modest number of employees found in most restaurants—rarely does a restaurant have over one hundred employees—
workers know each other by name, often have learned vast amounts
about each other's biography and interests through personal narratives
and shared experiences, and see themselves as linked.

The communal aspect of an organization—as a place where people
meet, share, and care—recognizes connections between an organizational analysis and an interactional one, a view evident in contemporary symbolic interactionism, neo-Marxism, and the new institutional-
ism. This connection can be recognized in organizational culture
through the realization that culture is fundamentally linked to a power
structure (Lamont 1989). This culture, coupled with the demand for
belonging or collective selfhood (an organizational self), is both cause
and effect of this culture, tethering people to organizations. The concept of organizational culture (Deal and Kennedy 1982; Peters and
Waterman 1982; Smircich 1983; Ouchi and Wilkins 1985) emphasizes
that customs, traditions, values, artifacts, jokes, and sagas are as im-

portant as formal structure or explicit goals. Organizational culture is a key means by which a negotiated order is established and reified by workers—making the workplace personally central, preventing alienation (Fine 1984; Ouchi 1981; Martin 1992). Organizational culture provides rules for negotiation (Kleinman 1982), techniques by which hierarchy is made real (Hodson 1991; Burawoy 1979), and legitimation for external contacts (Schwartz 1983; Kamens 1977).

RESTAURANTS AS CLOSE ORGANIZATIONS

For an organization to function efficiently and for workers to contain alienation, participants must feel that they belong: that the organization matters. One effective strategy of connecting workers to their work is for management to propound the metaphor that the organization is a family, a primary group providing personal self-image, community, and local culture. Organizations advance the claim that the chief executive officer is father (e.g., Clark 1972). Sometimes this metaphor is explicitly proclaimed by the organization itself in a self-serving or sincere attempt to increase worker loyalty; on other occasions workers will make this point themselves. Of course, organizations prefer voluntary commitment, and, from my observations, workers give this commitment more often than might be expected:

> I like the closeness that you have in the kitchen. I love people in kitchens. . . . It's like a family. You can tell each other exactly what you think. It's like all your brothers and sisters.
>
> (Personal interview, La Pomme de Terre)

GAF: What does the phrase "a chef is many things" mean?

JON: He's a dad. You look in the sense that, from Paul's side, we're Paul's second family. Paul spends every night with us. He works with us, and he knows all our hang-ups, what we like and what we don't like. He knows about our personal lives as much as we'll let up and about our problems and vice versa. We know all about him.

> (Personal interview, Owl's Nest)

> [After telling me that Stan's was very close-knit and very friendly, one cook comments:] This place at one time was very much something like one big happy family. At one time it was even more closely knit than it is now.
>
> (Personal interview, Stan's)

Not every worker used the metaphor of the family, but many named the tight friendships in the kitchen as a pleasure of work. The danger in using rhetoric emphasizing the emotional closeness of workers oc-

curs when the rhetoric is used by those managers who are resented by
workers—a problem of large or mismanaged organizations. For example, the Blakemore Hotel attempted to promote this closeness and car-
ing. Some unhappy workers felt that this was a con perpetrated by an
organization that had very little interest in them: "I just think [the
kitchen is] poorly run. . . . When Bernice [a pantry worker] started,
[the chef] came up to me and said that I want you to go up to Bernice
and say, 'I'm glad that you're working for the Blakemore.' Like I'm a
personnel director [sarcastically]. I looked at him and said, 'Are you
serious?' and he said yes. 'Now,' I said, 'wait, I'm not going to do
that.' How cornball" (Personal interview, Blakemore). An easy request, which co-workers might do spontaneously, has become an indicator of managerial disrespect and cynicism, because the emotional
basis for communal concern is absent. Yet, even at the Blakemore, although there is little support for management, workers are friendly.

Feelings of personal closeness occur despite, and perhaps because
of, the diversity of kitchen workers. The personal backgrounds of
waitresses, cooks, and pot washers vary widely, as do their ethnic
backgrounds. While for some this diversity is a barrier to communication, for others it is a benefit:

> I was working with real cooks. Black chefs from Washington who had been
> cooks for a long time, and I enjoyed the ambiance of the restaurant work.
> . . . Meeting people from different backgrounds, in addition to the middle-
> class people I was used to. Working with waitresses, raunchy waitresses
> who cursed like sailors.
>
> (Personal interview, Minneapolis cook)

GAF: What's the most satisfying thing about what you're doing?
DANA: For me, mostly it's the personal relationships that develop. With
        other cooks and the waitresses. Some people fade in and out, but
        they become friends. For a while a lot of Cubans worked there, and
        I became close friends with a lot of them. Kinda neat to work in a
        hotel like that, because you kinda become acquainted with an inter-
        national cast of characters. [The food and beverage manager] is In-
        dian; one of the waitresses is Irish.

        (Personal interview, Blakemore Hotel)

The sense of community is evident both within and outside of work. I
noted that cooks occasionally arrive at work early or stay late to insure
that they will complete their tasks smoothly and with a minimum of
pressure. More surprising is that some workers "hang out" at the

workplace, where they talk with friends, even though they are not "at work." Indeed, a merging of workplaces and "third places" (Oldenberg 1988; Marshall 1986)—places of sociality—is common in many work scenes. Lounges are not only used by those on duty. Of all the places that workers could be, they choose to be at their place of employment because they can use resources at hand for their own enjoyment and because that is where their friends are. The former is more understandable from an instrumental point of view: "Ron is sitting in the chef's office, using the restaurant calculator, doing homework for his chef-training course at a local technical college. I ask Ron why he's here, and he answers, 'The calculator is here.' He is not scheduled for work today" (Field notes, Blakemore). On other occasions cooks drop by to be served a "free lunch" at times that they are ostensibly off duty. More notable is the visit for sociable purposes, such as when a cook stays for three hours after his or her shift is over or when he or she is in "the neighborhood." The restaurant becomes a staging area for the interpersonal relations that transcend the doing of work. In fact, many best friends (Fine 1986; Putnam and Mumby 1993) are contacts at work.

Work-based friendships blossom outside work, and at each restaurant cooks, servers, and sometimes other staff share leisure, such as parties, fishing, concert going, or sports:

> One cook at the Blakemore regularly organizes an "Annual Booze Cruise." Staff pay $10 to ride a boat on the Mississippi and drink. However, partying is also less formally organized. Another cook invited co-workers to a party at her house. The hotel workers also play on a softball team.
> (Field notes, Blakemore Hotel)

> Cooks at La Pomme de Terre socialize, both drinking after work and playing flag football. Relations in the organization are sufficiently close that one of the cooks asks the owner if he would referee their football game.
> (Field notes, La Pomme de Terre)

Sometimes the kitchen friendships—as in all workplaces (Fine 1986; Parkin 1993)—transcend the platonic, becoming horizontal as well as vertical connections, although such relationships were not obvious at any of the four restaurants during the period I observed. If workplaces can generate liking, they can also spark love: "I think that there's a lot of hanky-panky between waitresses and cooks, and waitresses and bartenders. I don't think it's bad here at all, but I worked here during the days when it was bad. I think that the divorce rate is very high in this

business, because there's too many opportunities. Everybody gets
through with a busy night or something. They want to relax, and they
go and have a couple of drinks, and the next thing you know they're
checking into a motel" (Personal interview, Owl's Nest). He focuses on
heterosexual play, but in many scenes—including the restaurant
scene—homosexual ties are common. While I did not observe flagrant
relationships or public intimacies,[1] the workplace is an arena with a
full array of social ties.

RESTAURANT CULTURE AS
INTERPERSONAL CONNECTION

Max Kaplan (1960) noted of leisure that "matters of taste are the social
property of small groups, and as such they may provide useful indica-
tions of group boundaries." This is echoed in Robert Freed Bales's
(1970, pp. 153–54) comment that "most small groups develop a subculture that is protective for their members, and is allergic, in some respects, to the culture as a whole. . . . They [the members] draw a boundary around themselves and resist intrusion." I have termed the culture
of small groups an "idioculture" (Fine 1979, 1982), defined as "a system of knowledge, beliefs, behaviors, and customs shared by members
of an interacting group to which members can refer and that serve as
the basis of further interaction. Members recognize that they share experiences, and these experiences can be referred to with the expectation
that they will be understood by other members, thus being used to construct a social reality for the participants" (Fine 1987c, p. 125).

What has been demonstrated for families, sports teams, criminal
groups, and others is equally relevant for organizations (e.g., Roy
1959–1960; Ouchi and Wilkins 1985; Schwartzman 1987). Small,
closely knit organizations such as these restaurants may have a robust
culture. More than fifty years ago Thurmond Arnold (1937, p. 350)
detailed the cultural dimension of the "folklore of capitalism": "When
men are engaged in any continuous cooperative activity, they develop
organizations which acquire habits, disciplines, and morale; these give
the organizations unity and cause them to develop something which it
is convenient to describe as personality or character." The existence of
organizational sports teams and beer busts testify to this feature of organizational life. As Alice Waters suggested, restaurants have different
values as organizations, different styles, and varying cultures. In mak-

ing this argument, I ignore the existence of a restaurant "subculture"—those sets of cultural traits and actions that transcend individual restaurants and characterize large swaths of the industry and its associated occupational orders.

In each restaurant where I observed, cultural traditions were known by the kitchen staff, which they used as points of reference. For instance, nicknames were common. At La Pomme de Terre one maître d' was nicknamed "Young" because he had once called himself "*Young* Christopher Doane." At the Blakemore, Kate was called "Cates" (and she wore a nametag to this effect) because the food and beverage manager once called her that. Argot also developed. Much industry jargon is uniform across restaurants, even across regions (Gross 1958, pp. 386–87), but whether local or subcultural, this language facilitates communication. At the Owl's Nest dishes needed immediately were labeled "downtown," and dishes and products were given shorthand names, such as an ivory salmon, shortened to "ivory." On other occasions argot had a more expressive character, as at Stan's, where walk-in customers—those without reservations—were known as "Hessians." I witnessed a chef scribble a swastika on a ticket to indicate that it was for a "Hessian."

Work culture goes beyond nicknaming and slang to capture shared experiences. At La Pomme de Terre the former chef served as a reference point, even though he had left the restaurant several years before and was now the chef-owner of a competing establishment:

> I had eaten at Bruno's restaurant one night during this research, and I was closely questioned about what I was served. I mentioned that three dishes that my wife and I ordered were served with Cumberland sauce. This proved to be immensely humorous to the staff, because Bruno was known to use Cumberland sauce on *everything*—it was his signature. Tom, one of the maître d's, mimicked Bruno's Germanic accent: "It's cheap too." Howie, the sous chef, added sarcastically: "Open a can of currant jelly and slide it into a pan." Denny, one of the waiters, commented: "Add an orange and a piece of the peel so that it looks authentic."
>
> (Field notes, La Pomme de Terre)

During his tenure at the restaurant he hired his wife as pastry chef, and I was told that the cooks would delight in smelling her cakes burn, not telling her, in order to hear him berate his wife for "incompetence." References to this man were common, as dishes were compared, usually favorably, to the dishes that he had them prepare when head chef.

A COMMONWEALTH OF JOKES

Often organizational culture is connected to expressions of humor (Sykes 1966)—the threads of traditions are jocular. This form of discourse is crucial for binding organizations. Humor, with its attacks on fellow workers (Seckman and Couch 1989), is critical for determining the boundaries of the community and, thus, who can be trusted. Jokes reflect for the moment the willingness to accept a shared view of the world. Everett Hughes (1971, p. 341) notes that "among the most important subject matter of rules is setting up of criteria for recognizing a true fellow-worker, for determining who is safe . . . who must be kept at some distance." New workers are often tested through humor to see if they can take it (Haas 1972). Despite not being serious, the audience response becomes highly consequential. The recognition of implicit values suggests a common core of belief. Cooks, like other workers, have finely developed justifications for play (Marshall 1986, p. 33). While they argue sanctimoniously and sincerely that play and joking should not block the instrumental demand of "getting things done," they believe play should be extended as far as possible to strengthen community, drain excess energy, or relieve boredom. Humor is alleged to contribute to the satisfaction of working; for example, one cook told me that joking was "half the fun of working in the kitchen" (Personal interview, Blakemore Hotel). Others speak of the need "to keep everybody's spirit up" or "to keep the tension down" (Personal interviews, La Pomme de Terre)—emotion work through discursive practice, a key feature of organizational life. One cook explained:

> I think that [humor and joking] is essential. You have to [joke] in order to have a relaxed atmosphere. . . . There has to be the calming, relaxing, goofing around. Bruce and I do it a great deal. We goof around and kid around with each other. That's just our way of keeping relaxed and not letting things get to us. . . . I'm not saying me and Bruce are screw-offs and we don't do the work. That's not true. I'm saying that there has to be that sense of relaxation. . . . That's why Bruce and I get along so well when we work on the line: he on the stove and I on the broiler. There's that sense of relaxation. We know each other is there, and no matter how busy we get, we're always relaxed.
>
> (Personal interview, Owl's Nest)

While an observer might question the accuracy of this cook's assessment of his state of relaxation, he reflects how workers wish the workplace to be. They want to enjoy the circumstances of their labor and, in playing, establish a "joking relationship." Through a series of speech acts and behavioral traditions, workers tame the job's instrumental requirements and the strains that might otherwise occur because of conflicting interests.

Most organizations develop a robust joking, teasing culture, providing a forum intersecting the desire for interpersonal closeness and the creation of shared memories. Talk becomes the interactional glue that binds colleagues in a community (e.g., Grimshaw 1989). In examining humor in organizations I examine three genres—horseplay, teasing, and pranks—which, although they do not exhaust all the possible forms of humor, represent the main forms of interpersonal humor. Few formal, set jokes are found; humor creates and is responsive to circumstance. I exclude humorous remarks or actions that are not directed toward co-workers, such as sarcastic remarks about the restaurant, customers, or the working situation in general although these remarks also help to establish (or, in some cases, undercut) community.

Each genre can be understood by reference to the involvement of the interactants and by their awareness contexts (Glaser and Strauss 1967). Horseplay depends for its successful completion on the knowing involvement of multiple participants. Solitary horseplay is structurally impossible. Horseplay involves an open awareness context. Teasing, likewise, depends upon the parties to the teasing being aware of the frame. However, unlike horseplay, which is necessarily joint, teasing can be either asymmetrical or reciprocal—with one teasing act following another. Pranks differ in that, like their close kin, practical jokes, the target needs to be firmly wrapped in a tight, opaque cocoon. The target resides in a closed awareness context, enmeshed, for the moment, in a fabrication of which he or she is little aware. The direction of the humor is unidirectional although, of course, there is typically an audience beyond the perpetrator and target. While all three forms of humor are communal, they differ in their structure and how knowledge of the interaction is shared.

HORSEPLAY

Whether because of the spatial tightness of the kitchen and the intensity of the relationships among this group of young kitchen workers, mostly young males from working-class backgrounds, I found much boisterous camaraderie. Horseplay is common, thoroughly enjoyed, even though in some cases, given the presence of knives and hot pans, the jocularity can be dangerous. This physical activity contrasts with the boredom that workers might otherwise experience (Molstad 1986).[2] Work cannot easily be separated from leisure activity (Bowman 1983; Bell 1984). Work and play blend into each other, with play filling large or small temporal cracks (Fine 1990).

Much of the horseplay found in restaurant kitchens is centered on food. Food, the focus of the instrumental aspects of work, also is the focus of the expressive culture. Foodstuffs are the dominant reality of cooks—the source of frustration and satisfaction. At Stan's cooks played catch with a steak; at the Blakemore they threw a cauliflower. At a pizza restaurant the employees played "a make-believe game of baseball . . . where a rolling pin was used as a bat and pizza dough was used as a ball" (Bowman 1983, p. 109). Tools are also incorporated into this play:

> Doran and Lew are waving kitchen knives at each other, insulting each other. When Gene, another cook, tells them not to joke with the knife, Lew sarcastically responds: "OK, Dad," but they do put down their knives.
>
> (Field notes, Stan's)

> Paul, the head chef, pretends to chop my arm off with a large meat saw. Later Phil, the owner, throws an empty soft drink can at Paul's back. Paul then briefly locks Phil in the cooler.
>
> (Field notes, Owl's Nest)

An extreme example of collective horseplay occurs when one's body becomes the object of humor, as in a case of mooning reported by a female cook: "One Sunday we were cooking brunch, and it was really hot, and me and this guy John and another guy, we took our pants off, and we were standing at the counter, and the waiters . . . handed orders in, and when the three of us turned around, and our butts were sticking out of the back of our aprons. It was really cute. I really like that. Just a little comic relief. A lot of things like that go on" (Personal interview, La Pomme de Terre). Cooks, sometimes with other restaurant employees, transform their work space into a playground, sharing in the enjoyment and satisfaction of breaking from the primary work frame. When this is achieved collectively, it is especially effective in generating satisfaction within a structure that does not have worker satisfaction as an explicit goal.

TEASING

Teasing is one measure that a workplace—or any social system—is harmonious. Teasing is a marker of community; its existence recognizes that there is enough looseness or "give" in relationships that one person can make a joke at another's expense without the belief that those sentiments are real. That is, a play is *built into* the stable relationships among actors, based on sympathetic role taking. Situations establish those frames that are tied to them (see Gonos 1977; Fine 1983). In workplaces, a set of semiformal teasing ("kidding") relationships are important in that they mean to participants that they trust each other sufficiently that they can rely on them for work-related tasks. New workers are expected to tease in return, becoming part of the group. Proof of friendliness is critical for interaction; teasing provides a clear indicator of this attitude.

With the exception of the rush (see chapter 2), kitchen environments are filled with interpersonal joshing. The organization of talk can be defined as primarily expressive. Laughter is provoked by conversational mechanisms, grounded in shared understandings of the production of talk (Jefferson 1979; Sacks 1974). This teasing may be work related, but anything can trigger a teasing episode:

> The cooks tease Doran about his thick curly hair. Craig, one of the busboys, calls him Annie, after Little Orphan Annie, adding "We'll buy him a big red dress for Halloween." Doran responds good-naturedly.
>
> (Field notes, Stan's)

> Bruce, a cook, says to Denise, a young pantry worker who is pouring oil: "Don't spill that." As he says this, he jiggles her arm. Bruce continues his joking, pointing to Denise's neck:

BRUCE:	Oh, I thought that was a woodtick on your neck.
DENISE, believing him, yells:	What?!
BRUCE:	It's only a louse.
DENISE:	I don't have any lice.
BRUCE:	You do now.
DENISE jokes:	I must have got it from you.

> (Field notes, Owl's Nest)

On occasion people joke about absent others, for example, when the owner of the Owl's Nest jokes about his wife in a manner that reveals both his willingness to bask in the teasing and a racial insensitivity: "Dan, the owner, asks Paul, the head chef, for a can of oyster sauce to take home to his wife, saying: 'She drinks oyster sauce like it was pop.' Paul responds, 'She isn't Chinese.' Dan replies, smiling: 'Sometimes she acts gooky'" (Field notes, Owl's Nest). That an owner would be willing to make his spouse a target of jokes suggests that he is—for these workers—a "good guy," someone for whom these workers should wish to work diligently, despite low wages, poor equipment, and difficult working conditions. This owner also shares a reciprocal teasing relationship in which he and his head chef lock each other in the cooler and refuse to open the door. This teasing relationship permitted these men to finesse their disagreements and the strains of their positions.

Not all teasing is easy, in that it depends upon relationships of trust. Sometimes when cooks tease status inferiors, trouble brews. On one occasion several cooks considered placing trout heads in the pockets of a mildly retarded potman, but they let the matter drop for fear he might be angered. These cooks tease the other mildly retarded potman, who doesn't anger as easily, but even here, a certain discomfort exists because of the difficulty of having Ray give as good as he gets: "Dan, the owner, blows the horn of Ray's bicycle. When Ray returns from checking on his bicycle, he reports: 'I won't say nothing, 'cause I know who it is.' The other cooks tell Ray that he should blow the horn on Dan's car. Later, Paul, the head chef, jokes to Ray about Jon eating a scallop: 'We'll take it out of his paycheck. That will be five dollars.' Ray seems somewhat nervous, unsure whether Paul is kidding, and tells Paul: 'He took two.' Paul says: 'We'll take ten from his.' Ray turns to me and says nervously: 'We have a lot of fun back here.' " (Field notes, Owl's Nest). Teasing demands a belief in equal status; my observations suggest that this belief is not always possible to maintain, despite the benefits to all if it is accepted. One female cook at La Pomme de Terre, shy and feminine, was unable to participate in this banter, and that, coupled with her inexperience as a working cook, led to her termination.

Teasing is endemic at work, providing a temporary stigma, which others address and ignore at will, suggesting that we are all "passing"—that there is more than enough stigma to go around. That we agree to create, play with, and bracket this stigma suggests we care enough about each other to demonstrate that our propinquity measures communal feeling.

PRANKS

We reside in a world of *Candid Camera* and other manufactured and mediated practical jokes. In reality, this represents the desire to entertain ourselves by making the lives of others temporarily miserable. The willingness of these others to play along with this misery, making themselves uncomfortable for the satisfaction of others, suggests the power of social bonds. That pranks should be central to the establishment of interpersonal closeness is strange in that on their surface they appear opposed to the establishment of friendly relations. Of course, there are advantages gained from being a target—being considered a "good sport" and having the opportunity to return the misery. Like teasing and horseplay, being the butt of a prank (e.g., sending a new worker to the storeroom for a can of steam) is a marker of trust. That victim is expected to be a prank initiator in the future, becoming part of the economy of pranks. While pranks are not immediately reciprocal, in the long run they should balance. The danger, often found at camps and other preadolescent locales, is that a victim will receive more than his or her share of pranks and deliver less in return.

In the work culture "classic" pranks often have a lengthy "referential afterlife" (Goffman 1981): they are remembered and reported long after their original occurrence. One good prank can serve for many, and major pranks, as opposed to minor physical teasing, while rare, were vividly described in interviews. Memories and reports of memory are shared by workers; this sharing connects them in a powerful web. They have a humor culture.[3]

As with horseplay, pranks frequently involve symbolic manipulations of food, causing embarrassment or discomfort to co-workers: reordering the mundane character of the kitchen, polluting the food. Paul, the head chef at the Owl's Nest, was known for the scope of his pranks:

Jon describes one of Paul's pranks: "I was working the line once. It was very hot there, and so I had a Coke and took big swigs from it, about half the can. He loaded it with Tabasco sauce, and of course I had drunk about half of it. I could hear him giggling around the corner." Denise adds: "You know what he did to me. He had been peeling some fresh garlic. He said, 'Do you want an almond?' I bit down once." They report one of Paul's most memorable, if cruel, pranks. Jon explains: "Some lady brought in a duck. [Paul] was having everyone pet the duck, before he killed it. He snapped its neck before he brought it over to Denise." Denise continues: "I started petting it, thinking it was alive, and all of a sudden he let the neck drop. I almost got sick. I wish I could get even. . . . He's too suspicious. He smells everything before he eats it. . . . You should do something to him, Gary [the author], he'd never suspect you."

(Field notes, Owl's Nest)

This extract depicts the tension involved in this joking. Paul's memorable prank was mean, and Denise remembers it still, as did other workers who mentioned it in their interviews. While there is real affection for Paul, the desire for revenge is real, made difficult by his status and his suspicion.

Other restaurants have prank cultures, focusing on food products. The kitchen is a workplace in which situational looseness (Goffman 1963) characterizes the doing of work—differentiating it from more tightly controlled and observed places (e.g., Borman 1991):

GAF: Are there any really classic pranks?

EVAN: Putting meat juice in a glass and saying that it's black cherry and giving it to a dishwasher. I've done that. I've put vinegar in place of someone's ice water. We deep fried a little chocolate Easter egg and gave it off to a waitress. Fooling with the food, I guess.

(Personal interview, Stan's)

Mickey was sautéing one night, and he mixed himself a brandy and Coke. He was just finishing up the last order, and he went downstairs, and I dumped about a cup of Tabasco in his drink there, and he came back up, and he was drinking, you know you're not really supposed to be drinking brandy and Cokes while you're working, and I said, "You better drink that, here comes Tim," and he just tossed it down without even looking or smelling or anything and his eyeballs just popped out of his head. That was pretty neat because it almost killed the guy. It was obvious that his eyes were watering, but I thought it was pretty funny.

(Personal interview, La Pomme de Terre)

The success of the prank is a function of the trust among co-workers. They are willing to leave drinks available to co-workers and then not become irate when sabotage occurs. Some pranks do not involve personal discomfort but create the illusion that work tasks are complicated or difficult. In practice they undermine the routine grounds of everyday life, not trust: "We had some shrimp in the steamer, and Dale took the shrimp out, and he puts [in] all this baby shrimp, so when the steamer went off, Kate opened it up and saw all these baby shrimp, and she said, 'Oh, my gosh!' " (Personal interview, Blakemore Hotel). Other pranks play off specific work demands—manipulating the tickets—creating the illusion that much work is to be done:

It's a standard [prank] to turn in a bogus order with a million things on it. Juan did that once to me. I fell for it. It's funny now, but I was so mad at him at the time. He put down a whole slew of things on one ticket, and I produced every one of those orders. He got a charge out of that. Everything was circled. I was so overloaded.

(Personal interview, Blakemore Hotel)

Sometimes when the head chef goes down to the bathroom, we grab a bunch of orders and put them up. We take a long string of orders [tickets] and hang them up, and he comes back and says, "Oh God!"

(Field notes, Stan's)

The virtue of this common prank is that it causes no real harm, is not seen as mean spirited, and is easily set right. Among adults, pranks are only played among friends. The hostile prank is rare. In fact, only once did I learn of a prank targeted at a co-worker who was openly denigrated for falling for the "joke"—in this case the only waitress on the staff: "Dane, a waiter, hands Jody a hot baguette without warning her that it is hot. She grabs it and slightly burns her hand. Lesley, a female cook, tells him: 'That's mean.' He replies joking: 'If the little fool takes it, it's not my fault'" (Field notes, La Pomme de Terre). Pranks by themselves do not carry any inherent social meaning but are given meaning by the personal, status, and structural relationships among the parties to them. Pranks are situated, and this situated quality relates to how pranks are understood. More than presenting incongruous events—in which the world becomes a radically different place from what it appears to be—the prank conveys a message of superiority, in that someone has tricked someone else, a process that becomes evident when the prank is made public for all to observe: "We used to take rubber dog doo-doo or bones of fish skeletons and put it on a plate and ship it out to the maître d' for dinner and have him open it up in the dining room" (Personal interview, Blakemore Hotel).

Perhaps the most subversive act, quite possibly the rarest and certainly the most disgusting to the reader, is revenge played on the customer. In that the customer is unaware of what is being done to him or her, it is not a prank in the same sense as discussed above, and it is grounded in alienation, rather than community. Here the service and professional relationship between cook and customer is undercut.[4] While these attacks were uncommon and lived in memory more than in fact, they reflect the potential backstage power of the cook. One wonders whether the following events actually occurred or were merely symptomatic of scorn to customers, mixed with a measure of homophobia:

DIANE: I know one story that's just so terrible, I don't know if I can tell it to
            you. It was one brunch in New York, and three old fags would
            come in every Sunday afternoon. The restaurant closed at five. The
            cooks were wiped out, and we were really tired. We got there at
            eight in the morning. . . . A long day. They always came in at 4:45
            and sat down at the table, and this one Sunday, one of the guys that
            I was working with was really pissed. The waiter came back and
            said, "I want to get out. I don't want to do this." So one of the fags
            ordered—he just said, "Tell the chef I want my special order
            omelette. He will know what it is." So the waiter comes back and
            says, "The guy wants a special omelette, and you know what it is. I
            don't know what it is." And John said, "I know what it is." So John
            went and urinated in a glass. . . . He took the sausage that he was
            going to chop up and make the omelette with and dipped it in the
            urine and put it into the omelette.

GAF: Did he notice?

DIANE: Oh, he loved it. Compliments to the chef. That's the grossest thing
            that I have ever heard of. . . . [The cook] got off so wildly on it.

                                            (Personal interview, La Pomme de Terre)

While the kitchen is a community—a culinary commonwealth—those
outside the boundaries are subject to attacks of whatever kind cooks
feel they can get away with in the presence of their peers. Even this de-
structive example of humor can be fundamental for building community. Further, should it lead to termination, the job market is such, not
relying on recommendations, that fired cooks can rapidly be hired.

KITCHEN DEVIANCE

As I described in chapter 1, the unofficial techniques of cooking exem-
plify the underside of work. Deviance is as much a part of occupational life as ethics. Much that goes on in the kitchen should not be reported to management and must be hidden from customers and their
representatives: health inspectors and journalists. Most organizations
encompass deviance. These deviant actions typically protect the organization and the doing of work. Regulations proscribing deviance are
established by "society," operating through their agents: health inspectors and local, state, and national regulations. Other regulations are established by a management that may or may not care if these rules are
enforced: some toleration of deviance is a technique to satisfy workers
(Field notes, Owl's Nest). Around every regulation exists a *penumbra
of enforcement;* the violation of these regulations is a perquisite that

workers may take for granted as part of their jobs. Cooks, like college professors and other laborers, are expected to pilfer some supplies; otherwise, they will steal more. They should be fed well; otherwise, they will connive to be fed well without management's knowledge (McPhee 1979, p. 70). During my months of observation, the amount taken was relatively minor, like most restaurant pilferage (e.g., Marshall 1986, pp. 39–40), and I only learned of two economically significant instances of theft:

> I finally left [a family restaurant] in 1982. They were having a bunch of manager problems. One of the stores was going down fast. A couple of ladies set people up. Like back then if people did not like working with you or they just didn't like you, they would set someone up to get fired. In my case I was doing my job, but I didn't want to play their game. They were kind of milking the company. Stealing food and stealing money. . . . I finally got set up in this one store, and I finally quit.
> (Personal interview, Blakemore Hotel)

> I was told that a former chef was fired from a subsequent job for stealing lobsters. Cooks joked that this was how he could afford such a nice house. That he was the head chef made it possible for him to engage in this scam.
> (Field notes, Blakemore Hotel)

More frequent than stealing food and money were the attempts of workers to violate health and safety codes that were perceived as infringing on their freedom without any clear benefits. Smoking is a domain in which rules are bent. At the Owl's Nest an ashtray was provided in the back of the kitchen; I learned that it was hidden quickly during a restaurant inspection. Cooks smoked at three of the restaurants. Hair nets were not always worn, and at the Blakemore a prohibition against nail polish was ignored: "Dana is wearing lilac nail polish today. When she sees that I have noticed it, she tells me: 'Don't write anything about my nail polish. I'm not supposed to have it on.' She continues to wear nail polish and never is reprimanded" (Field notes, Blakemore Hotel). Perhaps the deviance that the general public is most aware of, at least according to stereotypes, is alcoholism—a normative deviance. I cannot assess whether cooks have more alcohol-related problems than others; however, they believed that this was so. These young men and women, largely from working-class backgrounds, did drink after work, before work, and occasionally on the job, but I never observed any cook who was so impaired by alcohol that it significantly affected performance—I met no "stinking drunks."

Alcohol is part of the "community," part of the setting, and part of the pleasure of working at a quality restaurant (i.e., one with a liquor license). As one cook explained, exaggerating:

> Every cook that I've ever known, not that they are alcoholic, but I think that it's not a problem, but it is something that's very much a part of it, especially at nights. . . . Working at night, there's a feeling when you get off that you're just wired, and you've got to go and talk. You're with these people, and you're so close it's almost like you want to go home and sleep with them, but you can't do that, so you go out and drink with them. It's like you reach a point where you feel you've been through this thing together, and you reach a point where you do it. You want to fraternize, so people go out and drink, 'cause they don't want to go home and jump into bed.
> (Personal interview, La Pomme de Terre)

For this man alcohol is a sacrament that creates intense bonds of community. Collective imbibing is central to community. The social characteristics of alcohol, linked to its easy availability in restaurant kitchens and perhaps to the heat and strains with which workers cope, leads to communal drinking.

Cooks generalize from the alcoholic cooks they know, playing off the stereotype of the drunken cook, to assume that their occupation is overloaded with drunks, denigrating their work in the process. The stereotype, perhaps based on empirical reality, makes cooks sensitive to the consumption of alcohol. The magnificent culinary writer, M. F. K. Fisher notes from European experience that drinking may be a preferred form of deviance from management's perspective: "All her cooks drank, sooner or later, in soggy desperation. Madame took it philosophically; . . . [she said,] 'The only cook I ever had that didn't take to the bottle ate so much good food that her feet finally bent under when she walked. I'd rather have them stagger than stuff' " (Fisher 1976, p. 405). Cooks are sensitive in our addiction-sensitive age to the dangers of alcohol: "[Otto notes:] I've been known to drink four or five pink gins. Gin and angostura. If it weren't for my work, I could drink all the time. You simply can't cook and drink. You cut yourself and burn yourself. You lose your edge" (McPhee 1979, p. 59). I was told frequently about the high rate of alcoholism although cooks often asserted that the problem is less severe than it had been, perhaps because of greater sensitivity to alcoholism or because cooks now come from a higher social class. Most cooks knew of or had worked with one or two alcoholics. One cook told me that, although he had worked with only one cook who was a "drunk," he read a survey that suggested that cooks were second only to bartenders in their rate of alcoholism (Field notes, La Pomme de Terre). Another told me, improbably, that "about 95 percent of us are alcoholics" (Personal interview, Blakemore Hotel), a statement that reveals more about the success of the alcohol-treatment industry than about the extent of problems in the kitchen. Many cooks claimed that no problem existed in *their* restaurant, but it was present in the industry as a whole—accepting the universal validity of the stigma while denying it locally.

Cooks did drink outside of work, joshing about this passion. The joking was similar to remarks among many young males about their interest and prowess in drinking and their kidding about its aftermath, revealing in the mock machismo of simultaneous swagger and denial. When I asked one young cook about the most satisfying thing about his job, he laughingly replied: "A Bud at the end of the night" (Personal interview, Stan's). Or when the head chef left one evening at 7:30, his assistant reminded him: "Remember that the next time I come in hung over" (Field notes, La Pomme de Terre). Or when one cook carried two bottles of wine, the head chef quipped: "Drinking with both hands today. I thought you gave that up" (Field notes, Owl's Nest). Alcohol was part of the accepted culture of these restaurants. All agreed that drinking should not be excessive and should not infect the workplace, but short of this, drinking was tolerated.

Each restaurant had a liquor or wine license, and so alcohol was present although it was shared discreetly, occasionally, and at the end of the evening:

GAF: During the time you've been [at Stan's] has there been a problem with alcoholism in the kitchen?

LEW: Not alcoholism, but drinking beer. All of us have beer at the end of the night. It doesn't affect us at all.

GAF: Does [the owner] know about it?

LEW: Yeah, but when we see him coming, we won't drink a beer when he's there. We'll try to hide it.

GAF: Why?

LEW: He'll get mad, tell us not to do it anymore. . . . He knows we're doing it to a point, but not as much as we're doing it.

GAF: How many beers will you have on a Saturday night?

LEW: I'll have one. Gene won't have any. Al might have two or three. I mean it's not like we're drinking a case of beer a night. It's where it should be. There's no problem.

(Personal interview, Stan's)

This reflects the attitudes of many cooks: Drinking must be limited to permit the community to function. If it is, it is "no problem"; if not, the violator is tarred with the stigma of his deviance. The community is accepting as long as does not affect expressive or instrumental demands: the self-esteem needs of workers and the economic goals of managers. As Lew indicated, many managers recognize the utility of drinking as long as they can deny its existence, a view privately expressed by one owner. Proof would demand that they take action to correct a functional behavior that violates the rules.

THE BREAKDOWN OF COMMUNITY

When a social system doesn't work, either for a brief or long period of time, a crisis looms. While I selected these four restaurants because they were successful, small economic systems, positive emotions did not always characterize kitchen activities. Workplaces generate arguments and disputes from internal strains and external forces such as demands on workers by management or moods brought to work from outside. These locales are crucibles for emotion work.

Tension can originate in long-standing personal animosities. This hostility often derives from perceived performance inadequacies compared to one's expectations. The tension at the Blakemore between the head chef and his workers grew from their feelings that their boss was unwilling to pull his weight—operating as an "executive" chef, rather than a "working" chef. Several cooks were bitter because of what they perceived as his neglect of his culinary and community responsibilities. He was a "manager"—in their view, not a very good one—rather than a team leader.

Other less status-based sources of interpersonal friction also emerged: "Kate explains her disdain for a colleague: '[He] is an Aztec sun god with that Indian headband. A pathological liar. He doesn't do anything; he just goofs off'" (Field notes, Blakemore Hotel). Kate rejects this man culturally, personally, and professionally. At the Owl's Nest animosity existed between one hot-tempered cook and a pot washer "who didn't know his place." These personal dislikes were rare in these small organizations, but they had the potential for social pollution.

A more general question is how to cope with day-to-day friction, some of which was rooted in personal styles of workers, deriving from their class or cultural position. While most workers at the Owl's Nest insisted that it was a pleasant place to work, during the period that I observed, the head chef held a meeting to allow kitchen workers to express negative emotions in a contained setting. An effect of this meeting was that it became inappropriate to bring up those issues again, even if they were not fully resolved. The "feeling rules" of the organization (and many organizations) is that once an emotion is expressed, it is no longer an appropriate topic. The bad feelings were buried without being cured.

The one cook who was most angry expressed a belief in stern discipline, even though, as a young man who frequently provoked others to anger, he could have been the victim of the policies that he espoused. In a sense, he was criticizing himself in the guise of criticizing the head chef, who attempted to avoid conflict whenever possible. He explained:

LARRY: You have be strict, and I think that's something that Paul isn't—strict. You have to be able to put your foot down if something happens, and I think a lot of times Paul lets things slide by. I had an incident with Dean [the pot washer] one time. You were there when he was talking back to Paul, saying "Well, I have a right to say how I feel." If everybody had a right to say how they feel in this restaurant, what kind of restaurant would it be?

GAF: What kind of restaurant would it be?

LARRY: There wouldn't be a restaurant. . . . There'd be so much bickering and animosity and so many problems that you would have to close the doors. People would be throwing stuff at each other and the floor. There's people there that . . . [don't] like [each other]. I don't like them, and they don't like me. There's always problems in a restaurant, and that's just one of those things that is always going to happen.

GAF: What should [Paul] have done?

LARRY: He should've just said, "Dean, you say another word, and you're going home." And if he did, send him home. What I've seen in Dean, he's the kind of person where [if] you don't put your foot down and let him know how you feel, he's just going to keep doing it over and over. That's a problem with Paul. If something's not right, he's just going to say, "Boy, that really bugs me, but I'm not going to say anything. I'm just going to let it ride." Paul is immature in management ways. He can get mad at someone, and if he gets mad at them, he's not going to talk about it to them. He's just going to be immature in the sense that he's not going to schedule him for so many days. . . . Dean had an argument with a girl [pantry worker], Denise. Paul wanted to talk about it, and Dean said something like, "She's your pet, and you don't think of the rest of us," and Paul said, "Well, piss on it," and walked away from Dean. Then he made the schedule up, and Dean had three days off. Dean usually works five nights.

(Personal interview, Owl's Nest)

Paul, attempting to avoid conflict, had his own "folk" theory of personnel management that differed substantially from his cook. He disliked bureaucratic rules and wanted to treat everyone personally, not confronting structural dilemmas. He explains his theory of emotional management:

> Let's say a person was having a real bad day. It probably started even before they even came in. A person has a bad day, and whether they want to or not, it's going to affect their surroundings at work and in their environment. It's going to affect the people they work with, the food that goes out. Depending on the person. Some are more sensitive than others. . . . Some people you can say, "Now, listen, you're acting like a damn fool, knock it off or go home," and they'll understand. Some people you have to handle with kid gloves and pull them aside and say, "Listen. You're obviously having a bad day here somewhere along the line, and I don't know if it has anything to do with work or not, but its affecting the people around you, and its affecting the way the food is going out." . . . Bruce and Jon, you can handle just about the same. They're very easy going. . . . Larry is a totally different story. You have to handle him with kid gloves. He's very sensitive, and he takes everything personally. I've had quite a few long talks about it. I said, "One of your biggest problems here is that nobody can talk to you without you taking it personally. They send the french fries back and say they look terrible, you take it personally. You are angered by it. You put the french fries up, and you throw the plate up of new ones. There's no reason for that. Everybody makes a mistake, but you don't have to take the mistake personally. You're a professional."

(Personal interview, Owl's Nest)

Both men rely upon images of a properly functionally organization and upon images of professional behavior, but their theories of emotional management and how that emotional management fits into a organizational hierarchy differ substantially. To function efficiently, work organizations must not only have rules of emotional management (Hochschild 1983) but also must agree upon the means of negotiating their rules when differences of interpretation occur—a form of metanegotiation (Kleinman 1982).

Of course, disagreements are situated. While anger is found in kitchens, it often blows over like a squall at sea despite being memorable at the time. If a kitchen is a family, yelling is part of family dinners: "Irene mentions Gordon's terrible temper. . . . One day she was standing in between Gordon and a Cuban dishwasher, who were throwing dishes at each other" (Field notes, Blakemore Hotel). I witnessed cooks banging pans and throwing knives, glasses, utensils, letting their anger escape within the confines of their backstage community. Fortunately, work groups are sufficiently accepting that when the anger passes, the angered can be reintegrated—the emotional display need not be tied to the self, except when the display is too frequent or dramatic: *emotional role distance* operates. One cook explained hopefully: "Everyone screams at each other, and right away after work it's all forgotten and everybody's buddy-buddy" (Personal interview, La Pomme de Terre).

For those with structural responsibilities the linkage between emotional display and self may be seen as closer. A chef had been terminated at the Owl's Nest largely because of his wild temper: calm Paul represented a pleasant contrast. One cook described this previous chef: "He was obnoxious a lot, always yelling. Chewing people out. You could hear it in the dining room. He even chewed [the owner] out" (Personal interview, Owl's Nest). Another cook described a day this chef flung a hot pan across the kitchen into a distant sink. What might have been tolerable from workers could not be accepted in the supervisor—despite the reputation of temperamental chefs. Few chefs have sufficient status or credit to get away with this "emotional brutality" on a routine basis.

Emotions at work are tolerated to a degree because it is in everyone's interest that things flow smoothly and that conflict is papered over, so long as all seems well on the outside. Joking is one major way in which salve is spread; yet, expectations and beliefs in emotional stability must be heeded if a workplace is to be a commonwealth of friends: a place where all strive for common ends.

NETWORKS OF KITCHENS

If an individual kitchen is a community, does the restaurant industry consist of a community of communities? While the answer to this question is a matter of degree, the close-knit connections that one finds in art worlds and other professional subsocieties are not evident here. While cooks could establish relationships because they share tasks and interests, in fact, such connections are rare. Because of occupational mobility, culture is spread, but no subcultural consciousness seems to have developed about food preparation.

Had this research been conducted in New York, Paris, San Francisco, Lyon, or New Orleans, a tighter network would surely have been discovered among the better restaurants. Similarly, some evidence suggests that owner-managers are in contact with their colleagues (Schmelzer and Lang 1991), scanning the organizational environment through social networks (Aldrich, Rosen, and Woodward 1986), a practice less useful to employees.

Cooking, like many occupations (Bucher 1962), is segmented. Some segments might be constituted like an art world with its tight social network. So, in Paris: "Among today's bright young chefs there is both competition and camaraderie. It is not unusual to spot one of them on his closing day enjoying a meal in a colleague's establishment, testing his own performance by comparison and gaining a bit of inspiration for a culinary takeoff when he gets back to his own kitchens" (Berry, 1979, p. 35; see also Wechsberg 1977, p. 128). Elite French chefs, like impressionist painters before them, sometimes vacation together, cook jointly, and trace their culinary lineage—activities absent in Minnesota, isolated from cultural elites.

Despite the possibility of the development of social connections, in fact, little networking occurred. Only once did a cook from another restaurant visit the kitchen of a restaurant that I studied: a cook from the hotel kitchen where two cooks from the Owl's Nest had previously been employed. Employers never visit former employees. Kitchen friendships might be intimate, but they are also transient. One cook commented: "One of those things about cooking, friendships are so transient. You meet somebody, you work with them, you become inseparable buddies, and then, all of a sudden, you change jobs, and you never see the guy" (Personal interview, La Pomme de Terre). While this cook did maintain contact with some past co-workers—important for job searches—these friendships are latent. Yet, although these contacts are relatively inactive, they can be activated. One cook at the Blakemore previously worked with a cook who had worked for the Blakemore's chef at a Ramada Inn, so she "got the scoop on him" (Personal interview, Blakemore Hotel). Another source of contacts for these workers are cooking-school classmates. Networks radiate from trade-school kitchens, unlike in elite French cuisine where young, ambitious cooks will move as apprentices from grand restaurant to grand restaurant, expanding networks of social contacts.[5]

Cooks do not discuss culinary experiments with those outside their kitchen. A gifted *pâtissier,* the pastry chef at La Pomme de Terre reported she did not know other pastry chefs in the Twin Cities, not even her predecessor. When dining, cooks do not announce their occupational standing. They pay full price, receive no special treatment, and do not visit the kitchens. In fact, at one restaurant the manager prohibits complimentary meals for fellow chefs. At best, they might get a special appetizer or dessert, but this was a hypothetical question. The chef at the Owl's Nest emphasized that he had never eaten there before being hired. Further, as I note in chapter 7, cooks do not dine at the top restaurants, where they might be inspired, but at restaurants where they feel comfortable. Cooks eat like average middle-class and working-class residents of the Twin Cities, not like gourmets or foodies. They do not eat like artists but like customers.

One local occupational organization operates in the Twin Cities: the Midwest Chefs Society. This group includes primarily those involved in trade education and institutional cooking. Only one cook at the four restaurants regularly attended meetings of this group, and he was a trade-school student whose instructor was then president. What might have been an occasion for chefs and cooks to socialize and discuss aesthetic and practical problems was primarily an opportunity for organizing charitable events and for cooking instructors to meet with institutional cooks, providing a network for students to find a niche in the job market. There was little recognition of shared or collective problems. The closest the group came to occupational debate was their desire for certification of cooks—a boon for culinary training programs. The young cook who attended meetings of the group emphasized its ability to provide a network, but most cooks to whom I talked had little interest or time to participate. One cook, who described himself as "pretty insulated" (isolated), explained that he sees his job as a job and sees activities such as the Midwest Chef's Society separate from his interests (Personal interview, Blakemore Hotel). The head chef at La Pomme de Terre felt that he should participate, that he would like to meet more chefs, but that "it takes three consecutive meetings in order to become eligible for membership." His schedule, and those of other cooks, made attending evening meetings costly for cooks who do not teach or cook in institutional venues.

The existence of a social network was most evident for job placement. Personal contacts are an effective means of uncovering employment opportunities (Granovetter 1974). Although networking was not critical in the Twin Cities restaurant industry, latent networks could be activated when a cook was searching for new employment:[6]

I talked to the chef [at his previous job], who was a friend of mine. I told him I wanted to leave. I wasn't sure where I was going; I just wanted to get out of there. So he said he'd talk to Tim, because Howie used to work there before [moving to La Pomme de Terre]. And he thought maybe he could bring me over here. So he talked with Tim.

(Personal interview, La Pomme de Terre)

Jon had worked at Winfield Potters before moving to the Radisson South. He moved because one of his instructors at his cooking program was hired as head chef. Later he moved when Paul, a colleague at the Radisson, became head chef at the Owl's Nest. Apparently there is still a connection between the Radisson South and the Owl's Nest. Jon tells me that someone from the Radisson had called, asking if there was an opening.

(Field notes, Owl's Nest)

These network ties indicate that the culinary world is not entirely anonymous; yet, the connections are limited and insufficient to build the occupation's professional or artistic status. Even managers do not have much contact with other managers, seeing themselves in overt competition with nothing to share. I do not argue that social networks in the hospitality industry will inevitably have this thin character, but that thin networks are common because of the economic organization of the restaurant industry and the operational structures within kitchens.

CONCLUSIONS

Workplaces are communities by necessity: workers share a common space and so must cope with each other. Like all communities they are governed, with workers recognizing the existence and legitimacy of some form of hierarchy as long as it does not interfere overly with the successful and pleasant doing of their work. Typically workers need each other to help with tasks that their bosses and the requirements of their occupation demand. This is a compelling motivation for the existence of a strong culture and a tight community. Of course, workplaces can be more or less successful, more or less close, and need to be examined individually if one wishes to advise management. Communities establish local cultures—workplace idiocultures—which emerge from jocular relationships. These relations are of particular importance because, unlike merely being shared, they require that each person sacrifice himself or herself for the amusement of co-workers. Individual costs produce collective benefits. The emotional rules and ideology of the kitchen set the tone for what can and should be done—how the

kitchen and the restaurant in which it is embedded—should be organized. In this, workplaces do not differ from families and sports teams,
even if the commitment level may be attenuated. Emotional ideology
belongs to workplace culture and connects directly to theories of organizational culture. All workplaces, but small workplaces in particular,
have cultures that emerge from the doing of work and cannot easily be
constructed by management. The culture becomes a reality for all
those who are a party to it. Even though organizational sagas (Clark
1972) and other management-inspired traditions are possible, values
and norms become sedimented because of the occupational structure
of the workplace. When work is smooth, generating commitment to
the organization, the culture is supportive and not subversive to organizational goals.

Finally, communities participate in larger communities. In the case
of the restaurant industry, this larger community is not well organized.
The temporal organization and competitive structure of the industry
makes such a community doubtful, and the lack of a clear ideology
that emphasizes subcultural values also decreases the perceived need
for such organization. No matter how strong the kitchen community,
an overarching community is not evident. Small, locally run restaurants operate under the aegis of "pluralistic ignorance" (Matza 1964),
whereby groups simultaneously face problems without awareness that
others are confronting similar problems. Whether this will be overcome remains to be seen, since today restaurants operate as if they
were isolated islands, rather than a part of an archipelago.

FIVE

The Economical Cook

Organization as Business

As soon as experience showed that a well-made *ragout* was
enough to make its inventor's fortune, self-interest, that most
powerful of incentives, kindled every imagination and set
every cook to work.

—*Jean-Anthelme Brillat-Savarin,*
The Philosopher in the Kitchen

Business organizations cannot be understood as independent islands,
as privately constructed worlds of meaning. They belong to a robust
economic system. Conditions of political economy influence the doings
of workers (Burawoy 1979). For instance, technological change within
an industry affects the dynamics of worker interaction, even though
workers (or individual entrepreneurs) had little input in the planning
and implementation of these changes or their economic impacts (Finlay
1988). De-skilling has profound and surprising consequences on the
structure of occupations, increasing some workers' status at the expense of others (Grzyb 1990). For instance, the structural and interorganizational needs of Hollywood production companies channel individual choices and shape the final "artistic" product (Faulkner 1983).
These structural alterations influence owners and managers as well as
the workers who are supposedly the "victims" of these changes.

The external, industrial constraints under which workers struggle
affect their doings and their culture (Prendergast and Knottnerus 1990;
Zukin 1989). Behavior cannot be disentangled from the political economy of society, a point recognized by those interested in meaning as
well as those concerned with structure (Blumer 1990; Denzin 1977;
Farberman 1975). How do restaurants, as service and production
units, fit into an economic structure? How can cultural production be

made profitable, and how do macrolevel decisions—both those of many small organizations, collectively considered, and decisions of institutional actors—affect personal action?

THE ECONOMIC NEXUS

Restaurants constitute hybrid industrial organizations, a cross between expressive entrepreneurialism and rational economic institutions, increasingly affected by organizational isomorphism (Dimaggio and Powell 1983). These organizations face the structural conditions that Coser, Kadushin, and Powell (1982, p. 7) describe for the publishing industry, suggesting similarities among cultural industries:

> (1) The industry sells its products—like any commodity—in a market, but a market that, in contrast to that for many other products, is fickle and often uncertain. (2) The industry is decentralized among a number of sectors whose operations bear little resemblance to each other. (3) These operations are characterized by a mixture of modern mass-production methods and craftlike procedures. (4) The industry remains perilously poised between the requirements and restraints of commerce and the responsibilities and obligations that it must bear as a prime guardian of the symbolic culture of the nation.

As documented in the introduction, the restaurant industry is a significant sector of the economy. Yet, most restaurants have a fragile economic base. Few freestanding restaurants have large profit margins (Miller 1978). As the owner of Stan's joshed, "There is a saying in the restaurant industry, which I think is right, that you lose on every sale, but you make it up on volume" (Field notes). The owner of La Pomme de Terre told me privately that they were "marginally successful"— they made money but not much. He had heard that several of his major competitors were in trouble, and in the next few years several closed. His business manager indicated that their profits were due to low overhead because of their relatively peripheral location, producing a low debt service.

In 1987, the census reported over 300,000 eating places with sales of nearly $150 billion dollars (*Statistical Abstracts 1990*, p. 769). What Jean-Anthelme Brillat-Savarin exaggerated in 1825 still applies today: "Gourmandism also has considerable fiscal importance; toll dues, customs duties, and indirect taxes thrive on it. Everything we consume plays tribute, and gourmands are the chief mainstay of every nation's wealth" (1970, p. 134). Despite the economic power of the industry, the mortality rate of restaurants is astounding. According to one report, of the 3,000 restaurants that open in New York City annually, nearly 2,000 fail within a year: "It is estimated that sixty-five percent of the restaurants that open in the city will fail in the first year, largely from three causes: not enough start-up money, squabbling among the operators, and inexperience in selling food for profit. And the restaurants that do succeed tend to last only five years" (Tharp 1980, p. 37; see Bennett 1982). National figures are not this high, but whatever the precise numbers, few restaurants become well established. This trend seemed exacerbated in the recession of the early 1990s, in which many prominent, classic New York French restaurants closed, with only the less expensive, "bistro" type restaurants surviving (Gopnik 1992, p. 128).

By the 1980s, opening a restaurant had become a popular fantasy among some sectors of the upper-middle-class, who hoped to become arbiters of aesthetic taste.[1] Yet, often it was a fantasy that became a nightmare, particularly if the owners hadn't determined the size and character of the potential market niche they were entering. As of 1980, it was estimated that to open a restaurant in New York City one needed $40,000 in start-up costs, or, according to some, enough money to pay expenses for a year (Tharp 1980, p. 38). These costs underline a crucial reality: freestanding restaurants, not tied to chains or corporations, tend to be undercapitalized, in view of the competition and the sometimes unexpected bureaucratic hurdles that state agencies enforce.

When the owner of La Pomme de Terre planned to open a new "superexclusive" restaurant, he negotiated a deal with the developers of the building in which the restaurant would be located: they would provide the capital, so that if the restaurant folded (as it did within a year), he would be protected. They had deeper pockets than he. Since many restaurants are opened by "entrepreneurs," they operate on a financial tightrope for years. Because of the number of competing organizations (12,000 restaurants in New York City alone), substantial profits are unlikely in this highly competitive free market. This financial reality has consequences for how restaurants are structured: to cut losses, rather than to make large profits.

That segment of the hospitality industry that is better capitalized, such as hotel restaurants, tends not to have the problem of immediate bankruptcy, but other problems, such as customer loyalty, employee satisfaction, corporate meddling, and management emphasis on the bottom line, are evident. These organizations cannot easily enlist workers and customers in perfecting the illusion that a restaurant meal is a private dinner party. Corporations, not as caught up in the "romance of a restaurant," tend not to have the commitment to culinary quality of smaller entrepreneurs, unless gourmet dining is the market niche to which they aspire. This suggests a plausible explanation for the lack of large corporations in haute cuisine dining. While some cities have several upscale restaurants with a single owner (the owner of La Pomme de Terre owned three other restaurants in the Twin Cities), these restaurants are typically different in style and rarely do "chains" of upscale restaurants extend beyond a single metropolitan area. Haute cuisine dining is assumed to be a unique experience, an expression of an auteur-chef, rather than a fungible and reproducible experience.

Because of small profits and the difficulty of maintaining stable cash flow (from variable customer loyalty), upscale restaurants have largely remained the province of the small entrepreneur, with hotel restaurants representing the oft-maligned corporate edge of culinary involvement in the industry. Hotels have an important role in the restaurant industry as their financial support of and influence over training centers such as the Culinary Institute of America indicates (Desens 1979, p. 60).[2] Both individual entrepreneurs and large corporations have advantages in their competition.

Restaurants are economic organizations on several dimensions: (1) their attempts to set prices and cope with customer demands on the output boundary; (2) their control of workers, conditions of work, and labor costs; and (3) their attempts to control material costs, the input boundary of the organization.

PRICES AND CUSTOMERS

Organizational ecology, a green and charming term for the red tooth and claw of industrial competition, provides a compelling image for the workings of businesses (Hannon and Freeman 1989). The expression reminds us that industrial organizations do not just succeed or fail, but rather they succeed or fail *in context*. One makes choices in light of the external constraints that one confronts. Decision makers at a restaurant, or other organization, must be aware of what is occurring in social fields that affect its ability to achieve its instrumental and expressive goals.

An organization is part of a "macrointeraction" system, in which the choices each actor selects have an effect on others. Kitchens are only possible because of diners, just as diners are only possible because of kitchens; and both are only possible because of an economic system based on choice of employment and consumption. This linkage of macro- and micro- through mediating processes is what symbolic interactionists refer to as the "meso" level of analysis (Maines 1982).

Customers are judged both by quantity and quality. Whatever the hopes and desires of workers and managers, they shape their products to the preferences of their audiences (e.g., Arian 1971; Martorella 1982; Coser, Kadushin, and Powell 1982, p. 226), who are often more conventional and less sophisticated in taste than producers and may be scorned (Gillon 1981, p. 49). The reality for every restaurant is the number of customers and the size of their checks; without a client base and monetary flow, a restaurant will quickly be bankrupt. Establishments that are adequately capitalized (Miller 1978) can survive slow sales for a while but not forever, particularly when competitors are thriving. Restaurants can manage slow Tuesdays but not many slow Saturdays; slow Januarys but not slow Decembers; slow Independence Days but not slow Mother's Days. One mechanism of control is to request or demand reservations. Management plan their labor needs on estimates of patronage, making the best of a bad lot, since labor costs typically comprise about 30 percent of management expense. For this structural reason cancellations pose a major problem, sufficient that the house manager at La Pomme de Terre calls large parties that do not arrive within thirty minutes of their reservations. Some upscale restaurants now demand a credit card deposit. Staffing the kitchen based on a reservations book can produce strain in the kitchen: "Tonight was a strange night in that there were twenty-five cancellations, or 'no-shows.' This included a table of ten, a table of five, and two tables of four. The owner tells me that cancellations really annoy him, and that people who do not show up or cancel at the last minute 'have no understanding of the restaurant business. . . . We had to send one waiter home tonight.' Cancellations also hurt the take-home pay (tips) of waiters. Cooks tend to be less affected than waiters, but if the turnout is really light, a cook will be sent home early as well" (Field notes, La Pomme de Terre). When one considers that at this point in the mid-1980s the average check at La Pomme de Terre was about $30–$35, these no-shows have real consequences. Even at the Blakemore and the Owl's Nest, with average checks between $20 and $30, each customer mattered. Stan's had a lower per person check, more turnover, and more walk-in business, so no-shows or cancellations were less critical. Still, they too guessed how many cooks and, especially, servers to schedule.

It is not simply the number of customers but the size of the checks that determines a restaurant's success. A party that orders the cheapest items on the menu, doesn't order appetizers or desserts, and avoids wine will not generate profit, just as consumers who only purchase loss leaders or car buyers who avoid add-ons do not help the bottom line. In contrast, some parties "make" evenings:

> One night the Owl's Nest had a party of thirty. Paul informs me: "That ticket's as much as they used to have in a whole night. First night I worked we had thirty people. They told me it was an average night." He estimates that the check for the entire party will be $1,000, but when he learns that almost everyone in the party ordered wine, he increases that estimate to $1,500. He tells me: "A party like that is a good evening, just in itself." They generate more profit for the restaurant than some parties twice as large. This night offsets many slower evenings, giving the owners a cushion, and increasing the likelihood of staff bonuses.
>
> (Field notes)

While the number of customers increased since Paul had taken over, it was below their best years, when this traditional, businessman's continental restaurant was a dominant culinary force—one of the two or three best restaurants in the Twin Cities. The city culture had changed. Mel, a longtime cook, told me that they used to serve several hundred people for lunch whereas when I observed, one hundred at lunch was considered a good day. While weekend evenings were busy, they were not chaotic; one hundred people was considered profitable. One weekday night with sixty-eight customers was considered "a good money night" (Field notes, Owl's Nest). The large party described above was a throwback to the days, a decade earlier, when large groups dined on steak and wine, and when restaurants that provided this in an elegant, if florid, setting were considered haute cuisine. In the mid-1970s, new establishments that were French or nouvelle cuisine or nouvelle American (La Pomme de Terre) emerged, some elegantly muted like La Pomme de Terre. During this time, some old warhorses, like the Owl's Nest, fell out of favor. The New Class had taken over from business elites as culinary tastemakers. Paul emphasized serving fish and seafood, attempting with some success to capture health-conscious customers. This restaurant, which had once made its reputation on its beef, was now serving mostly fish. The organizational ecology and the culture had changed, and the Owl's Nest had changed with it. By the mid-1980s, two other "grand" Twin Cities restaurants had closed.

The number of customers is not important per se, but it is correlated with total spending. While some restaurants—those that focus on high turnover (such as Stan's or the archetypical McDonald's)—are less concerned about the customers they recruit, upscale restaurants aim for a particular target, using customers as part of the ambiance. These establishments typify their customers, both in general strategic discussions and in describing particular parties. La Pomme de Terre attempted to recruit affluent urban professionals—the stereotypical yuppie. These diners had considerable cultural capital in the culinary realm (Bourdieu 1984, pp. 174 ff.), having had experience dining at fine restaurants and a "well-developed palate." They also desired "unique" creations; monkfish with peach sauce or basil-cantaloupe sorbet were seen as creative, not merely bizarre. Consuming novel combinations marked one's status. In contrast, the Owl's Nest had less interest in these consumers, and appealed to those who were older, more traditional but equally well-heeled. These diners were no longer wedded to traditional steak, beef, and pork dishes; yet, these items remained on the menu. Female consumers from this group were more likely to order fish than were their male counterparts. These customers lived well but were more likely to stay close to their previous gustatory experiences. The Blakemore, a hotel restaurant in a chain that did not emphasis its cuisine, located in a downtown venue that was deserted in the evening, tended to rely upon hotel guests: businessmen and some families. Decisions—such as the installation of a display kitchen—were made by central management and, perhaps for this reason, never attracted an audience. For the Blakemore the precise number of customers was not critical, because the hotel would always need a restaurant and, hence, cooks. At Stan's the problem of a customer base was less severe, because it was essentially a neighborhood steakhouse, situated in a lower-middle-class community in which there were few other quality restaurants. On a busy Saturday night Stan's could serve over five hundred customers, and there was a continual struggle in the kitchen for three hours to keep up with customer demands. Their clients demanded steak, served without sauce or other fancy treatment. As long as the beef was of high quality, which it was, and priced competitively—about ten dollars each—customers would leave satisfied and return. They had established a profitable market niche that had served them for decades. A few years after this research the restaurant faced a challenge as the local bridge across the Mississippi was closed for two years for repairs. This hurt the restaurant, but the construction encouraged locals to avoid downtown.

Each restaurant had its own targeted market, segmented by age, income, gender, residence, and culture. Within these segments different customers patronized the restaurant at different times. For instance, at Stan's: "Eve, a waitress, describes the Sunday afternoon customers as the 'cardiac crowd.' She noted that these senior citizens typically leave small tips. On Saturday she received $85 in tips but expects half of that on Sunday" (Field notes). While few restaurants are open Sunday afternoon, Stan's profits because its management has selected a target audience that wishes to dine then. At this time they sell fewer steaks; many senior citizens select chicken. One cook notes that "a hamburger, a turkey sandwich, and a roast pork" constitute a typical Sunday order. Their customers affect their cuisine.

The Blakemore profitably caters to prom-night couples, since many high school proms are held at or near the hotel. While the hotel must cope with the challenges of adolescent awkwardness and hormones, the hotel management values those nights although the waiters complain about small tips. In contrast, La Pomme de Terre misses out on prom business. The Owl's Nest finds conventions desirable because these customers order steaks and liquor on their expense accounts and leave big tips. Convention season is profitable for the Owl's Nest but has little effect on Stan's. For the Owl's Nest, being advertised in convention programs is important for business whereas neither Stan's nor La Pomme de Terre is much interested in such promotion. Even though each restaurant has a substantial middle-class appeal, each market niche differs.

COOKS AND CUSTOMERS

The relationship between cooks and customers is complex, mediated by others, notably servers or managers. Yet, despite this mediation, some customers gain the status of "regulars" and become part, however tangentially, of the restaurant community, relied on for the organization's continuing success:

Four years ago the Mitchells discovered Travestierre on 83rd Street [in New York City]. "We really liked it, so we went there seven nights in a row," he says. "By the end of the first year, we had eaten dinner there a hundred times. Now we know the whole family, so when they opened Latanzi's down in the theater district, we started going there too. I like it best when Paolo, my favorite brother, does the cooking. I call up and say, 'Paolo, I am coming over tonight. Save me some porcini mushrooms.'" . . . [Another customer comments,] "Today you are judged by the kind of foie gras you eat and the kind of restaurant gossip you speak. Throughout the ages, the status symbols have changed. There was the library, the swimming pool and the wine cellar. Now it is status to be a personal friend of a three-star chef."

(Morrisroe 1984, pp. 47, 49)

One restaurant critic argues that repeated patronage is necessary to get the best food and service—he speaks of gaining the "home field advantage" (Jacobs 1980, p. 16). At the Owl's Nest a few regular customers are invited back into the kitchen, an honor that servers don't always receive because of tight space. A house captain at La Pomme de Terre speaks for all staff: "After four years we have ever and ever more regulars you treat kinda like friends and kinda like customers. People differ on that. Some like to be called Mister all the time; while with others you can become almost friends. One of the rewards is dealing with regulars" (Field notes; see also Marshall 1986, p. 41). While the primary relationship is between maître d' and customer or server and customer, cooks become aware of regulars through narrative accounts from maître d's, servers, and owners. Keeping a regular happy and returning is a substantial economic benefit for any restaurant. A regular who brings guests can also help generate new regulars.

Once one has established a market niche, change can be precarious. Paul explained that when he was hired at the Owl's Nest, he realized that they had to change but not too rapidly, for fear of losing regulars. He realized that he had to educate these customers to his style of lighter cooking, which he felt could expand their customer base. Yet, for financial reasons, he simply couldn't jettison the old customers. After Paul left the Owl's Nest, his replacement expressed similar goals:

[The new chef] has instituted subtle changes in the award-winning restaurant's tried-and-true favorites, with help from the [Owl's Nest] veteran corps of cooks and servers. "The old way is fine," he told them, "but let's approach it with a new twist." By building trust with both staff and long-time customers, he's made progress. "When a frequent patron would order his usual New York strip, I'd send out two or three sauces—anchovy, green peppercorn—and say, 'See what you think.' By setting up the customers to enjoy the food by having the staff explain and present it properly, you gain their confidence."

(Waldemar 1985, p. 154)

Trust is an important element connecting customers and workers. It becomes an instance of "joint activity" in a market environment (Prus 1989). Service providers must cultivate a sense of closeness, loyalty, and community from those on whom they depend (Bigus 1972). For André Soltner of New York's famed Lutèce the relationship is "like a doctor-patient relationship built on trust" (Burros 1986, p. 23). One chef explained: "When I travel in France and visit my celebrated colleagues, I have great expectations. I never order; I ask the chef what he is going to do for me. Often I would like to tell my guests to please leave their worries with their coats at the door. We like demanding customers, provided they know what they want" (Wechsberg 1980, p. 36). The cost in accepting customer demand is that one gives up a portion of one's hard-won professional authority to those who are less trained (Hughes 1971, p. 346). Yet, the possibility exists of establishing an ideal economic relationship based on mutual respect and friendly regard. This is evident when regulars ask for special dishes without inquiring about the price or when they ask waiters to bring them what is "good" that night. Misused, this could lead to inflated prices and the serving of foods that are not selling—a mild "con" involving fabrication (Goffman 1974), used on some naive customers when management asks servers to "push" a dish. The goal, however sincere the friendly feelings, is to have the customer return and bring others: "A female regular, celebrating her birthday, didn't order dessert, so Davis, a server, puts a small candle in a strawberry and surrounds it with mounds of whipped cream. Davis jokes to me: 'It's the little things we do that keep them coming back for more'" (Field notes, La Pomme de Terre). A reality of many occupations, particularly applicable to cooks, is that workers must please clients who do not share their taste. One frustrated chef fumed: "We have to please everyone. You're at their mercy. [Customers] don't have much taste" (Field notes, La Pomme de Terre). At Stan's customers are referred to as "assholes" (Field notes).[3]

The establishment of illusory, or "parasocial," relations is required to prevent a sense of alienation. As Lutèce's André Soltner points out, "Between the cook and eater there is an invisible string. He is pleased because I gave him something from me. I want love from my customers" (Burros 1986, p. 23). However, cooks' hopes for respect are often not satisfied because they lack direct ties to customers. To cope with this, several of the restaurants prominently displayed notes from their customers in the kitchen—a means of sharing the compliments that servers hear but that are only indirectly known to cooks, building some measure of loyalty from cooks to those they serve. For instance, a letter posted in the pantry of La Pomme de Terre commented that the meal the writer was served was the best meal that he had ever had. The head chef tells me: "That's what makes it worthwhile" (Field notes). The cook risks his reputation by serving his food to customers (Charpentier and Sparkes 1934, p. 97), and, in turn, he wants respect, esteem, or even love. As one cook explained: "I got into [cooking] because I like people's reactions to eating food. I like to serve people. . . . I still enjoy creating dishes. I very much enjoy talking to people that truly like my cooking" (Personal interview, La Pomme de Terre). The ultimate compliment, a rare one, is receiving a tip directly from a customer. This happened once or twice at La Pomme de Terre and was memorable for the workers involved. The standard mediated economic relations was, for that moment, overturned.

As noted above, some cooks hope to "educate" customers, raising the level of their taste. This is evident in remarks made by the new chef at the Owl's Nest and was an issue at La Pomme de Terre, where the cooks were more adventurous than their customers, who were, admittedly, more adventurous than most. The nineteenth-century chef Escoffier claimed that the cook's first duty is to satisfy customers and the second is to teach them (Sanger 1980, p. 53). These two goals—satisfaction and education—encapsulate the dilemma of cooks as service providers and professionals. This model can be found in all occupations that strive to be role models for their customers—jazz musicians, barbers, gardeners, dental hygienists, and the like.

ROUTINE VERSUS INDIVIDUAL TREATMENT

Many businesses based on repeat patronage desire to treat their customers as acquaintances—to create the illusion of community, asking employees and managers to know these strangers "personally"—establishing a relationship of loyalty and trust (Bigus 1972; Prus 1989). This model is in direct conflict with that of interactive service establishments such as fast-food chains that strive for fully interchangeable personnel and routinized transactions (Leidner 1993). Personalized treatment increases transaction costs, in contrast to routinized, rationalized treatment that maximizes efficiency. Further, the former provides a measure of autonomy to those who interact with clients. In practice, some customers—those defined as regulars or those designated as "big tippers"—receive special treatment. Restaurants are prestige markets and use special treatment as a means of encouraging the "right" customers to return: "Waiters were reported to 'size up' customers and base their level of service on the anticipated gratuity. . . . [Restaurants] encourage the patronage of businessmen, professionals, the successful, and the affluent. Regularity of patronage may be rewarded through the allocation of good tables, personal courtesy and attention, and the waiving of reservation requirements" (Schiller 1972, p. 137). This special treatment also extends to the food served. In all cases these benefits involve the provisioning of scarce goods. Special treatment requires that not all are entitled to the same public treatment, and so some customers may notice that they are not treated equally. Since restaurants are prestige markets, providing opportunities for conspicuous consumption (Finkelstein 1989), they publicize their clientele as well as their own products. Clients become part of the theater of the restaurant (Shelton 1990), as well as an end in themselves.

Each of the freestanding restaurants made special provision for their best or most favored customers:[4]

> The cooks are working on a salmon order when the server returns to the kitchen and tells the cook to "hold on with the salmon. Charles [the owner's son] wants to pick it out." Charles enters the kitchen, explaining "That's my parish priest out there. [He chooses a salmon steak.] Don't overcook it. Don't undercook it." The cooks prepare it very carefully.
>
> (Field notes, Stan's)

> One customer always receives special treatment. Cooks prepare a special, large salad with lettuce, carrots, zucchini, and onion. Denny explains: "If we don't give her enough, she'll ask for more, so why not please her the first time." She insists on having half an orange squeezed on her salad, served with a side order of Caesar dressing. Her server reminds Denny: "When you make [her] vegetables, no wine. She just can't have wine. You can put in herbs but just no wine or salt or anything like that." I felt that the cooks were frustrated in having their aesthetic standards compromised, but they make her food as ordered.
>
> (Field notes, La Pomme de Terre)

While special treatment has an instrumental effect in increasing tips, it also benefits the establishment by keeping a regular returning. This preferential treatment is in the interest of the establishment, no matter how much it violates the canons of equality. Similar treatment for all customers would not be justified economically in that the likelihood of their returning is low. One needs a core of clients on whom the economic stability of the restaurant can rest.

Difficult Customers. Just as special customers require stroking because one wishes them to return, difficult customers must be dealt with as well. Here restaurant staff use diplomacy to satisfy these individuals and in extreme cases decide whether to "cool them out" or to be willing to lose their business. Diplomacy is key to handling "troublesome" customers because of the belief that the way in which disruptions are handed can affect repeat patronage (Prus 1989). Tact is necessary not just for that customer but because a complaining customer becomes the center of attention. Thus, even though management may believe that it is right, it often accedes to the demands to create a loyal and compliant client and to demonstrate publicly to all present that they are reasonable. Complaints, properly handled, can be good business.

Cooks, of course, don't see the situation as it develops; they often have to solve a problem, relying on the server's narrative to describe its character and the type of person involved. When the culinary quality is at issue, cooks have no authority to defend themselves. They must accept the decision of the server or manager. Servers and managers must be diplomatic toward the customers and the cooks if they are to remain on good terms with everyone. Since servers are not always diplomats and their immediate loyalty lies with the tipping customer, it is not surprising that cooks can vent their rage against fellow workers, in lieu of attacking the ignorant customer.[5]

The easiest solution to a culinary dispute is simply to recook food according to the customer's taste or to present something different. Cooks must grin and bear the insult to their food and what it implies about their competence. Servers assuage the temper of the cooks by boisterously demeaning the same customers with whom they are schmoozing in the dining room. The friction seemed particularly intense at Stan's Steakhouse, where customers were not well enough socialized or lacked cultural capital to treat cooks as professionals, simultaneously defining themselves as competent judges:

> One customer is served a shrimp salad and refuses it because the tiny shrimp are not deveined. Robin, her waitress, tells Doug, the head chef, that "we don't have deveined shrimp. She doesn't want them. Pfft." Charles, the owner's son, asks Beatrice, who is working in the salad area, to see if the shrimp are peeled and deveined. She does check, although she is not pleased about the request, and reports that "there's nothing wrong about it. It's

peeled. It isn't deveined, but that's just a little bit of black in there. It's always like that." Robin explains: "That lady almost had a coronary." Charles comments that "you'd have to use a microscope." Robin tells Charles that "she wanted me to pick all of the shrimp off and replace it with chicken. I told her we're out of chicken. That's not sanitary." Charles ends the discussion by telling Beatrice: "Would it help if I told you she was pregnant?" His sexist remark is taken to mean that management supported the kitchen staff, and the incident is closed, although nasty remarks are made all day.

(Field notes, Stan's)

Robin had a problem with a woman at lunch today who was "a bitch . . . a biddy." She ordered the same steak as her friend, but she felt that the two steaks were cooked differently and differed in size. Robin reports: "She said, 'I'll learn enough to bring people in here at lunch' . . . I'd like to throw her out the door." Robin supports Lew, who cooked the steak, and comments that the woman is a troublemaker. The owner instructs her to take a dollar off the woman's check.

(Field notes, Stan's)

The restaurant staff, including management, must demonstrate collective solidarity, however they might feel privately. These "unreasonable" attacks from customers cause workers to cohere. I never heard servers attack cooks for their errors, but they frequently berated customers.

Negative Special Treatment.   On rare occasions cooks attempt to sabotage the dinners of difficult diners. The narrative from chapter 4 in which a customer's sausage was supposedly dipped in urine is an extreme instance of backstage revenge. Spitting into a customer's soup is not unknown if a cook is frustrated and feels that he can get away with it (Orwell 1934). Typically, cooks prepare dishes in a sloppy or inadequate fashion as retaliation:

Maggie, a server, comes back into the kitchen really annoyed and tells Gene about an order of top sirloin: "I want you to split these tops. I want small ones. Those people don't deserve them. I told them they couldn't split them, but they insisted on them." Gene finds the smallest tops he can.

(Field notes, Stan's)

Steffi tells the cooks that a steak has been returned: "Can you put this on more. He says it's not well-enough done. What can I say?" Charles, the owner's son, adds: "We got a real bitcher out there. Cook the hell out of it. What the hell."

(Field notes, Stan's)

The problem at Stan's, more than the other restaurants, is that customers at a steakhouse believe that they have the legitimate right to
complain about how steaks are cooked. As a high volume restaurant,
the patronage of any given customer is not critical for their economic
survival, and as a result, cooks need not care as much about repeat patronage. When a request that is perceived as unreasonable is coupled
with a hectic, frustrating evening, sabotage is possible.

Since food preparation occurs behind closed doors, cooks have the
opportunity to perform depredations with the customer none the
wiser. Their expressive acts never become public; the food is presented
as "normal," prepared "as requested." In principle, customers have little bargaining power except for their tips and the possibility of their return. Once a complaint has been made, restaurant staff may believe
that these customers will not tip or return, thus, reducing the customer's bargaining power further. Fortunately for customers, the
moral dignity of these workers is usually sufficient to stay the bitter
hand of revenge.

In fact, customers are the source of a restaurant's success. Creating
a market niche, positive relations, and a reputation are crucial for survival. To survive, establishments must assume that their potential customers are a mass and must be able to reach those they do not personally know, through mass media outlets and word of mouth through
urban networks. While organizational success is based on the sum of
idiosyncratic decisions, these decisions can be predictable in some measure from structural and cultural features. Each restaurant has a strategy for survival that may be implicit but is operationalized through
customer recruitment and media relations.

MEDIA RELATIONS

Perhaps because they are small businesses competing in a highly differentiated market, none of the three freestanding restaurants I observed
advertised widely. They had signs outside—a modest form of point-of-
sale publicity—and they paid for notices in city magazines and restaurant guides. The Blakemore Hotel placed advertisements throughout
the hotel but did little beyond this to encourage customers to dine.
These businesses are too small to make radio, television, or billboards
wise investments. These restaurants waited for customers to find them
through word of mouth or free media notice. Since Stan's, the Owl's

Nest, and La Pomme de Terre were all relatively successful establishments, with the first two in operation for decades and the third for nearly a decade, customers had found them. Yet, the lack of control over their reputation proved to be a continual threat.

Industries are linked, serving each other's interests. By the 1970s, the mass media had learned that food news is popular, and by working with restaurants, they could publish features that draw readers. For some restaurants—those that hope for a sophisticated, metropolitan clientele—a good review stimulates business and can "make" a restaurant, bringing a flood of customers (Hall 1985, p.1). For instance, at La Pomme de Terre the owner had been concerned about appointing Tim head chef, while still in his early twenties. Shortly after his appointment a glowing review in the *Minneapolis Tribune,* suggesting that the restaurant was the best in the Twin Cities, indicated that the choice was successful, and patronage increased (Field notes, La Pomme de Terre). Later a weekly entertainment guide named their poorly attended Sunday brunch as the best in the Twin Cities, an announcement that brought great cheer to the kitchen. Before that review the management had been thinking of eliminating the brunch because of low attendance. Business picked up temporarily; but even reviews have their limits, and later the brunch was ended.

Feature stories also affect sales, and chefs may agree to provide recipes when asked by newspapers or magazines, even if they must recreate recipes that were never written down or alter those otherwise impossible to prepare at home. Stan's received a boon—a mixed blessing for the cooks—when a television magazine show featured the restaurant. Viewers were told that for the next week, if they mentioned the feature, they could receive a discount on certain steaks. That weekend the restaurant was flooded with over six hundred customers. To keep the kitchen under control, all steaks had to be ordered medium. Charles, the owner's son, explained that with the discount, they barely broke even on the cost of the meal and, therefore, were losing money, but he valued the television exposure and would gladly repeat it, believing that the restaurant would gain returning customers.

Just as good reviews help, negative reviews can be painful:

For years the Coach House restaurant was awarded four stars—the highest rating—by the *New York Times'* food critic. Then one Friday early last year the paper published a scathing review that found fault with nearly every aspect of the restaurant. . . . "We had 186 reservations for that night," recalls

Leon Lianides, who has owned the restaurant for 35 years. "Eighty people didn't show up. They didn't even call." In the weeks that followed, patronage at the Coach House fell about 50%.

(Hall 1985, p. 1)

The gain or loss of a Michelin star is a momentous occasion, whose repercussions are financial but also devastating to the honor of the chef. . . . in 1966 the owner of a Parisian restaurant which lost both of its Michelin stars in a single year committed suicide.

(Clark 1975, p. 204)

These are bitterly extreme examples to be sure, but the economic consequence of a widely read unfavorable review provokes sympathy for the restaurateur who wishes to kill the critic, extracting revenge for destroying his or her livelihood.

Critics, and media reports in general, perform a "gatekeeping" role. With an abundance of businesses in the same industry arena, customers search for some basis on which to select. Word of mouth is important, but this publicity depends on the activity of some customers who have already tried the restaurant. While restaurants can generate their own publicity, the main institutional basis by which the public learns of a restaurant is through the media. This applies most dramatically in the world of elite establishments, although a similar process operates in local markets. Elite critics become tastemakers, just as critics influenced the acceptance of abstract expressionism in the New York art world (Wolfe 1976; Guilbaut 1984). In the culinary world this process is most clearly demonstrable in the acceptance of nouvelle cuisine in France: "Most credit for the success of the Nouvelle Cuisine must go to Henri Gault and Christian Millau, whose support for the adventurous chefs and the gusto with which, in the columns of their annual guide and monthly magazine, they are prepared to lampoon any restaurant which is both reactionary and bad, has enabled the new philosophy to filter down from the rarified atmosphere of the great restaurants to the general public" (Gillon 1981, p. 11). Gael Greene, the restaurant critic for *New York* magazine, argued that a handful of powerful New York critics popularized spicy Chinese food: "About 10 or more years ago, Szechuan become very important to New York. . . . It was the passion of [food critic] Craig Claiborne and [*New York* magazine's] underground gourmet, who was the combination of Milton Glaser and the late Jerome Snyder. The passion of those three for very spicy food developed an extraordinary following for Szechuan cooking" (Winegar 1985, p. 18). Of course, trends ratified by elite critics may be too expensive, unusual, or spicy for consumers, who want the illusion that they are patronizing the "hot" new restaurants (Finkelstein 1989). As a result, some restaurateurs find a market niche by taming these new cuisines so their middle-brow customers will feel they are getting the experience while consuming palatable food. Cultural innovation has been modified for a mass audience.

The process that occurs in elite venues is also evident in local markets. To a degree, the restaurants found in a particular area will be a function of local critics. Minneapolis had critics with adventurous and sophisticated palates, and perhaps for this reason Minneapolis's restaurant scene expanded during the 1980s from its sleepy senescence of the decade before. In contrast, without adventurous or sophisticated critics—without any regular critic for much of the decade—St. Paul never did develop a viable restaurant market. While other explanations might be given, the fact that Minneapolis critics were more likely to review and praise Minneapolis restaurants, and the reality that most of their readers resided in that Twin City, influenced the two restaurant communities by affecting audience knowledge.

From one perspective the critic has a duty to develop a culinary audience, indirectly increasing the number of restaurants from which the critic can choose, because the audience's increased interest in dining out has led to a larger number of patrons of new restaurants (Fine and Ross 1984). Since critics are also read by restaurant management who complain vociferously if they receive a negative review, perhaps hurting a publication's advertising, a strong push operates in local markets, such as the Twin Cities, to write something favorable about most establishments, particularly those owned locally. Criticism of national chains seems to come more easily.

Yet, critics, like cooks, see their task to educate the public. Before Craig Claiborne joined the *New York Times* in 1957, restaurant reviews were linked to the newspaper's advertising and promotion department (Buckley 1982, p. 46). By developing a culinary discourse and rating restaurants, Claiborne helped to change that. The food revolution of the 1970s spread culinary discourse from New York to the hinterlands (Hanke 1988) as restaurant food became a "prestige good" and knowledge of cuisine became part of cultural literacy for young urban professionals (Zukin 1991). The creation of a shared discourse may be integral to the establishment of legitimate occupations and stable organizations.

The mass media is integral to the organizational environment in which restaurants compete and, by affecting the success of a restaurant, has an effect on the lives and positions of kitchen workers. Positive notice creates a buoyant kitchen, whereas criticism affects not only the bottom line but also the relations within the kitchen as blame must be assigned and changes must be plotted.

THE INTERNAL STRUCTURE OF RESTAURANTS

THE DYNAMICS OF PRICING

A key element in choosing and competing in a market niche is pricing. Consumers of any product or service wish to know how much they will be charged. In the case of restaurants and many other enterprises, no "fair" price exists. Prepared food has substantial price elasticity, although in any market niche there are expectations of what price is reasonable. Thus, a "steak" might sell for anywhere from $5.00 to $25.00. While there are differences in quality and quantity of the meat—the accompaniments, the atmosphere, and the skill of the preparers—a steak is essentially a steak. Chefs, in conjunction with managers, must decide how much to charge for a particular product. While occasionally the chef will "cost out" the dish, trying to keep food costs near 30 percent, a magical figure, these calculations are approximate. I observed little discussion or computation of how "specials" should be priced. Typically prices are selected off the "top of the head."

Restaurant management must price a dish in a range so that customers can afford it and will find the price legitimate. This means that the price of some dishes can be set much higher than their cost, while others are set lower because of customer expectations. Chicken will typically be priced less than beef, because beef is considered culturally more valuable than chicken. A fair price is not an objective measure of the cost of the dish but of its perceived value—its use value. For example, the Blakemore, more careful than most about calculations of cost, attempts to price its dishes so that the *average* food cost is 31 percent, but items are treated very differently. Rack of lamb, even though it is one of the most expensive items on the menu, has a food cost of 65 percent; while chicken Oscar, a much less expensive item, has a food cost of 27 percent. The diner who wants his or her money's worth should choose the rack of lamb, a dish on which the hotel loses money. The server will not object, in that to the client the cost of the lamb is higher than that of the chicken, and the tip should be higher. Management and chefs who receive a bonus for minimizing food costs feel that servers should push the chicken—the lamb is a "loss leader." Management depends on the organizational loyalty of the servers through their "salesmanship" to insure that not many loss leaders are ordered, even though servers are not formally critiqued on their orders. At one point the chef was forced to return to his suppliers an order of racks of lamb that cost eleven dollars each, because the dish had a total food cost above 100 percent. He found cheaper lamb of poorer quality (Field notes, Blakemore Hotel).

Restaurants generally keep prices on the menu within a modest spread between some higher- and lower-priced dishes. They decrease the spread between the dishes that cost more to make and those that cost less, lowering the prices of the most expensive items and increasing the prices of the least expensive items. Paul, the head chef at the Owl's Nest, explained to me that all dishes need to be priced similarly, and so meats may sell at a loss; however, this is balanced by the higher profit margins for some fish. Some popular dishes pose economic problems: "The ivory salmon I'm losing my butt on, but I'm making it up on other items. . . . I should charge $35 for the ivory salmon. Since I need $25 to break even, I need to make it up on other items." Most vegetables are inexpensive and are not often considered in the financial equation (Field notes, Owl's Nest).

Because many dishes at La Pomme de Terre are specials and are off the menu, they are priced daily. When the restaurant served an appetizer of fresh chanterelles with marsala in puff pastry, the chef explained that he will maintain his 35 percent food cost. He uses only three ounces of chanterelles in each appetizer, which sells for $8. These mushrooms were purchased on the spur of the moment from one of his distributors. After they prepare the appetizer, they use some of the remaining mushrooms in veal leg with sliced chanterelles, for which they charged the high price of $21.50. The leftover mushrooms are used for a chanterelle omelette at lunch and for a Perigueux sauce. By using every mushroom piece and pricing dishes accordingly, the chef can recoup the nearly $100 per case that the mushrooms cost. La Pomme de Terre relies on a clientele that accepts the price elasticity of food costs; yet, even at this restaurant, dishes were never priced at over $25.00, which would have been defined as beyond the legitimate range of what food should cost in this market in the mid-1980s.

While it is nearly impossible for customers to negotiate with servers on the cost of particular dishes, restaurants negotiate the price of a banquet. Each restaurant has a banquet or party service, and the prices of meal service are set directly with customers. Costs depend on the size and status of the party, whether the restaurant is busy, and the clout of the customer. Once the price has been arranged, the chef must minimize his labor and food costs to make a profit. While restaurants such as the Blakemore may have a price list, in fact, arrangements are flexible in practice. The price list is only a guideline, a maximum, for negotiation. As one Blakemore cook told me, "Obviously many other places have better food than we have. . . . [Management has to] say, 'Why don't you bring your party of fifty in, and we can give you a deal' " (Personal interview, Blakemore Hotel).

Cooks and managers believe that "reasonably" priced items—whatever that means in a particular context—sell well. Thus, the Owl's Nest sells a lot of liver—perhaps surprising to the legions of liver haters—because it's one of the cheapest items on the menu.

For restaurants that have many customers, one technique to increase or stabilize profits is to raise the profit on each individual dish. Stan's, strained to capacity on weekend nights, raised prices, increasing each item by fifty cents. The owner's son, commenting on the over six hundred customers they had one night, explains: "Our prices are too low. Our food is good, but it's not that good" (Field notes, Stan's). The cost of a meal, over time, controls the flow of customers, in management's attempt to obtain an optimal number for efficient operation and maximal profit.

Obviously, the income of restaurants reflected in the number of customers and the amplitude of their checks reveals only half the picture. This income is only meaningful in comparison with the costs incurred. Two restaurants with the same income may vary greatly in success. Restaurants must deal with three classes of financial obligations: fixed costs, labor costs, and food costs, leaving enough room for a profit margin, usually set between five and ten percent.

Fixed Costs.   Each restaurant has its own equation of fixed costs, depending on its location, equipment, debt service, and rent or mortgage. The business manager of La Pomme de Terre claimed that they could survive financially because of modest overhead costs. They were located on the ground floor of a condominium in a residential area, away from downtown, popular with young urban professionals, near an art museum and theaters. While this area was not quite "gentrified," it was home to gentry. Their overhead was manageable. As the business manager pointed out, "If we had to pay the debt service of some of those places downtown, we could never have made it" (Field notes, La Pomme de Terre). For many freestanding restaurants, bankers are the silent partners.

Place and the costs associated with space become essential to the cultural meaning and recruitment of clientele (Zukin 1991). Significantly, the three freestanding restaurants I observed were located away from both the central business district and the most exclusive residential areas. La Pomme de Terre is located in an artistic, cultured area, permitting its location to be a part of the consumption experience. The Owl's Nest is located, as it has been for twenty years, on a major industrial and down-at-the-heels business thoroughfare, which makes obtaining a dinner crowd challenging. Stan's, a neighborhood restaurant, is situated on a main commercial street in a lower-middle-class residential area. Place influences consumption and audience. Selecting a relatively inexpensive location permits upper-middle-class individuals without investing large amounts of their own capital to obtain financing to open their own restaurants. A banker's choice to finance such an enterprise depends, of course, on his or her own financial balance sheets and estimates of the potential market.

A frequent tactic of restaurateurs to reduce expenses is to purchase the space of a restaurant that went out of business. In this way, one can obtain the equipment needed for a restaurant at a bargain. Once a space becomes a restaurant, it is likely to remain one. Yet, this pattern shows that some owners have ignored the reality that some establishments have failed because of location, not incompetence or lack of potential diners.

The internal space of a restaurant can be as important as its external place. As described in chapter 3, conflict often erupts around the quality of equipment. Management desires to limit costs, and cooks desire to cook well and easily. The choice of what kitchen equipment to purchase is tied to each goal; it is sometimes dictated by bankers' limits as well as chefs' preferences. The cooks at La Pomme de Terre and the Owl's Nest wanted new stoves, but management continually postponed that decision. Many restaurant kitchens are not air-conditioned because management is not convinced that this major expense would improve efficiency or food quality. The benefits and the costs are not seen as linked. A minor, but still troubling, dispute at La Pomme de Terre was the head chef's desire to have the owner pay for his cook's uniforms, which cost thirty-two dollars each. The chef told me that a uniform is worn out within six months, and that cooks let the uniforms become tattered to avoid the replacement cost. His solution was to let the bills slip through, so that the restaurant does, in fact, pay for the cook's uniforms, although how long that will continue is uncertain. La Pomme de Terre, in contrast to the Owl's Nest, paid for cooks' knives. In each restaurant the responsibilities and rights of cooks were negotiated and sedimented into routine practice, sometimes through union contract but other times informally among the cooks, chef, and management.

Labor Costs.   All restaurants are staffed—otherwise, why go out to eat? But how many people are needed and at what salary? Historical and economic circumstances bring changes not only in technology but also in the size of a workforce, depending on the needs of diners for what service symbolizes. For instance, a minor effect of the French Revolution was that nobles let most of their kitchen staff go, leaving others to work in the increasingly popular public restaurants (Willan 1977, p. 134).

At each restaurant in which the head chef has budgetary authority over labor (among those I observed, all except Stan's), he must decide how to allocate his budget. While there is no fixed limit on labor costs, chefs realize that if they are under budget, they will receive a substantial bonus. Thus, their personal interest diverges from that of their cooks. In general, labor costs should be less than food costs. For instance, at the Blakemore Hotel the chef tried to keep the labor costs of the cooks to about 10 percent of the restaurant and banquet service income.

Immediately prior to my observations the Blakemore Hotel had experienced layoffs. The popular sous chef and two or three other workers had been terminated, and cooks were concerned that others might follow because of poor business. The restaurant was not generating sufficient income, and management attempted to balance their budget by trimming labor costs. By the end of my observation, although the restaurant was still not attracting customers, the budget was balanced, and no further layoffs were threatened. With fewer workers, more convenience foods were used. One cook justified his restaurant's use of instant mashed potatoes by commenting: "Instant potatoes will come in handy if you don't have the help. If you want to run everything fresh, then you need that help. That's another big, major problem of restaurants. There's never enough help" (Personal interview, Blakemore Hotel). The control of labor costs affects the cuisine, reflecting once again the linkages between economic choices, work lives, and consumption choices. Reducing labor, leaving a thin line between adequate performance and incompetence, can produce failure. Cooks expressed frustration—and sometimes grim satisfaction—that cutbacks had affected the food quality:

> Dana relays the "disaster" with the deli platter yesterday: "We were late as usual. They had Ezra do these platters, and he had never done them before, and they looked like garbage." She claimed too few competent cooks were employed. She described herself as totally overwhelmed. She said that originally Kate was the baker, but now she is, and she is also supposed to prepare soups and vegetables, a division of labor that she describes as "sick. . . . If I had to do the soups and the special and the bread, that would be OK, but I can't do that and the banquets. . . . I'm leaving [today] with no chili for tomorrow. Like today, it's nonstop. They expect you to work overtime, then they don't pay you. . . . They don't say thank you or anything. It's sick."
>
> (Field notes, Blakemore Hotel)

While Dana is particularly bitter, her complaints exaggerate the frustrations of others. Management works cooks as hard as possible while keeping wages low. Cooks do work overtime willingly without pay (see chapter 2), but this can lead to the perception that employers use them, particularly in the absence of a strong community.

In addition to reducing the size of the workforce, restaurants are notorious for paying cooks low wages. Obviously, the "proper" wage is a matter of debate, as it is for all occupations. During the period in which I observed (1982–1983), the average annual wage for a head chef was approximately $30,000,[6] with the average starting hourly wage set at about $6.00, rising to $9.00 to $10.00 for more experienced cooks. A 1984 analysis suggested that chefs earn from $18,000 to $45,000, with a starting salary for cooks (in the form of hourly wages) from $9,000 to $12,000 (*Chronicle Occupational Brief* 1984, p. 2). A chef in the Twin Cities is a middle-class occupation, but other cooks receive working-class wages. Because most cooks are paid hourly, restaurants trim labor costs by sending cooks home, telling them not to come in, or simply shortening the number of hours that they are there while demanding the same output. For instance, Jon was asked to arrive at the Owl's Nest at noon, instead of 11:30 A.M. I asked Jon why the chef made this change: "He wants to see if I can get the same work done in half an hour less time, or [he says jokingly] he thought my last paycheck was too big. . . . or [he adds more seriously] business is slacking off" (Field notes, Owl's Nest). An alternate approach, practiced by the Blakemore, is to close the dining room early. If no additional reservations are on the book, the Blakemore closes the dining room thirty minutes ahead of schedule, cutting labor costs, even though they may lose customers.

From the standpoint of management—including those chefs who receive a bonus for keeping labor costs under budget—the more they can produce with less labor, the better. This economic reality must be balanced against the social reality that by cutting too much, as happened at the Blakemore, they can lose the sense of community, loyalty, and willingness to work diligently or provide overtime voluntarily. Labor process theory can be pushed too far, ignoring the subjective, emotional commitments of workers even in the face of management control and low wages.

Some restaurants fail because management is unwilling to hire until business improves, not realizing that the food will never reach the necessary quality without sufficient staff:

> I [was hired] at the Ramada Inn. Little did I know that I was the only cook that would be [there] at night. I was the night chef basically. I was the only one in the kitchen. There was nobody around, nobody under me, just the food and beverage manager was up in his office. So you'd have a banquet of two hundred people plus [that] you'd have to dish and serve while you're feeding everybody in the restaurant. . . . There was no one else working the line, and the orders are coming in, and you'd have to stop everything, catch up a little bit, go back. [The food and beverage manager] didn't want to hire anybody else because we have to get the business going in order to be able to hire someone else. We were trying to tell him the business isn't going to get going, because you don't have anybody else.
>
> (Personal interview, Owl's Nest)

Perhaps the food and beverage manager decided that no matter what he did, the business was not going to improve enough to hire another person, and so his concern was to balance the budget with fewer expenses.

Low wages are integral to the economic structure of cultural organizations to keep these luxury goods priced at a point that consumers are willing to pay for them (Phizachlea 1990). Even haute cuisine restaurants in New York minimize labor costs (e.g., Claiborne 1982, p. 144).

One technique, common throughout commerce, is to replace well-paid, experienced workers with low-paid, inexperienced ones:

> It sometimes happens that a young [worker] who has started as a dishwasher and has learned the skills of the cook actually replaces an older cook, the younger forcing out the older by his willingness to work for a lower wage.
>
>   (Herman 1978, p. 42)

> [The previous chef had been replaced.] In the company I was the only obvious choice, but he [the owner] could've gone outside too. To get an experienced chef is fairly expensive, and his operation was a little bit questionable at that time, but I think he made a very wise move, just speaking from a third-person point of view. I think he made a wise move in choosing me, 'cause he could get me cheap, and I knew what was going on.
>
>   (Personal interview, La Pomme de Terre)

This choice, critical for the restaurant's survival, was based on the reality that Tim, the sous chef, could be hired cheaply. Fortunately, this decision contributed to the restaurant's aesthetic growth, but it was based on its economic survival. Labor costs set a firm reality, demanding a level of customer patronage and a sufficient profit per customer.

Food Costs.   Food is the raw material of the culinary industry. Even for restaurants that maintain their own gardens, such as Berkeley's Chez Panisse, food is not free and must be priced "realistically." To examine the food industry thoroughly requires a global analysis (Bryant et al. 1985, pp. 243–324). The foods that Americans consume are produced throughout the world, and consumers rely on the efficiency and economic choices of multinational producers such as United Fruit or Castle and Cook, and their distributors, to revel in the culinary choices that they insist upon (Enloe 1989). The demand for food choices by diners connects the small freestanding restaurant to the world economy. Political instability, global weather patterns, and ecological alterations—all affect what is served, as when coffee or oranges are suddenly perceived as too expensive, causing changes in menus or in the quality of products served. Or, alternatively, when new foods come on the market at reasonable prices, cuisine changes. The coming of truffle farming and cultivated morel mushrooms will soon alter gourmet dining. As I describe in chapter 6, in discussing the constraints on culinary aesthetics, food costs, influenced by conditions far distant from the restaurant, affect aesthetic production. Food costs, chained to the political economy, are a reality that is central to kitchen life.

On occasion chefs attempt to negotiate with purveyors, but this was relatively rare. In practice, each trusted the other, and I was surprised that typically when orders arrived, they were not checked. This trust may not always be warranted, and one purveyor, in the midst of a labor dispute with the Teamsters, delivered beef tenderloin instead of rib-eye steaks. The problems that one organization has with another may infect its relations with a third, influencing its economic and moral standing. Restaurants exist within a web of interorganizational relationships that have consequences for organizational survival.

Chefs compared distributors to gain better prices or quality; each restaurant I observed used several purveyors and switched on occasion. Purveyors know, as do restaurants, that by providing an overly expensive or substandard product or by not delivering as promised, they might be paid once, but since the market is competitive, there is no certainty of further patronage. This problem, of course, is not unique to restaurants, but purveyors have comparable relations with their suppliers. While restaurants are looking for stability and positive relations in their dealings with food providers, they know that there are others to whom they can turn. In the Twin Cities several dozen food wholesalers compete for restaurant business, not counting purveyors from outside the area; restaurants also had the possibility of purchasing directly from farmers, farmers' markets, and grocery stores.

In addition to negotiating with purveyors, restaurants employ several strategic techniques to control costs: illusion, downgrading, reusing, and reducing. Each links the economic needs of the organization for survival with issues of impression management. For these techniques to be successful, they must be limited to the backstage, for otherwise customers would feel cheated, even if it could be argued that they are being treated fairly.

Illusion. One way in which food costs can be reduced—a technique that borders on unethical behavior and sometimes crosses it—is to serve one item as another. A particularly dramatic challenge, one vigorously denied, was made by a chef visiting the grand New York haute cuisine palace Lutèce: "He examines Lutèce's coquelet à la crème aux morilles. 'It's juicy and good,' he says. 'It isn't squab. It's Cornish hen, you know—Frank Perdue. There has been a certain sacrifice of quality for volume. Prices are higher. Rents are higher. I mean, the guy's a businessman.' . . . If you're supposed to have truffles or morels or cockscomb and you cheat—that's reprehensible" (McPhee 1979, p.

88). This was also evident in one Twin Cities restaurant that was supposed to use truffles in its dishes but used "artificial" truffles instead. There were no complaints. Fortunately, no consumer advocate exposed its secret.

Downgrading.   Different brands vary in quality and cost. Each restaurant must select the quality of the products it will serve. If a restaurant cooks with wine, does the vintage or vineyard really matter? Can anyone tell? Isn't the final taste the criterion? But suppose the taste *is* affected; how much of a difference is too much? In some sense, the answer depends on the market—will customers return? However, customers rarely make decisions to return on a single comestible (steak and wine are exceptions); and even if they do, they rarely announce it. Every restaurant must compromise between the ideal and the economic reality, and this reality is linked to its perceptions of the market niche.

To survive is to attempt to save money when possible, using "downgraded" products—even if using them does not by itself deceive the customer. An excellent gourmet restaurant like La Pomme de Terre chooses to purchase the cheapest salt, plastic wrap, and even pecans, assuming that the difference in taste is not noticeable, but the difference in price would be. The chef at La Pomme de Terre struggled to decide the proper mix of cheap and expensive coffee to include in their after-dinner mix, finally selecting five parts expensive coffee mixed with three parts cheap coffee (Field notes, La Pomme de Terre). The Owl's Nest has always had brussels sprouts and hash on the menu, but as these are not popular (ordered perhaps once a month); they are never fresh but merely defrosted when needed. Likewise, when mold is found on artificial truffles, it is merely trimmed, and the truffle chopped and served (Field notes, Owl's Nest). The higher the cost of the foodstuff, the more likely it will be served, no matter its quality. Too much has been invested to let taste determine use. The cheaper the food, the more likely it will be perfect.

These decisions also affect how dishes are prepared. Cheap ingredients are often used in place of relatively more expensive ones.

When Gordon has to make cherry cobbler, he asks Denver, the head chef, about using butter:

GORDON: Can I use melted butter?
DENVER: With what?
GORDON: With the cobbler.

DENVER: Use shortening.

GORDON: Why?

DENVER: All the butter will do is make it a little richer.

(Field notes, Blakemore Hotel)

This discussion was perhaps a little more explicit than usual, but cooking decisions regularly depend on such choices. This does not mean that the cheapest will always be used, but it is always an option—the best choice in the absence of compelling reasons.

Food that is prohibitively expensive is likely to be dropped from the menu when an alternative is judged equal. La Pomme de Terre changed from serving sparkling water to noneffervescent water because of cost, and it used to offer a complimentary chocolate truffle after dinner but eliminated that touch for economic reasons. Likewise, a restaurateur notes a change in his menu for reasons of cost: "We have to be bottom-line conscious these days. You can't make money serving lobster . . . and swordfish isn't much cheaper. So we look at the lowly sea bass and try to make something of it" (Demerest 1980, p. 87). Menus and recipes respond to marketplace costs. As demand increases—for example, for the once-scorned redfish—prices change, and blackened redfish is more costly as a result, with the possibility of overfishing that "trash fish." Supply curves affect price as well, as when shrimp or snail farms decrease the cost of these formerly luxury items.

Reusing.   One effective way to reduce food costs is to insure that nothing goes to waste. As some say about farmers' use of hogs—everything is used but the oink. Leftovers reflect "poor management," guessing wrong about the demands of customers and not being able to use the remaining food. In discussing pricing I described the number of dishes into which La Pomme de Terre was able to incorporate chanterelle mushrooms, thereby increasing the price of each. Tim, the head chef, was particularly proud of the fact that he used the remaining pieces of chanterelles, just turning brown, in a beautiful, delicious, and expensive mushroom tart, which he proudly announced is "all made from leftovers" (Field notes, La Pomme de Terre). Creating specials using leftover food is common but sometimes sneered at: "Howie asked me what I would eat if I dined at La Pomme de Terre. I tell him probably the specials. Diane agrees, 'I'd order the specials. That's what the chef wants to cook.' Howie adds sarcastically: 'That's what the chef wants to get rid of. I was talking to the chef at La Tortue, and he was telling me that the special was veal tips *en croûte*. Who would want to eat frozen veal tips' " (Field notes, La Pomme de Terre). While I did not observe uneaten chili or soup thrown back into the pot, bread was occasionally reused, as were condiments. Restaurants refilled half-used bottles of ketchup and steak sauce (Field notes, Stan's), a technique well known by bartenders who marry half-empty bottles, sometimes mixing cheap liquor in more prestigious bottles, so the prestige of the label can rub off on the alcohol.

Reselling cooked items that didn't sell is common. One night La Pomme de Terre served beef Wellington as a special. However, only two orders were sold; the other six were sold for lunch at $10.50, rather than the $16.50 at dinner. Had it not sold at lunch, it would have been used for the employees' meal.

When La Pomme de Terre purchases lobster, they may use most of the meat for a dish (e.g., lobster Navarin with mussels), the remaining shreds of meat for a bisque, and the shells for a stock. In fact, the employees meal is often transformed leftovers—hamburgers made from the end pieces of pork and beef tenderloin (Field notes, La Pomme de Terre). Rendered fat is used for french fries or broth (Field notes, Owl's Nest and La Pomme de Terre). Restaurants use everything, diminishing purchases, but they avoid, in most cases, serving food that has gone "bad" to unsuspecting customers.

Reducing.   The final technique is among the simplest: serve less food or reduce food inventory. The former reduces one's cost directly, the latter indirectly by decreasing up-front costs.

Few restaurants explicitly promise customers the amount of food they will receive. Obviously, if a customer is promised a quarter pounder, a dozen oysters, or a sixteen-ounce steak, restaurants have to deliver or come sufficiently close so that the customer can't discover the fraud. More often customers are told that they will get a "jumbo" steak or a "heaping" platter of fries, but what does this mean in practice? When budgets are tight, it may mean that they will receive less than they had received the week before.

Sometimes the amount of food is explicitly set by management; in others it is a matter of judgment and is negotiated in practice:

> Bruce is cutting steaks from a big piece of meat, but he is not certain how large they should be. He asks a fellow cook: "What are we cutting our Queens [steaks] at? Twelve [ounces]?" Although the cook he asks is not certain, they decide to cut the steaks at twelve ounces.
>
> (Field notes, Owl's Nest)

Jon asks Bruce if he should use seven or eight shrimp for the sautéed shrimp. Bruce tells him: "Use eight, they're smaller."

(Field notes, Owl's Nest)

This concern with food costs sometimes appears unseemly, and cooks rarely criticize others but use humor as a form of social control (Sacks 1974): "Tim, the head chef, jokes with Howie, his sous chef, about the number of scallops Howie puts on the plate, commenting: 'Boy, you're generous.' Although the remark is in the form of a compliment, it clearly has a control function to remind Howie to cut back on the amount he serves" (Field notes, La Pomme de Terre). Or chefs may ratify the concern with food costs by transforming their enterprise into satire:

> Denver jokes about the approximate number of vegetables he is dishing out. He comments: "One carrot too many." Kate joshes: "You should believe me when I say we have enough." Denver: "We should have a scale around here." Willy, the food and beverage manager, jokes with Denver about Denver's putting vegetables on the wrong plate: "Wasted three ounces of vegetables." Kate adds: "Write him up. Write him up." Denver counts the number of vegetables in three ounces: "That's seven and a half carrots and five zucchinis."
>
> (Field notes, Blakemore Hotel)

Taken together, food, labor, and fixed costs determine whether a restaurant survives or fails; yet, chefs receive little training in making these decisions. They do no more than guess, cutting wherever they think that it will be unnoticed. As a result, chefs are not given final financial authority but have a management supervising and mediating their relationship with the external economy.

MANAGING COOKS

At their best, managers are friendly strangers in the world of the kitchen; at their worst, they are hostile intruders. In some restaurants, such as the three freestanding ones I observed, management is generally well liked and respected—even when lines are drawn between kitchen workers and management. In the hotel kitchen, management is resented, but their dicta are obeyed. In turn managers praise their cooks when possible, hoping to foster organizational loyalty and trust.

The Dynamics of Autonomy and Control.   As with all instances in which work spheres abut, autonomy and control over the shared arena are critical. Occupations constantly attempt to expand their sphere of authority (Hughes 1971, p. 293; Abbott 1988). Degrees of autonomy are negotiated between the specific interactants and also between those organizational actors—state agencies, professional organizations, labor unions—that stand behind the immediate occupational arena. Not surprisingly, participants look to their local circumstances and personal relations for enacting change. Thus, Paul described his relations with Dan, the owner's son, who has the daily management responsibility:

> Dan and I have a very good open line of communications. He has given me more of a free hand than any other chef in the past has. The last chef was really watched very carefully. I was watched when I first came in. They didn't know me from anybody. You've got a nice résumé, and you've got some experience. But does he know? Can he handle a kitchen? As time went on, I had to prove myself first. . . . They'd watch my sauces. Watch me make it, taste them. Everything I did. Anything I did they watched. They weren't staring at me, but they'd check on me. How I handled the people, how the food came out of the kitchen.
>
> (Field notes, Owl's Nest)

Perhaps because of their positive relationship, this head chef admitted that the owners should have final authority. He adds, "I have a free hand to do as I please in the kitchen, but if there's something they don't like, I will honor their professionalism and their etiquette and say, 'Fine, if you don't like it, we won't do it'" (Personal interview, Owl's Nest). This is the ideal relationship, and even though another might be generally positive, some aspects may chafe. Yet, despite the desire to make the web of authority personal, it is ultimately based on the rights of those with property and capital over those they employ and can, under most circumstances, fire.

Division of Knowledge. Workers resent managers because of their belief that their managers are not sufficiently skilled or knowledgeable to understand the problems that workers face. Thus, some managers, particularly in small organizations, attempt to learn about work tasks, to participate in the same discourse. For instance, the owner's son at Stan's has a cooking degree from the local technical vocational institute, and although he has never cooked professionally, "if a cook suddenly gets angry and decides to walk off the job, I can come back and cook" (Field notes). This skill not only increases rapport but also provides an extra layer of social control, should that be needed. The owner's son at the Owl's Nest actually worked in the kitchen for two years, which he modestly described as "a humbling experience."

These men can communicate with cooks on an "equal-status" basis, since they are aware of some of the routine problems of the kitchen.[7] Knowledge can be acquired by managers if they make the effort.

The Politics of Autonomy.   The savvy manager tries to convince workers that he will treat them with "a velvet hand in a velvet glove" (Burros 1986, p. 25), and that he will permit them as much autonomy as possible or at least its *appearance* (e.g., Burawoy 1979; Hodson 1991). Managers may permit cooks to listen to a radio in the kitchen and occasionally, as on Super Bowl Sunday, a television. Although the manager may enter the kitchen frequently, the shared illusion is that the visit is "merely" social, and that the cooks are in charge.[8] For instance, when Dan, the owner's son, visits the kitchen at the Owl's Nest, the cooks occasionally provide him with a taste of the special dishes that they are testing, ostensibly to share the dish but also to give him the opportunity to express his judgment. Indeed, in many small, seemingly friendly organizations, it may be difficult to know whether a manager is monitoring or just socializing. When the owner's son casually ate a vegetable from an order of veal Parmesan, was he testing the dish or snacking? (Field notes, Owl's Nest).

The chef must negotiate authority over the kitchen, as it isn't given at the outset and can always be limited. He must demonstrate competence before effective negotiation can begin. When the negotiation is unsuccessful, problems result, as a chef at a natural foods restaurant explained: "Part of it is the situation at the restaurant wherein management responsibilities aren't clearly delineated, and so I've had to deal with a lot of recurring problems that were never solved, because nobody grasped them and solved them. I didn't have the energy or the mandate from the owner to take over entirely, and so it was sort of a frustrating situation" (Personal interview). Ideally, the two parties should respect each other, allowing greater leeway. As the head chef at the Blakemore explained:

DENVER: In the ideal situation it would be the two heads [the chef and food and beverage manager] combining and saying, "I don't want this because," and the other one saying, "I like this because," and just work it out between them. It works successfully in both ways, depending on who's stronger in food. If the chef is a knowledgeable, creative individual, he should be given free reign. If the [food and beverage manager] is more experienced and traveled than the chef, he should have some input.

GAF: How does it work here?

DENVER: If he wants something done which can be totally asinine, and I prove to him that he's wrong, on occasion I can reason with him and say this is why I don't want it done . . . and other cases he just comes out being just so stubborn, and I just back off so I'm not fired, and I say, "Fine. Do it your way." I really don't care. I don't want that hassle.

(Personal interview, Blakemore Hotel)

Autonomy, while based in structural relations, is not absolute but must be acquired by the chef over time. Management, however, will not give up its *right* to control, even when it doesn't exercise that control.

The Dynamics of Control.   At each restaurant where I observed, the owner, his representative, or the manager visited the kitchen on an almost daily basis. Even if the chef was in charge operationally, the owner wanted to know what was happening, "managing by wandering around." Each of the freestanding restaurants was the main source of income for the owner; therefore, he (and in two cases, his son) was directly concerned with the profitability of the kitchen. Cooks know that, and, in a capitalist system, properly, managers have the final say, although they should not push the point. As one cook told me, "When you own your own restaurant, you can do things your way, and you can pay people what you want, and you can run the shifts the way you want. When you work for someone else, you can't do that" (Personal interview, Blakemore Hotel). Understandably, many cooks dream of owning their own establishment.

Owners see their presence as critical to the restaurant's success—micromanagement is part of their management ideology. For instance, Charles told me that the element that makes Stan's successful is the hard work that he, his brother, and his father put into the restaurant and the fact that they are constantly present, insuring, in his view, consistent quality. They established a system of oversight, controlling the keys and double-checking the tickets. Charles ordered meat, although he permitted his head cook to order fish. Every night he checked the inventory to insure that the restaurant will not run out of food.[9] Their control was so tight that cooks felt continually observed: "Evan asks me, 'Are you reporting all this to the [owners].' After I emphatically say no, Evan responds, 'That's good.' Al laughs, 'They've got the whole kitchen microphoned'" (Field notes, Stan's). In fact, the owner's son admitted that his presence is an indicator that something needs checking, has gone wrong, or needs to be corrected: "When I don't come back [into the kitchen], it's a compliment. When I come back, it's usually for a reason. Because of my background [being trained at trade school], I know what's going on back there. I'm reading plates. I'm talking to the waitresses. It's complimentary for me not to come back here. It's better not having someone breathing down their back" (Field notes, Stan's). Since his presence indicated the perception of a problem, it is understandable why Charles was not entirely welcome. When the staff would see him, they assumed that he had seen something that displeased him. Cooks at Stan's resented that owners ordered them about, for instance, making them perform meaningless jobs unrelated to cooking, such as watering the trees in front of the restaurant. One cook reported, "If I say anything to him, he says, 'I pay you seven dollars an hour. You can do anything I say to do' " (Personal interview, Stan's). This perspective is not limited to Stan's management; at the Owl's Nest one cook told me that the son of the owner treated him "like a slave," and the restaurant was "like a prison" (Personal interview, Owl's Nest). Even at La Pomme de Terre a cook scorned the owner for not knowing as much as he pretended and for being unable to judge culinary quality. Such resentment, the measure of alienation implied, seems endemic in that these workers were attempting to carve out their own rights and responsibilities from the shadows of management control. By contending that their employers are deficient, workers preserve their rights and underline the injustice of a lack of autonomy.

Union Control.   The union has traditionally been a bulwark against "excessive" control by management. Of the four restaurants three—all but La Pomme de Terre—were unionized. These restaurant unions were weak, and complaints were numerous about their ineffectiveness or corruption. Significantly, none of the union representatives was a cook. Of the nineteen cooks who commented on unions in the interview, eight (42 percent) were in favor of unions and eleven (58 percent) opposed. In practice, unions had little daily effect; they were not a presence in the workplace. In such personalistic organizations in highly mobile job markets, unions cannot have the power that they have in some large organizations, where the membership is large, the labor pool more stable, and the market competition not so keen; where companies are more concerned with labor peace than cost cutting (Burawoy 1979).

Many cooks, even some in favor of unions in principle, felt their own union did nothing, and several used obscenities to describe their frustration. However, union supporters believed these institutions could protect workers from a hostile management:

> There's a lot of places in the restaurant where you need someone to repre-
> sent you. Managers have a lot on you if you don't have someone to repre-
> sent you as far as paywise and working conditions. The manager can say if
> you don't like your conditions here, you're fired. . . . They can always get
> someone else to replace you. When you're in a union, you're more or less
> protected from that.
>
> (Personal interview, Stan's)

> I think a union is a good thing for anybody really. . . . Because my boss can't
> fire me just because he doesn't like me. . . . The union will fight for people.
>
> (Personal interview, Blakemore Hotel)

Others commented on increased benefits from union representation:

> I filed a grievance [at a previous workplace], and I needed a union. They
> were right behind me, and I won. They were screwing me out of fourteen
> cents an hour for nine months. Without a union there to do anything about
> it, your employer says, "Well, tough." It's nice to have an equal with your
> employer. It's nice to have someone behind you to back you up.
>
> (Personal interview, Owl's Nest)

> I've worked nonunion and I don't like it. Too many people take advantage
> of these people that don't have some sort of strong backing behind them.
> The union gives you benefits.
>
> (Personal interview, Blakemore Hotel)

Other workers oppose unions not only because they are weak but also
for philosophical reasons—mostly because they limit the freedom of
businessmen who in the restaurant industry have a difficult time surviving. These workers see unions protecting lazy employees, not allowing better employees to be promoted on their skills. They believe that
unions violate a sense of equity and put a roadblock between management and their employees:

> It gets to the point where the unions tell the businessman how to run his busi-
> ness in terms of what he should pay and so forth. I don't think that's right.
>
> (Personal interview, La Pomme de Terre)

> I think that if you do a good job and are a good cook, I think you don't
> have anything to worry about, and you don't need a union really.
>
> (Personal interview, Blakemore Hotel)

For these workers, unions are an institutional barrier to judgment and
promotion based on merit. Unions serve as a buffer against management's attempts at control; yet, in doing so, they reduce the autonomy
and sense of self-worth of workers by treating them as a class without
regard to their abilities. In the guise of protecting workers, they have
instituted a bureaucratic barrier to individual treatment. If strong,

unions have the power to shape relationships in the restaurant, causing some restaurants to fail by raising labor costs.

Corporate Control.   My generalizations about corporate control are limited since I have examined only one hotel kitchen. However, it was clear that the hotel kitchen had problems and frustrations not shared by the others. While this involved personal characteristics of staff and management, stories told about other hotel kitchens suggest that these problems were not unique to this establishment.

I began observing at the Blakemore shortly after some layoffs, when headquarters had insisted that labor costs be reduced. The layoffs were not well received. Some of those laid off had been popular, but even more important, the layoffs increased stress in the kitchen. The resentments and frustrations were real and were coupled with the recognition that management was always watching and could, if it chose, control every aspect of kitchen life, such as "writing up" workers for swearing, or banishing vegetables from the menu: "I ask Denver why they don't serve red cabbage anymore. He explains that '[the restaurant manager] doesn't like red cabbage. It's a nice vegetable out there at night. It's almost luminous on the plate.' One day the hotel manager told Denver that he was using too much broccoli and cauliflower, so they started using cabbage, cheaper and easier, but 'one day Sanjay ate dinner here, and he said, "I don't ever want to see it in here again" ' " (Field notes, Blakemore Hotel).

Many kitchen workers truly disliked the hotel corporation. The head chef explained:

DENVER: I'm not a big corporate fan. I don't like corporations.

GAF: What is the most difficult thing about your job?

DENVER: Coming to work. I said [to the hotel's general manager] I don't mind coming to work and busting my ass, and there were times before that we did. . . . That was fine, but at least when you're here you get a smile from someone or a joke, and you didn't mind working hard. But now it's just drudgery to just walk into the door in the morning. Everybody's chin is down to their shorts, and nobody's smiling. Every time you turn around somebody is lacing into you for some reason or another. I'm tired a half hour after I get here. Just from the atmosphere of the drudgery.

                                    (Personal interview, Blakemore Hotel)

While this chef claimed that he was working up to ninety-six hours a week, his cooks often saw him come in late and take off early, and didn't believe that he was concerned. They felt used; one pantry worker told me that she was exploited, adding "that's one thing about working for a corporation." Others spoke of poor benefits, poor pay, and poor equipment. The cooks felt that the cutbacks indicated that management didn't care and didn't understand that the cutbacks would hurt the quality of the food. One cook believed that good cooking was against management policy: "The Blakemore doesn't want to have good chefs. They want to have someone they can use. They want someone who will jump when they say jump. They don't want someone to run that kitchen so great and do better things and make their food stand out from other places" (Personal interview). Another emphasized that all the corporation wanted was "the dollar. You're expendable." Still another felt that the corporation believed that "if you work in the kitchen, you have minus intelligence" (Field notes).

I was told a story of how management accused a housekeeper of stealing, which was indicative of its attitude toward employees. She allegedly had a mental breakdown after being accused of the theft of five thousand dollars and after the corporation sent the police to her home at two in the morning. The next day the money was found in the guest's room. The story indicated how little the corporation cared about or trusted their employees.

This perspective bred intense sarcasm, a pervasive form of organizational behavior (Seckman and Couch 1989). When a potman didn't show up, one of the cooks sarcastically commented that "if they [management] want a pot and pan washer, they can get Sanjay [the manager in charge of the restaurant]." The cooks simply worked without pots and pans getting cleaned. Once the restaurant manager nearly slipped on a wet patch of floor. After he left, Denver cursorily examined the floor, shrugged his shoulders, and ignored the problem: it didn't matter.

In this restaurant the kitchen workers felt that the corporation was not on their side, and that the managers were not part of their community, which bred alienation. While this attitude is not found in every corporate environment, and some hotels are run well, I heard other, similar accounts of hotel life. The cooks were unable to understand the structural demands placed on the managers, and the managers were unable to communicate effectively with the cooks about their decisions. The structural web in which the hotel kitchen was enmeshed was never adequately explained to workers, although such an explanation might only have increased the alienation.

CONCLUSION

It is impossible to separate the reality of a organization situated in economic space from the reality that it is also a group with localized patterns of interaction. The culture of the organization responds to the culture of the community. In this chapter I have attempted to demonstrate some of these linked realities. Organizations must survive in a structured environment that demands minimized fixed, labor, and food costs with the maximization of customer patronage and profit per customer if the organization is to survive. Achieving these ends has consequences for the structure and culture of the restaurant. Cutting costs makes work life less pleasant and more demanding, either because the resources on which workers can rely are poorer or smaller, or because the amount of work that they must do within a period of time is increased.

In this chapter I hope to have demonstrated that an interpretation of work, grounded in culture and interaction, is congruent with a structural, organizational, and economic orientation. Behaviors of actors within the kitchen are constrained by external forces. In turn, the efficiency of joint action in the kitchen is linked to organization success within its competitive arena. Hovering beyond this, influencing how one can influence potential, targeted customers is the broader economy and the amount of competition from other organizations. We expect customer patronage to decrease in a recession, but if enough competing restaurants fail, the surviving organizations may profit and expand. These connections between macro- and microunderstandings of an organization are complex, but to ignore them would be to abandon explaining the dynamics of the economy.

SIX

Aesthetic Constraints

De gustibus non disputandum.
          —*Latin proverb*

In view of workers' demands for autonomy and organizational constraints on that autonomy, how is "good" work possible? Sociologists of work have been little concerned with questions of how work gets done, as that doing relates to questions of style and form: the aesthetics of work. The conditions that produce "quality" have been ignored, while the technical, functional, and goal-directed doings of workers and workers' attempts to undercut authority in the workplace have been emphasized (Fantasia 1988; Hodson 1991). This approach treats work worlds as instrumental systems, downplaying that what is useful to the management or consumer may or may not be elegant to the workers. How do organizations facilitate and restrain occupational aesthetics?

During the past two decades sociologists have attempted to understand the creation of cultural products through a "production of culture" approach (Peterson 1979; Becker 1982) that analyzes cultural production through the same tools as "industrial" work. This perspective emphasizes that: (1) issues of quality are central to production, and that process involves "aesthetic choices"; (2) aesthetic choices are a form of organizational decision making, can be negotiated, and are not fully reducible to organization demands; (3) organizational features encourage, channel, and limit aesthetic choices; and (4) organizations can define their own aesthetics, taking into consideration their placement within a market niche and clients' definitions. In contrast, I wish to demonstrate how options and constraints produce the expressive form of work products: what might be termed the *culture of production*. Organizational, market, and client constraints affect the qualities of work products.

In speaking of the expressive side of production, I select the slippery term "aesthetics" to refer to the sensory component of production.[1] Why aesthetics? This concept is the broadest of a cluster of terms that involve the sensory qualities of experience and objects: beauty, creativity, elegance, goodness, and the like. An aesthetic object, or act, is intended to produce a sensory response in an audience (Shepard 1987; Wolff 1983). No special brief exists for this definition other than its utility and general reasonableness. It captures the cognitive ("satisfaction") and affective ("sensory") components of aesthetic judgments and includes the intentional quality of human action. Aesthetics emphasizes that these choices are distinct from purely instrumental and efficient choices: that workers care about "style," not only about technical quality. Although form and function are typically intertwined, aesthetics refers specifically to the production of form, not only function. Attempts to produce "good work" often involve an intimate linkage between form and function, and functionally perfect objects may be seen as having perfect form. Judgments of quality derive from both, although my focus here is on the former. In cooking, and other work arenas, the sensory characteristics of objects and services have a special standing among workers and the public.[2]

The practical creation of industrial objects is a fundamentally social enterprise, constructed through interaction and organizational constraint.[3] As a result, the feeling for form or creative impulse, and its limitations, needs to be emphasized in theorizing on the structure of work and occupations. Not doing so gives a distorted picture of the workplace, making it alternatively seem too instrumental, denying a sense of identity and craft to workers, or filled with conflict, emphasizing how workers are separated from their work and their supervisors. Work matters to workers, and workers have craft standards by which they judge work products and performance that transcend the narrow goals of producing things efficiently and to bureaucratic specification. This connection between the worker and the work is central to the occupational identity of workers. Craft is a part of all work life (Forrest 1988).

First, cooking, like all occupations, involves an aesthetic concern that takes its form from decisions about the sensory components of food. Second, the practical doing of cooking is an everyday accomplishment and is negotiated in practice by workers. Third, culinary production is channeled by social and economic constraints and by occupational segmentation.

DOING AESTHETICS

All work is socially situated and constrained environmentally and organizationally. No matter how idealistic the worker, in fact, goals are embedded in the negotiated compromises of work. Aesthetics is activity, rather than a doctrine (Becker 1982, p. 131)—it is an everyday accomplishment. Theory only flickers around the edges of the consciousness of workers. Following from this, most workers are not explicit about (or even conscious of) their aesthetic decisions. They desire to produce objects or services that are pleasing sensually, but typically their awareness of the basis for this desire is vague. For example, a hotel cook told me: "When I make my soup . . . I try to make it look as nice as possible, and to taste. I feel I take a lot of pride in it. When other people make soup it doesn't always look like mine" (Field notes, Blakemore Hotel). This worker has a generalized sense of "niceness" that includes looks and taste, but the analysis does not transcend this partially inarticulate sentiment.

The content of this sensibility varies in each cook and restaurant, and is further complicated by the realization that cooking involves situated choices. Still, all cooks hope to present dishes of which they are proud—food that will appeal to their customers' senses, not merely food that will satiate them or make them healthy, the functional characteristics of food. This culinary evaluation involves numerous senses. The head chef at La Pomme de Terre responded when I asked what he liked best about cooking:

> Making something that I think is just the greatest. I did a bouillabaisse . . . and I thought it was just the greatest. . . . It had a lot of seafood in it, a lot of shellfish, shrimp, lobster, mussels, clams, and about six other seafood items in it, and the sauce was a somewhat thin, primarily lobster-based sauce, lots of butter, and very, very rich, and the thing that was best about it was everything was made to where, typically if you have bouillabaisse, you have to hold onto something with the tongs and dig meat out of the shell and stuff like that, but I prepared it so that everything was done for you. . . . It was not only tasty and unusually fantastic as far as flavor, smell, and sight; it was easy to eat.
>
> (Personal interview, La Pomme de Terre)

The range of senses is invoked in this cook's sense of his culinary triumph.[4] Lest one believe that this sensory concern applies only to tony
restaurants, where some might claim the cooks *really are* artists, it applies to the steakhouse as well. The chef at the steakhouse responded
to my question about what a piece of baked salmon should be: "It
should be just very lightly, you should see a tinge of brown on the outside, but it shouldn't be overcooked. It should be just done. Nice and
moist" (Personal interview, Stan's). Again, a range of sensory modalities affects the evaluation of food, even where one might assume that
such interest is limited.

An aesthetic evaluation may involve more than the production of appealing products: it may also derive from the doing—an experience of
"flow" (Csikszentmihalyi 1975). Some cooks speak of themselves as
artists through their actions (Clark 1975, p. 33), making cooking a performance art. For some the criteria for quality labor are primarily in the
product: the sight, feel, taste, or smell; for others they are in the performance; but for each the work has a style, a sense of form, an aesthetic.

Ideally this evaluation should be grounded within the occupation—
although products are typically also judged by clients and on occasion
performance is as well, as in demonstration kitchens. The evaluation of
production is not only a result of demands of customers and managers
but also of cooks' independent standards of judgment. Certainly these
independent standards cannot radically vary from customer demands,
even for elite chefs (Kimball 1985, p. 18), and there are critical situations in which clients' demands take precedence, but cooks have their
own judgments that are not reducible to organizational requirements.
Management and customers do demand aesthetic production and, so,
are in sympathy with the goals of the cooks, but the constraints from
these demands and standards of aesthetics may limit what cooks are
able to produce. All parties value "good work," but the meanings and
the external considerations differ.

The salience of evaluations by cooks are evident when workers are
creating "unique" items. This follows from the observation that the
more unique the product and the less routine the task, the less an organization can rely on formal rules, and the greater the autonomy that
must be given to workers (e.g., Woodward 1965; Faulkner 1971;
Coser, Kadushin, and Powell 1982). Individualized production tech-
nologies lead to choices but simultaneously can lead to a recognition of
the lack of autonomy because of constraints. When cooks can create

without pressure, they do and are proud of the results. For example, one cook preparing a wedding dinner carved a pair of birds of paradise from apples and sent them to the bride and groom as *his* gift for their marriage (Robert Pankin 1987, personal communication). Likewise, after making a chocolate cake, the pastry chef at La Pomme de Terre added four raspberries and drizzled chocolate sauce over them, commenting "I'll put some fruit on here so it looks a little more abstract" (Field notes, La Pomme de Terre). Although she was expected to create "beautiful" desserts, her touch was not a result of management policy; rather, her standards developed from a sense of what it meant to be a competent pastry chef and an artistically literate person.

Although cooks have some control over the sensory characteristics of the food they prepare, the doing of this aesthetic work is a daily achievement, not merely grounded in theoretical choices. The production of "high quality" items, as defined by cooks, depends on a balance of culinary ideals (e.g., using natural ingredients, adding delicate garnishes) and of production constraints. The ends direct production choices, as in two discussions of the color of a sauce:

> The head chef at the Owl's Nest pours a considerable amount of Gravy Bouquet in his brown sauce to make it "richer." He then adds white pepper and stirs the sauce. He explains: "Black pepper shows up and looks like mouse turds. Little black specks. So I use white pepper." White pepper is also added to the restaurant's mashed potatoes.
>
> (Field notes, Owl's Nest)
>
> The head day cook is preparing cheese sauce, using powdered cheese. He adds a capful of orange food color to the pot, saying that this makes the sauce look more like cheese, and, if you were actually to add cheese, "It gets too sandy."
>
> (Field notes, Owl's Nest)

These cooks are making decisions in practice. They believe, correctly, that the visual appeal of the food, the first thing that both cooks and customers notice, affects the way the dish tastes—sensory realms are interconnected (e.g., Moir 1936; Pangborn 1960).

Cooks can be admiring or critical toward what they prepare, depending on their evaluation of the outcomes, both in terms of sales and customer appreciation and in terms of occupational standards. This evaluation implies a realm of objects that do not meet the criterion of ideal or acceptable objects. No occupational world can long survive if participants judge everything equal to everything else.

For collective judgment, differentiation in the evaluation of produced objects is essential.[5] In cooking, this judgment may involve any
of the relevant senses. For example, one cook criticized a bunch of
grapes as having "bad lines." An outsider might wonder how grapes
can have bad lines, until it is learned that the ideal of a bunch of grapes
is a pyramid, and that other bunches better meet this criterion. Crepes
can be described as "lopsided," implying agreement that crepes should
be circular. A more detailed example is the condemnation of a dish
that "doesn't work": "Howie and Tim taste the beet fettucini that they
planned to serve with a tomato sauce—an orange-red sauce on top of a
crimson pasta. Tim says to Howie: 'There's something that didn't
work. It looks like puke.' Howie adds: 'It tastes like Chef Boyardee. It
tastes like SpaghettiOs. It tastes like snot rag.' They decide not to add
the sauce" (Field notes, La Pomme de Terre). This judgment is predi-
cated on their view of what constitutes proper food presentation—
which colors go together, and what the taste and texture of a properly
made sauce should be. Such standards, while tied to occupational standards, must be echoed by customers. Although the judgments of cooks
should never be far from their sense of the customers in their market
niche, when being creative, they use themselves as guides:

> You have the idea in your mind of how something should come out and
> you have to use your hands and eyes and taste and nose. You have to make
> it come out the way . . . you want it.
>
> (Personal interview, Stan's)

> The thing is to just have the guts to go in and do it. Just try it. Not worry
> about, Is this thing going to work or not. . . . It's color, flavor, texture,
> smell. It's all those things put together, and somehow I have a sense of or-
> ganizing these things and putting them together.
>
> (Personal interview, La Pomme de Terre)

Cooks do not discuss these judgments in terms of their customers, but
in terms of what they believe "works," even if they lack a formal theory of the activity (Sclafani 1979). A set of aesthetic conventions exists
that is based on occupational standards (Becker 1982), separable from
organizational demands, but which must be fitted into the constraints
imposed or believed to be imposed by external sources and by the
structure of the occupation itself. Occupations struggle to gain control
over criteria for judgment from regulators, employers, and clients. Although the recognition of this struggle has been a staple of the analysis
of "professions" and other occupations, it applies equally to control of
aesthetic choices at work.

CONSTRAINTS AND NEGOTIATIONS

With claims of independence within an occupation on the one hand and structural limits on the other, how do workers produce objects that they consider satisfying and of high quality? What are the dimensions that channel how workers do good work? Three forces external to occupational autonomy limit production choices, leading workers to cope with these constraints. In cooking, as elsewhere, organizational constraints determine not only the products but also shape the values of workers. On some occasions, cooks chafe under the restrictions of the workplace, but often these restrictions are taken for granted and treated as merely an occupational reality.

Cooking, like all occupations, is grounded in negotiation and compromise. Cooks strive to control the means and circumstances of production, both to make their day passably pleasant and to permit them to be satisfied with what they produce. The proximal source of constraints is a restaurant management that depends on the loyalty of its customers, and this pressure is filtered through the head chef, who is given an annual or monthly budget with which to work. Management supports and encourages aesthetic presentations as long as good work remains profitable. To satisfy management the chef must manipulate the staff to make a profit (and receive a bonus) and to produce good food. Control is furthered by most cooks' internalized acceptance of these economic and temporal constraints.

The most difficult dilemma for cooks is the recognition that often they must serve "bad food"—food that they believe is not up to their own standards of quality, but they have no choice.[6] It is difficult to propose a set of rules that will predict when "poorly prepared" food will be recooked: the cost of the food, the time for cooking, the pressure in the kitchen, the status of the customer, the conscientiousness and mood of the cooks, what is wrong (and if it can be partially corrected without recooking), and the status of the restaurant—all affect the decision. These decisions are negotiated among the kitchen staff and with management on the spot, but all cooks must recognize that they must serve food that they know is not up to their standards. Cooks shrugged when they sent substandard food to unknowing customers and responded sarcastically when, at times, servers announced that they had been complimented on these dishes.

One cook described her frustration with a rack of lamb: "I've racked some lamb. . . . that was just an abortion. It was just awful; I rolled the pastry too thin, and the lamb was overcooked, and . . . it came out looking not like it was supposed to. That makes me feel bad, even though that's fine, and you have to use it. You can't throw it away, but I feel really bad" (Personal interview, La Pomme de Terre). Cooks are dismayed when they have made food of poor quality, and like so many workers they deny that they really care by turning the offensive food into a sick joke, engraving role distance in their performances: "The watercress sauce created for the salmon appetizer has separated. Tim, the head chef, says sarcastically: 'Oh, well, they all look like shit. We don't have to worry.' Gerry, his co-worker, jokes: 'The room's dark'"(Field notes, La Pomme de Terre). Such joking is legitimate in that cooks have other occupational rhetorics besides that of artist to rely upon; for that moment they can constitute themselves as manual laborers, as alienated as any. In occupations such as cooking that can draw upon several occupational rhetorics, workers can strategically employ these to preserve their self-integrity. They identify with the food they produce and see a reflection of their inner qualities in the outcome. When the food does not meet their standards, they must use techniques for backing away from the linkage of self and product. The strategic use of occupationally acceptable rhetoric is a means by which workers can cope with the personal tensions of presentation of self.

Recognizing the constraints in preparing high-quality dishes, I examine three processes that limit cooks from achieving their occupational ideals: customer taste (client demands), time (organizational efficiency), and the economics of the restaurant industry (the resource base of the occupation). These factors cause cooks to compromise their own taste.

CLIENT DEMANDS

The restaurant cook prepares food for an audience that does not belong to his or her occupation, and that may not have the same standards or even be aware of their existence. Yet, cooks and customers agree that restaurant food should be aesthetic, whether or not they agree on what is meant in practice by this term.

Because of market demands, autonomy is yielded to the expectations of the audience (Arian 1971). As a result of the loss of autonomy, workers may resent those who do not have their standards of quality and competence—not just bosses, whose sin is cynicism, but clients, who are seen as culpably ignorant.

Unlike occupations (e.g., beauticians, housepainters, plastic surgeons) in which workers negotiate directly with those who ultimately judge them, cooks rely upon a typification of the audience, derived from their understanding of the restaurant's market niche.[7] Their evaluation is mediated through managers and servers. Those standing beyond the output boundary are not easily known (see Hirsch 1972; Dimaggio 1977): they are absent others. Dishes are cooked for typifications, not persons; yet, persons have the option to complain. Customers judge the dish, whereas cooks have difficulty judging the customer.

As a consequence, cooks develop techniques for dealing with the vagaries of customer taste. At the steakhouse and the continental restaurant cooks routinely undercooked beef. This allowed for correction if the customer wanted the meat more well done. Steaks can never be cooked less. Still, these cooks became annoyed when customers insisted on eating steaks well done. One Friday night at Stan's a large number of steaks were sent back to the cooks' frustration: "One waitress says to the head chef, referring to the customers: 'Are those steaks burnt up enough?' The chef responds: 'I hope so. I don't want them.' Later another cook comments about the evening: 'Bunch of assholes out there. They don't know what they want.' He means that they don't want what he wishes to serve them" (Field notes, Stan's). This problem is equally relevant at La Pomme de Terre, where the canons of nouvelle cuisine emphasize not overcooking food to preserve its "natural" taste. These cooks, too, became annoyed when their "perfectly" cooked dishes (pink duck breast, translucent fish) are returned for additional work. The cook's ability is not only questioned by the customer, but also cooks believe that by accepting the motto The Customer is Always Right, they are prostituting themselves,[8] even though they hope that they may eventually educate their customers (viz., Becker 1963, pp. 79–100). By pleasing the customer, they deny the validity of their own standards. The legitimacy of their aesthetic standards are invalidated by external demands.

Spices and condiments pose a similar problem. The head chef at the Owl's Nest notes: "You season things but not completely seasoned. The first thing the customer does is see the salt and sprinkle it on, pepper and etc. Takes a bite and puts it down and says this has too much salt on it, and take it back. He was the one who put the salt on it; we didn't. So we underseason things. You have to think for the customer. . . . You have to think of everybody's taste" (Personal inter view). Even if cooks feel that some foods are unappetizing, they must serve them to customers who enjoy them. Further, even though they personally feel that some foods taste "bad" (e.g., fried liver, spinach), they must learn how to cook them so that the customer who likes them will know that they are cooked correctly, that they represent the best professional practice. They must role-play their clients. This concern for customer taste, and its limits on cooks, is evident at La Pomme de Terre in the selection of fish specials: "I ask Tim how they select the two fish specials each night. Tim tells me: 'We try to have variety. If we have an unusual one, like with perch, we'll have a conventional one, like the monkfish' " (Field notes, La Pomme de Terre). Customer taste is always taken into account, often explicitly by cooks. This differentiates them from contemporary practitioners of the fine arts, who, rhetorically at least, deny obeisance to client demands, which is considered subversive to occupational standing.

ORGANIZATIONAL EFFICIENCY

Organizations are expected to produce a certain number of products or services in a set time period (Lauer 1981). As a result, as described in chapter 2, temporal demands constrain production decisions in restaurant kitchens. Customers will wait only so long for any dish, and cooks have limited time in which they can prepare, given the size of the staff, affecting what can be served. These temporal constraints suggest why, discomforting as it may be, when food falls on a dirty counter or floor after it has been cooked, cooks will wipe or rinse it, and then serve it, the customer being none the wiser. The illusion of quality demands hidden affronts. Since cooking is a backstage occupation, innumerable depredations to the foodstuffs are possible (e.g., Orwell 1933, pp. 80–81). A steak that takes thirty minutes to cook must be served because of customers' temporal expectations; customers would never wait for a "second try." Likewise, if a fillet of fish breaks while removing it from the pan to the plate, cooks rearrange it as nicely as possible but still serve it. The production features of the kitchen and, ironically, the demands of the client permit no alternative.

Time also affects specific tasks in the kitchen, which, although they would make the food more appealing, cannot be tried because of time constraints. One cook explained that he wishes to do a "French cut" on a rack of lamb but added, "I'd never have the time to do it" (Interview, Blakemore Hotel). On another occasion, while rushing to make a cherry cobbler, the head chef told one of his cooks to use shortening rather than butter in part because of preparation time (Field notes, Blakemore Hotel). Likewise, cooks do not have the time to improve poor-quality produce: "Martha, the day cook, says to Doug, the head chef: 'The radishes are bad, but I don't have time to clean them up. . . . These look awful.' They are dirty, discolored, and misshapen. Doug sorts through them and throws out a few of the worst ones, and they serve the others" (Field notes, Stan's). The problem of timing was particularly acute at Stan's, which serves more customers than the other three restaurants. Often plates were not wiped off if sauce spilled. As one cook joked on a busy evening, "I'm going for numbers, not for quality." Although this is not always true, it is often true under less than ideal circumstances. Production is a necessity, but *quality* production is a luxury.

Time constraints apply not only to particular dishes but also to the creation of more elaborate food presentations. As one cook remarked: "To be creative you need time. You can't always have a deadline behind you. Because when you do, you're in a rush. And then when you're in a rush you tend to fail with the creativity. 'I need this by such and such a time,' and then you start getting out the same old thing" (Personal interview, Blakemore Hotel). The head chef at La Pomme de Terre had learned the day before that he must prepare a large press party for his employer. The chef confided to me that despite an impressive menu (sole turban, smoked goose breast with port wine and fruit, goose liver mousse, and duck galantine): "It's not going to be as good as I'd like. I only learned about it today. I'd like to make a grandiose first impression. . . . It's a matter of pride. The artist's pride is at stake" (Field notes, La Pomme de Terre). Ideas for a large display with fresh lobsters and a lobster mousse had to be shelved for lack of time. Although the owner felt that the party was a great success, the head chef was disappointed because it didn't measure up to the quality of which he felt they were capable. While the organization was technically efficient—it did produce *something*—it was not sufficiently aesthetically productive, by the standards of the chef. Indeed, the demand for organizational efficiency led to a disaster with one of the dishes: a sole turban, whose mousse filling didn't set properly:[9]

> Howie tells me that the problem with the sole turban was that "the mousse wasn't made correctly. We could have corrected the problem, but there just wasn't enough time." Throughout the afternoon, while preparing for the buffet, there is joking about the failed dish—joking reflecting an underlying

tension. Half-joking, Howie says to Tim: "I put the fish on the outside. Look how perfect that is." Tim comments: "This isn't life or death." Dane, a waiter, jokes: "It's just your job." Howie adds, kidding: "Your reputation is on the line. . . . I hope you make it back [from the reception]. . . . I hope they don't lynch you. I'd wear a neck brace if I were you."

(Field notes, La Pomme de Terre)

All those involved recognize that a mistake had been made, and through their jokes, they are attempting to "process the tragedy." Yet, such processing is not as easy as it might appear, because the failure speaks directly to their sense of themselves as competent professionals and artists (Bosk 1979). Only the reality that the reception must begin with whatever food is available ends the jokes. Even so, and even though the owner considers the reception to be a succès d'estime, the failure of the turban becomes a part of the culture of the kitchen.

RESOURCE BASE

The final constraint is the cost of materials. Cooks must not forget that in fact they are part of corporate capitalism. In few other market segments does a free market operate as clearly as in the restaurant industry.

Price and quality combine to determine restaurant success, as judged by external publics. Restaurants are known directly by clients who learn about them through advertising, experience, word of mouth, organizational publicity, and institutionalized gatekeepers such as critics and journalists. On a basic level, price and quality conflict, and the manager and head chef must decide to which market niche to appeal, taking into consideration their perception of the organizational ecology. It is the rare restaurant of which one can report that: "One has no feeling of anything being measured or cost-accounted. Mounds of butter, jugs of thick cream and bottles of wine are everywhere and seem to be added to everything in unlimited quantities" (De Groot 1972, p. 116). Or in which a chef could report: "Sometimes we have to remake a dish three or four times until it is just right. Last week one of my assistants prepared a *gratin des langoustes*. The sauce was 'short,' too thick and not clear enough. The client might have been satisfied. I wasn't. I made him remake it three times. You cut down on your profits, but you can't run a good restaurant by keeping an eye on the cash register" (Wechsberg 1985, p. 204). Not living in the rarified precincts of French haute cuisine, the head chef at the Owl's Nest recognized the need for economic trade-offs: "We always have variables. The compromise in your mind is using the best you can use and still putting it into an affordable level for the average customer" (Personal interview, Owl's Nest). As decisions are locally situated, despite their structural implications, this trade-off involves specific decisions about particular products, rather than an absolute rule of thumb: "In theory the head chef of the Owl's Nest believes in using the best that is available. He explains: 'The customer may not be able to tell in the finished product. The finished product might taste the same, but it should be made that way.' However, when I ask later why he adds cheap American cooking wine to sauces, rather than expensive French wine, he claims: 'People can't tell the difference' " (Field notes, Owl's Nest). The question is always: Best for what? Imported truffles, beluga caviar, and Château Margaux add enormously to the cost but only slightly to the taste. For this chef, adding these expensive ingredients is not even considered until a sociologist brings them up. The economic reality of food preparation affects his aesthetic vision.

According to the staff at La Pomme de Terre, what distinguishes it from elite American restaurants is not the quality of the preparations but "the touches"—those extra garnishes that restaurants can afford to add if they have a large staff and a loyal clientele. They compare their restaurant to others and find themselves wanting: "The owner confides to me that one of the Twin Cities restaurant critics said that La Pomme de Terre was the best restaurant in the Twin Cities but not as good as Le Perroquet (Chicago) or Lutèce (New York). The owner explains: 'I asked [the critic] why. He said, "The touches.". . . They have more people in the kitchen. The difference is volume. They can count on being sold out every night of the week. We can't' " (Field notes, La Pomme de Terre). Timing, customer taste, and resources merge to prevent this restaurant from reaching its "potential," as judged by the owner's estimation of the local restaurant market. A year later he opened a more expensive and formal restaurant, which included "the touches." It failed; the market did not exist. Cultural products have different price elasticity, even within particular niches. Some food prices are simply considered "obscene." An obdurate reality prevents unconstrained aesthetic activity.

The skill in running a profitable organization is to provide goods or services that clients desire, and that appear to be worth more than they cost. Some foods seem expensive but are not. When the head chef at La Pomme de Terre created saffron pasta with lobster sauce, he noted that the food cost "is not all that high." Likewise, the head chef at the Blakemore explained that salami horns filled with cream cheese look elegant but are inexpensive.

A worker's ability to compromise on quality when his or her judgments conflict with the economics of the organization is crucial for advancement. The head chef at La Pomme de Terre had planned to promote his head day cook to sous chef but decided against it:

> Because he's such a renegade. I can't rely on him to do what I want him to do. . . . As an example, last week he's been doing that veal special that he came up with, and it's a real beautiful dish. He takes the veal roulade, and he puts prosciutto ham and goat's cheese with herbs and folds it over and sautés it and serves it with tomato sauce. It's a good dish. He had a couple in there that were getting a little bit dark. The veal starts to get a sort of gray when it gets old, but they were fine; they were just starting to turn gray. I looked at them, and I said they're fine. . . . and he was putting up a couple of veal specials, and I went in the walk-in, and those suckers were sitting there . . . I called him in and said, "What is that, for your mother or what? Come on and get moving. This is a restaurant." He's got such a paranoid pride over being criticized for something that he just took it upon himself to do it. . . . He doesn't have the concept that we're in business. He just thinks it's one big happy deal.
>
> (Personal interview, La Pomme de Terre)

This cook placed his standards of quality—standards with which in theory his head chef agrees—above the production needs of the organization and, being unwilling to negotiate, lost his opportunity for promotion.[10] Cooks must keep one eye on the stove and the other on the marketplace, balancing their sensibilities with what the hospitality industry will permit. While chefs and cooks negotiate, and chefs negotiate with managers about the boundaries of their decision making and their commitment to quantity and quality (e.g., the number of scallops to serve or the time at which food begins to be "off"), an economic imperative channels the kitchen staff's ability to produce.

THE SEGMENTATION OF AESTHETIC WORK

Although each occupation is concerned with the expressive quality of production, comparative analysis demonstrates that this concern is variable, not absolute; it is expressed in different forms that may be more or less central to the doing of work. Some outcomes and performances are seen by workers as having more value than others. Further, a determination of what constitutes quality is not absolute within an occupational or art world. No single "aesthetic" sense or unified set of conventions exists. Painters do not paint alike, and they do not believe that they should. The task itself influences one's orientation to work and the role that aesthetic or sensory concerns should have in production. Occupations are socially segmented (Bucher 1962). Cooking as an occupation is segmented on several dimensions; three of the most prominent are the status of the restaurant, the cook's career stage, and the work task—reflecting differences among organizations, actors, and events.

RESTAURANT STATUS

Cooks have different working environments—the types of restaurants for which they cook. Freeman and Hannon (1983), detailing the importance of market niche in organizational ecology, focused on the restaurant industry. As I noted in the introduction, restaurants are competitive small businesses in a segmented environment. In this free market, product differentiation is crucial. Restaurants and cooks have different standings and variable amounts of cultural capital,[11] due to the market niche to which the restaurant aspires and the cook's relationship to that niche (his or her habitus), producing variable amounts of cultural differentiation (Bourdieu 1984). When the cook and restaurant management do not share a cultural orientation, the cook must cook "up" or "down" to the level of the restaurant: the display of cultural capital involves impression management.

Some managers expect cooks to reveal a sharp sense of sensory or aesthetic concern: to be aware of the subtle permutations of smell, taste, texture, and looks, and to use these culinary senses autonomously. Cooks at La Pomme de Terre were more overtly concerned with individual choices than were cooks at the other restaurants, and they were given more leeway, since they were expected to be creative. These cooks did not cook from recipes; they created new dishes or cooked using accepted practice. Employees of the hotel kitchen and the steakhouse were less self-consciously concerned with aesthetic quality although they made creative decisions and felt pride in the appearance and taste of their food. Time and motivation in these establishments sometimes led to food being served that might not have been served elsewhere (e.g., onion rings with breading falling off)— they didn't have the time and resources for elegant and creative production.

The self-image and market niche of a restaurant affects how workers view the sensory qualities of their production. Although McDonald's and Lutèce have aesthetics associated with their work, the cooks
at the latter have more autonomy, and their aesthetic decisions are
more subtle and consequential. McDonald's maintains corporate aesthetic standards for the "design" of their food, set by a central office
(Leidner 1993). Worker "aesthetics" at McDonald's involves problem
solving of immediate production needs: following preset rules for style,
care, efficiency, and routinely coping with customer demands.

CAREER STAGE

A concern with aesthetic issues has different salience at different stages
of a cook's career. These stages often correlate with organizational position. Workers advance in the restaurant hierarchy as they demonstrate competency. Jobs change as individuals mature and achieve
higher status. Different values, goals, and opportunities influence how
aesthetic preferences affect production decisions.

Entry-level cooks are often required to perform routine manual
labor, unlikely to be defined in terms of aesthetic choices. They may be
asked to chop onions, peel potatoes, or de-string celery. As they
progress, they are given more responsibility, and with it comes the authority to know—that is, to be allowed to prepare and later to create
complex dishes (Mukerji 1976). This responsibility emerges when the
cook demonstrates talent, competence, and conscientiousness to his or
her supervisors. I asked a junior cook at La Pomme de Terre whether
she had created any dishes:

DIANE: I haven't been allowed the freedom to. I think I will.
GAF: Is there any dish you want to try?
DIANE: Yeah. I did a rainbow trout stuffed with spinach and mushrooms
          and chopped spinach with cream sauce [at home]; the trout is com-
          pletely boned and stuffed inside it, and it's wrapped in puff pastry
          and baked and served with a beurre blanc or *vin blanc* sauce. It's re-
          ally a beautiful dish 'cause you make little puff-pastry fish, and I'd
          like to try that.
GAF: Have you spoken to [the chef] about that?
DIANE: No. I'm just waiting.

                                        (Personal interview, La Pomme de Terre)

The more experienced chef and sous chef are routinely expected to create dishes. Even when cooks are permitted to innovate, they usually

check with their supervisors. I once asked the head day cook at La Pomme de Terre about dishes that had failed. He indicated that this doesn't often happen because "we play it pretty safe. If it's outlandish, we ask [the head chef]" (Field notes, La Pomme de Terre). Inexperienced cooks, with less autonomy, must acquiesce to the dictates of those higher up: "Bruce, a regular evening cook at the Owl's Nest, complains about how the head chef makes him cook asparagus: 'I hate lemon on asparagus. . . . It's all right, but it's not my taste, but it's what Paul likes. He puts a whole rind in [while it's cooking], and it falls apart and goes all over the asparagus' " (Field notes, Owl's Nest). Status and role direct the locus of aesthetic decision making. The objects of production reinforce authority relations. Occupational segmentation means that all do not have equal opportunity to participate in aesthetic choices. Although a possibility exists for negotiation within the kitchen, or at least a questioning of authority, a power structure determines what is served.

WORK TASK

Within any job tasks vary. Some tasks involve a greater consciousness of the sensory dimension of production than others. Painting the background of a portrait is less aesthetically demanding than painting the figure, even though some aesthetic sensibility adheres to both. Some surgery is routine, while other surgery requires a light touch. Buffets and platter work often involve close attention to appearances, while at other times preset aesthetic choices affect the work. One hotel cook distinguished between creativity involved in working the line (preparing food to order) and planning a banquet plate: "A line has no creativity to it at all. As far as working in the back, I think you must have creativity because you always have to think up something creative to garnish up your plate with or to make your food look nice" (Personal interview, Blakemore Hotel). Within an occupational routine, tasks differ in the attention given them, in part a function of the degree to which the cook has control over what will be on the plate or platter, and how it is arranged.

In many restaurants cooks have interchangeable jobs. They switch tasks depending on immediate needs; they are not specialists. Yet, specialty areas exist: notably pastry work, where the visual appeal of the dish is central. The pastry chef at La Pomme de Terre defined the difference between cooking and pastry work as the difference between two art worlds: "I think people that get into pastry really heavily and do a lot of fancy decorating, and that's an art like painting. Whereas cooking has more artistic talent in preparing it to the proper degree of doneness and, plus, its arrangement on a plate, so it's a little bit more like photography" (Personal interview, La Pomme de Terre). The great nineteenth-century French chef Carême linked pastry and architecture as one of the five fine arts (Revel 1982, p. 68). Pastry work, with more unpressured time for preparation and planning, permits more thoughtful attention to aesthetic concerns than "line" cooking.

The concern with the sensory qualities of products is a variable characteristic of occupations. While aesthetics is always present, its form and prominence differs. The status and market niche of an organization, the stage of one's career, and the particular task that must be completed each influence how workers address their aesthetic concerns. These choices cannot be reduced to organizational demands but are channeled and specified by organizational and occupational characteristics.

BEYOND THE KITCHEN

A concern with the sensory qualities of products and production applies to all work life, not just restaurants. Much of what we mean by "quality" has this sensory, or aesthetic, dimension; the object or performance transcends functional requirements. Even when unself-conscious about stylistic components, workers still care about what and how they produce. In this, all work has the components of artistic endeavors. House painters, portrait painters, and abstract expressionists have an aesthetic sensibility—a belief that the sensory characteristics of their products matter and that, ideally, the basis of evaluation should be from within the group.

This does not deny the power of constraints. Structural constraints mute an aesthetic centrality. The constraints may derive from one's position, from one's clients, from production dynamics, or from the organization's resource base. Art is like work and work is like art.

Examining aesthetic choices and constraints expands a production-of-culture model. Production decisions are socially organized but are not *merely* a function of this organization; aesthetic choices and decisions about quality are partly independent from production. This generalizes to other occupations, even though details differ. Most occupations confront demands of client control, organizational efficiency, re-source management, and segmentation.

CLIENT CONTROL

Practitioners realize that they labor for those outside of the occupation (Hughes 1971, p. 321). Even though clients rarely make explicit demands of the workers, the occasional complaint and the typification of the client constrain action. Lawyers, as well as their clients, are judged by juries; law clerks attempt to write beautiful briefs, barely read by put-upon judges (Riesman 1951). Dental patients care little about the dentists' standards for elegant fillings as long as they do not feel pain and think they look good. Jazz musicians must put up with the frustrating ignorance of their audiences and shape their notes accordingly (Becker 1963, pp. 91–95). Ministers realize that God is not the only one judging their sermons (Kleinman 1984). In these cases explicit demands are not made of workers, but messages filter through. After production is complete, evaluation begins, and the existence of audiences with different or ambiguous standards shapes activity. For some occupations clients continually judge subjects in which the worker has a greater expertise (e.g., cooking, hairstyling, selling dresses), and this affects whether they return; for others the client is unconcerned or ignorant about the aesthetics of the work, provided the outcome and cost is satisfactory (e.g., plumbing, surgery).

Clients act on judgments when they consider the sensory appeal of the product or performance, and use that as a basis for further patronage. This is particularly evident in cases where clients receive quick and complete information such as food preparation, as opposed to other services that are judged many miles down the road, such as auto repair. When aesthetic choices matter to clients, workers' decisions must address their taste; when clients do not care, these decisions are fettered by costs and efficiency. A crucial goal of "professionalization" is to insure that the primary source of occupational evaluation is internal, rather than external, and that clients accept this.[12]

ORGANIZATIONAL EFFICIENCY

The conditions of work, particularly temporal conditions, determine how much and what kind of things can be produced. Workers on an assembly line realize that the line keeps moving. One has a limited time to do it "right." Doing it right may be sacrificed to just doing it. Writers have a cynical rule: "Don't get it right; get it writ." Court dates and judges' limits on closing statements impose restrictions on attorneys. Patients can stand only so much anesthesia, and parishioners need to leave church to attend Sunday dinners.

Some nuances of a task may be sacrificed because of clients' lack of patience or because of the constraints on labor costs. The clock is a stern master, although the real master stands behind the clock. Workers in many venues negotiate to extend the time for completing work. While differences exist among occupations and segments of occupations, temporality has both a phenomenological and obdurate reality.

RESOURCE MANAGEMENT

The cost of materials sets a membrane around production. Ingredients, tools, and environments determine what can be done. The furniture upholsterer is at the mercy of the fabrics, the hairdresser at the mercy of the dyes, the sculptor depends on the quality of the marble, and the drill-press operator is limited by the machine. The quality of these resources is often out of the hands of the worker but is decided upon by someone else with separate goals. Work is set within a market. The fit between resources and organizational environment limits aesthetic choices.

OCCUPATIONAL SEGMENTATION

Although all occupations must deal with the challenges posed by the constraints described above, differences within occupations also affect the doing of work. What you pay contributes to what you get. Hospitals, repair shops, architectural firms, and universities differ in the style of their product and the competence with which it is produced. In offices and organizations some are newer to the job, some have more autonomy, some care more, and some have positions that demand more conscious care: home painters are more conscious of the sensory effects of their work than industrial painters, surgeons more than anesthesiologists, and jockeys more than stablehands. Occupations are socially segmented, and segments rely on different standards of judgment.

While aesthetic choice is a regular part of the doing of work, it is variable, not absolute. The centrality and amplitude of aesthetic inter-

est coexist with retaining one's job, keeping it tolerably easy, and gaining self-esteem and material rewards. While each occupation has areas
in which expressive choices are relevant, few totally lack such concerns. In contrast, no occupation is so devoted to the pursuit of form
over function that social constraints do not exist. Factory work has a
creative component (Bell 1984), just as the work of fine artists shows
constraints of market and control systems that affect the doing of ostensibly "purely" creative work.

THE CULTURE OF PRODUCTION

Management and labor are in firm agreement that work quality is crucial. Aesthetic production must be consistent with organizational goals
and not subvert them. Yet, the intersection of the expression of quality
with efficiency may produce friction. Workers wish they had more
time, co-workers, and resources, so they can be unhurried and untram-
meled. Management is likely to emphasize greater efficiency. Good
work is profitable to a point, and this point is connected to market
niche and price elasticity. Management has the direct problem of profitability, whereas for workers profitability is only an indirect concern.
As a result, value consensus may devolve into conflict or frustration.

To the extent that workers have and can maintain a craft orientation, they can extend their zone of discretion in production decisions.
To the extent that they are connected to a bureaucratic organization,
management makes the choices, solidified into rules and practices, that
workers carry out. A strain exists between the craft organization of
work, which vests authority in the members of the occupation, and the
bureaucratic organization of work, where decisions result from authority hierarchies and formal procedures. Occupations in which each
object is uniquely prepared reinforce the craft orientation; jobs that
emphasize consistency and efficiency tend to be found in bureaucratic
organizations (Stinchcombe 1959). Even in the latter arenas, management may tolerate, even encourage, some worker discretion, although
it may not maximize profits, if it reduces labor discontent and allows
for a predictable flow of production (Burawoy 1979). The role of discretion is indicated by the willingness of management to permit cooks
to take extended breaks, change positions, and choose which dishes to
recook. The effects of this light hand are seen in cooks' willingness to
work overtime or arrive early, fill in for absent others, and make special dishes for important customers—each beyond the limits of formal

job requirements. Further, when worker aesthetics are congruent with that of management, some flexibility on material and labor costs may be tolerated and passed on to the customer as the inevitable expense of "quality."

Producers, consumers, and managers—all value "good work" within the imperatives of monetary or psychic costs. When the system works, each will accede at critical points. The challenge for management, especially evident at La Pomme de Terre, the most explicitly "artistic" of the sites, is to have workers accept management's vision of material constraints as a given and to work within those constraints. Since a trade-off exists between quality and its cost, mediated by customer evaluation, the choices are not objective. Organizational success in expressive production involves a moving dynamic: to be good enough *and* cheap enough that one's targeted customers will return and recruit others.

While it is true that art is like all work, the questions are where, when, and how aesthetic autonomy and social control interpenetrate, and how they are negotiated? Under which circumstances are workers concerned about the sensory quality of their products and services, and when are they permitted control over this quality? The answer is shaped by the articulation of workplace negotiation and by the reality and typification of the market.

SEVEN

The Aesthetics
of Kitchen Discourse

Is there a philosophy of nourishment?
        —*Nietzsche*

Talk is poetry; sociological poetry, rhythmic webs of connotative meaning bound together within a social structural matrix. Meaning depends upon a community of shared understanding in which strings of lexical items are interpreted. When we talk about *things,* we do not directly refer to the whole of our thought; our language is necessarily imprecise and capable of variable interpretations. Much of what we know we must leave unstated—full explication is impossible (Garfinkel 1967; Pollner 1987).

In practice, however, speakers draw from each other similar evocations. We strive "to induce a sameness of vision, of experienced content" (Isenberg 1954, p. 138). When this shared understanding occurs, it is because we have had similar experiences and have been taught to understand them in similar ways. Symbols are only marginally precise. This circumstance was nicely captured by the pragmatist philosopher George Herbert Mead in *Mind, Self & Society:* "It is the task not only of the actor but of the artist as well to find the sort of expression that will arouse in others what is going on in himself. The lyric poet has an experience of beauty with an emotional thrill to it, and as an artist using words he is seeking for those words which will answer to his emotional attitude, and which will call out in others the attitude he himself has" (1934, pp. 147–48). This type of speech or writing applies especially to those forms of talk that have an aesthetic reference: that is, that attempt to present an argument of sensory appreciation about an experienced object or event. Thus, talk at work may fall into this category. When speakers wish to explain the sensory or aesthetic characteristics of an object or event, they rely upon role-taking skills and reflection (Mead 1938, p. 98).

Speech acts do not need to be flowery or "aesthetic," even within art worlds. While replete with metaphor (the claim that A resembles B, and this relationship is meaningful), the language can be mundane, routine, quotidian. Indeed, much occupational communication relies on abbreviated or profane images, assuming collective understanding. Talkers in such circumstances are rarely self-conscious about their talk. This is particularly true in communities in which extensive cultural capital is not a requirement for entry. Communities of talk are not limited to elite culture producers, although surely these producers are most self-conscious about what they do. The creation of meaning is found in communities of all kinds and is incorporated and expressed within the activities found in those communities (Schudson 1989, p. 153).

In this chapter I attempt to understand "aesthetic" talk, not to present a philosophy of language *(langue)* but to reveal a pragmatics of language *(parole)*: talk used by workers involved in the everyday creation of aesthetic objects. How is language used to create community standards—here, aesthetic standards? Sociologists have traditionally been hesitant about analyzing aesthetic judgments. Perhaps we have agreed with the philosophical position set forth by Kant that aesthetic judgment is a function of the "aesthetic attitude" (Shepard 1987, pp. 64–70), grounded in individual distance, disinterest, or perspective. When classified in this reductionist, psychologistic way, aesthetic judgment may seem outside the realm of sociological analysis: philosophers routinely ignore the social component of these choices. Sociologists such as Gans (1974) or Bourdieu (1984) who have examined "taste" see cultural choices as mediated through such classic social variables as class position or educational attainment, but have ignored or downplayed the interactional context in which evaluations are learned and expressed.

Sensory judgments are grounded in social relationships, face-to-face negotiations, social structure, and organizations (Mulkay and Chaplin 1982) and are found throughout society. These judgments, while they purport to present empirical statements for belief, present "feelings." By feelings I refer to the linkage of physical feedback and emotion talk. This talk can be analyzed through the sociology of the body and the sociology of emotion: how what one senses (felt reactions) is transformed into self-reflective cognitions about these sensory states.

A personal response is insufficient for building a "universe of discourse." These expressions are meaningful because speaker and audience are embedded in the same "moral community." The acceptance of talk strengthens the recognition of communal properties among the speakers. One of the key markers of community is the existence of shared constraints of language (Searle 1969; Grimshaw 1981, pp. 267–73; Cicourel 1974). Constraints are grounded in social organization and socialization, and they depend on the existence of common knowledge of linguistic rules and patterns (Swidler 1986). To talk "sense," those who converse must have an adequate notion of what each may and can talk about before the conversation begins.

The general category of speech events that captures the discussion of the sensory experience involves "tacit knowledge" (Polanyi 1958, p. 49): "[T]he aim of a skillful performance is achieved by the observance of a set of rules which are not known as such to the person following them." People routinely act with considerable competence and with a "sense" of what is right without being able to describe what it is that they do (Sclafani 1979). We know things we cannot explain (e.g., the sound of a clarinet [Wittgenstein 1968, p. 36, par. 78]). This complicates matters when individuals must describe their activity to those ignorant of the rules—socialization becomes a challenge and a hurdle. Language is a poor indicator of what techniques and sources of evaluation produce aesthetically competent products (Danto 1964). Frequently we can neither explain nor define, a point made by the philosopher Ludwig Wittgenstein:

> When we're asked "What do the words 'red', 'blue', 'black', 'white' mean?" we can, of course, immediately point to things which have these colours,— but our ability to explain the meanings of these words goes no further!
>
> (Wittgenstein 1978, p. 11, par. 68)

> Imponderable evidence includes subtleties of glance, of gesture, of tone. I may recognize a genuine loving look, distinguish it from a pretended one. . . . But I may be quite incapable of describing the difference.
>
> (Wittgenstein 1968, p. 228)

How, then, can meaning be established? The answer cannot be internal to the linguistic system of which the speakers are parties but must relate to outer criteria (the context and structure of the social system) (Wittgenstein 1968, p. 153, par. 580). It is the ability to "know in context" and to compare present contexts to past ones that permits aesthetic judgments and the ratification or criticism of judgments by others (Fine 1992a). This allows us to interact smoothly without recourse to the existence of impossibly precise definitions, in the face of "family resemblances" (Wittgenstein 1968, p. 32, par. 67). Even when the objects to be classed together have no one thing in common, they are still categorized together because we perceive a preponderance of similarity (Rosch 1978).

Talk in kitchen environments provides a fortuitous set of data for my argument, in that professional cooks routinely judge dishes that they produce and serve. While cooking involves the efficient production of foodstuffs for public consumption, these objects must be sensually pleasing, to both cooks and customers (Fine 1992b). As a result, a concern with flavor is central to the doing of professional cooking.[1] As the workers in a restaurant kitchen constitute a closely knit small group (Gross 1958; Whyte 1948), they rely on colleagues for advice, help, and judgment. Culinary talk is an integral part of cooks' work responsibilities and satisfies workers by persuading them that they are talented and competent craftsmen, even though most have entered the occupation without a self-conscious aesthetic sensibility (Fine 1985): they are aesthetically untutored.

In the more prestigious reaches of the occupation, the rhetoric of "art" is frequently encountered (Zukin 1991, personal communication; Charpentier and Sparkes 1934; Caldwell 1986, p. 38; Herbodeau and Thalamas 1955, p. 4); yet, cooking is also a low-paid, low-skill job for many who work at it. Even some elite cooks deny their "artistic" status (e.g., André Soltner in Burros 1986). Because of the range of images and the structural tensions associated with cooking, it is a particularly apt occupation in which to examine the creation of aesthetic talk. No widely accepted "theory" of food exists; food talk is not privileged discourse. As a result, cooks must continually construct and reconstruct culinary meanings for an unknowing or skeptical audience. Yet, all occupations try to some degree to produce objects and services with "style," however defined (Fine 1992b). For this reason aesthetic judgments in restaurant kitchens can be generalized to other work worlds.

TALKING ABOUT FOOD

English, in common with other Indo-European languages, does not have an extensive vocabulary to describe sensory experiences. Yet, the five senses are, in practice, expressed with varying specificity and clarity. The visual aspects of our world, temporally stable and which can be pointed to, are reflected in the largest and most denotatively descriptive vocabulary. We all can see simultaneously what we describe. When we describe something as empirically certain, we use visual terms—exclaiming "Seeing is believing" (Dundes 1972). Vision is culturally privileged among speakers of Indo-European languages. Tactile and auditory sensations have an intermediate position—measurable and easily shared by a community that feels and hears.

Reaching a shared understanding about taste and smell poses a greater challenge to audiences. For this reason cooks and those interested in food find it difficult to talk about things edible. If many foods are "good to think" (e.g., Douglas 1984), these thoughts are not always easy to express (Adams 1986, p. 26; Corbin 1986, pp. 6–7, 111). Scientists have not developed standardized measuring scales by which taste can be judged and discussed: taste has no widely shared equivalent of volume and amplitude. Further, an object to be tasted must be consumed—incorporated within the body.

Smell has some of the components of taste, but we lack an adequate scale with which to measure it, although scientists have attempted to develop one (Harper, Smith, and Land 1968; Burton 1976; Cain 1978; McCartney 1968). Often we are at the mercy of "experts" (Ackerman 1990), who create criteria by which smells can be classed. Yet, these classifications rarely transcend the laboratory. Because smell and taste do not have precise standards of judgment associated with them, they provide a critical case for the development of a sociology of aesthetics. Despite the difficulty of developing such a language, perfumers and gourmets do understand their colleagues. How? In the absence of a well-developed linguistic code that specifically denotes sensual—olfactory and gustatory—experiences, how can individuals believe that they share meanings? In the case of professional cooks, how do they become sufficiently confident that, as a practical accomplishment, they can use this knowledge as a tool in their occupational world?

THE "PROBLEM" OF FLAVOR

Whatever the reasons for this lack of differentiation of smell and taste, Western culture does not socialize people to these senses: there are no culinary appreciation courses in American schools;[2] going to a restaurant is not the same kind of event as going to a museum. Smell and taste are defined as secondary senses. They get no respect. Some suggest that the senses of taste and smell are not merely secondary but are also "lower" senses than vision or hearing, an argument made by Aristotle, Saint Thomas Aquinas, Kant, and Hegel. Taste and smell, they claim, do not involve sufficient portions of the intellect to involve contemplation. These senses do not go beyond themselves; they do not lead to theoretical insights. Colvin (1910, p. 357) suggests: "Sight and hearing are intellectual and therefore higher senses, that through them we have our avenues to all knowledge and all ideas of things outside us; while taste and smell are unintellectual and therefore lower senses, through which few such impressions find their way to us as help to build up our knowledge and our ideas." This is a social construction, for, in fact, any sense can be a window to the world. The limits on what one "sees" in taste and smell is culturally determined. Culinary standards are not universal (Mennell 1985; Mintz 1985; Bates 1968; Curtin and Heldke 1992). The Japanese tea ceremony is a potent aesthetic event, as significant for its audience as a painting. Likewise, one can discover in a bowl of bouillabaisse the economic circumstances of the fishermen of Marseilles, the zest of the French for sensual living, or the symbiotic relationship between the sea and the garden. That we typically do not think these thoughts is a cultural choice, not one inherent in our sensory apparatus or in the food. Yet, the cultural choice to downplay the gustatory and olfactory has effects, particularly in the development of language. A serious language of taste and smell would demand dramatic changes in our modes of description of foods. As the nineteenth-century gourmet Jean-Anthelme Brillat-Savarin (1825 [1970], p. 40) wrote:

> If it is granted that there exists an indefinite number of series of basic savours, all capable of being modified by an infinite number of combinations, it follows that a new language would be needed to express all the resultant effects, mountains of folio volumes to define them, and undreamed-of numerical characters to label them. Now, since no circumstance has so far arisen in which any savour could be appreciated with scientific exactitude, we have been forced to make do with a few general terms, such as *sweet, sugary, acid, bitter,* and so on, which are all contained, in the last analysis, in the two expressions, *agreeable* or *disagreeable* to the taste, and which suffice for all practical purposes to indicate the gustatory properties of whatever sapid body is in question.

A similar perspective is found earlier in the writings of John Locke (1700 [1975], p. 122):

The variety of Smells, which are as many almost, if not more than Species of Bodies in the World, do most of them want Names. *Sweet* and *Stinking* commonly serve our turn for these *Ideas,* which in effect, is little more than to call them pleasing or displeasing; though the smell of a Rose, and Violet, both sweet, are certainly very distinct *Ideas.* Nor are the different Tastes that by our Palates we receive *Ideas* of, much better provided with Names. Sweet, Bitter, Sowr, Harsh, and Salt, are almost all the Epithets we have to denominate that numberless variety of Relishes, which are to be found distinct, not only in almost every sort of Creatures, but in the different Parts of the same Plant, Fruit, or Animal.

In the centuries since Brillat-Savarin and Locke wrote, little has changed. Talk about food is decidedly constrained by the lack of vocabulary. As Jacobs (1982, p. 8) wrote recently, "How inadequate the language is in the service of palatal sensation, how hollow with overuse the few available modifiers!" Yet, this absence does not mean that individuals cannot express opinions and attitudes about food; rather, they rely upon a set of shared assumptions that they convey in an indirect and implicit manner.

Much discussion of foods is imprecise. Consider one cook's attempt to describe the taste of a salmon *sorbise:* "I thought it was excellent. I thought it was one of the better creations. It blends in with the fish flavor excellently. It's just super. It's not tart. Smooth" (Field notes, Owl's Nest). A person who had never tasted this dish could hardly learn from this description that onions are a central ingredient. Likewise, another cook commented about the soup of the day—lentil soup: "Yucky soup today. . . . I hate lentil. . . . I don't want to try it. There's probably nothing wrong with it. I just don't like it" (Field notes, Owl's Nest). When a particular dish is called "nice," "good," "wonderful," or "disgusting," we are in a world of shared assumptions: others will know *why* that adjective is used, even if they disagree. A community of meaning exists, which permits cooks to prepare competently those dishes that they find appalling so that others find them appealing. Part of this vagueness may be a consequence of the lack of training and cultural capital of these men and women, basically working class in origin. Bourdieu (1984, pp. 177–79) emphasizes the role of habitus in providing cultural categories for individuals of different economic and social stations to use to make sense of their worlds and express their identities; this formulation is comparable to Bernstein's (1970) class-linked elaborated and restricted codes. Yet, this explanation, which relies on a model of "culinary literacy," does not address the challenge of depicting gustatory aesthetics which exists throughout the class hierarchy.

A more direct and personal way to recognize the difficulty that people have when evaluating food involves a thought experiment. Select your favorite food, and then describe *why* you like it. Often the first answer will be straightforward and tautologous: "Because it tastes good." If so, ask again; why does it taste good? How could you describe the taste of the food to someone who has never tasted it? If one is rigorous in demanding an answer, one quickly discovers the failure of terminology—other than basic terms: sweet, salty, acid, bitter. Whether such terms have an "essential" meaning—as Wittgenstein doubts—they have a metaphorical meaning *in use* (Wittgenstein, 1968, p. 39, par. 116).

Fortunately cooks are not asked to perform this daunting task, except by intrusive sociologists. Consider these two representative inquisitions:

GAF: What is something that you really like?

DOUG: Stuffed green peppers are really good.

GAF: Why do you like them?

DOUG: The flavor of green peppers.

GAF: How would you describe that? What is it about green peppers that you like?

DOUG: I like fresh vegetables. I like green peppers.

GAF: How would you describe it to someone who's never had one?

DOUG: I don't know how I would describe it. I wish it was something easier like fish or something. I have no idea.

                                        (Personal interview, Stan's)

GAF: What are your personal favorite foods?

DANA: Pizza.

GAF: Why do you like pizza?

DANA: I really don't know. I guess I just like the taste of it.

GAF: What do you like about it?

DANA: It's spicy. Do people have answers for that question? I don't know. I've never really thought about it.

                                        (Personal interview, Blakemore Hotel)

In posing this thought experiment to academic colleagues, I found the responses were similarly inarticulate but phrased with more sophistication. Even those who can provide reasons for preferring a food typically borrow generalities and metaphors from other sensory modalities. One cook whose favorite food was lobster said he liked "the delicate taste to it, the nice flavor. It's really light. It's not overwhelming or overpowering" (Personal interview, Owl's Nest). Another claimed that her favorite food is French bread because it is "soft and crusty, slight bit of salt, salt is part of the great thing about eating French bread" (Personal interview, La Pomme de Terre). I asked people to explicate what had been taken for granted—everyone knows why a pizza can be said to be good; even if he or she didn't care for pizza, only a "cultural dope" would have to ask (Garfinkel 1967).

In discussing food one relies on metaphors or similes to describe taste, smell, texture, or looks (Mechling and Mechling 1983). These images can either refer to other foods or to some nonedible object: objects that, when the metaphor or simile is effective, are resonant within participants' life worlds (Schudson 1989, pp. 167–70). Food similes are the easiest constructions, even when the comparisons are surprising:

> Howie says to Tim, the head chef, about a batch of cheese puffs that Tim had just cooked: "Beautiful. These puffed up just like souffles."
> (Field notes, La Pomme de Terre)

> Diane tells me that they make their veal stock very thick, "like molasses."
> (Field notes, La Pomme de Terre)

These speakers take adjectival descriptions of the food (i.e., airy and thick) and apply them to other foods similarly typified.

Similes and metaphors extend beyond comparing one food to another. A food can be compared to anything if its symbolic value helps the listener understand its sensory characteristics: "Tom, one of the house captains, compliments Tim, the head chef, on a special of the evening: 'These scallops looked real good.' Howie, the sous chef, adds: 'That sauce looked like velveteen satin'" (Field notes, La Pomme de Terre). The shiny and smooth qualities of the sauce constitute the basis for the metaphors of velveteen and satin. Adjectives such as "mellow" or "soothing" describe foods that are well liked, even though these terms do not have any overt food relevance but can be linked to other objects similarly typified.

Using similes and metaphors to denigrate is more common and more likely to carry rhetorical force. Cooks frequently liken unsuccessful dishes metaphorically to "shit," in American culture a highly marked and generic term of opprobrium: "Ron says to me about their new dish, fillet of sole Santa Cruz, which the management of the hotel has added to their menu: 'The sole looks like shit now. Two half bananas on top. No sauce. . . . Real stupid' " (Field notes, Blakemore Hotel). This dish lacks the markings of a successful dish in color and textures. Other descriptions are more exotic:

> Howie jokes to Lesley about the salmon she has been preparing—a whole salmon *chaud froid* with green sauce and relish: "What did you do, throw up all over it."
>
> (Field notes, La Pomme de Terre)
>
> Howie remarks: "I went to [a trendy restaurant] and ordered lemon sole. I should have known better. It tasted like a plastic helmet. The fish was cooked to death."
>
> (Field notes, La Pomme de Terre)
>
> Kate is making a pink spread named Strawberries and Cream, served as a sandwich. Kate tells Don, who looks at the spread with some disgust: "We sell more of those than anything else." Don comments: "That's a gut bomb. It's like eating a rock. They're tasty, but you can't eat very much of it."
>
> (Field notes, Blakemore Hotel)

These judgments depend on expectations that kitchen workers have of successful dishes: dishes that mix colors appropriately or are "light" and fresh, fitting into cultural ideologies of food. These expectations derive from previous experiences in kitchens and as diners. Previous experiences provide the basis for comparative judgment, serving as points of reference or precedents for aesthetic evaluation (Lakoff and Johnson 1980). Cooks are continually learning; each judgment is modified by dishes they previously created and tasted, even as culinary theory is discounted in the face of pragmatic experience. The La Pomme de Terre sous chef comments on how he decides which ingredients will mix: "Well, half the time I think you don't know, you just guess. If you're a good cook, you guess right. There are certain things like I would've never thought of, like basil and cantaloupe. Basil is kinda spicy, peppery. But we made a cantaloupe and pink peppercorn sorbet a little while ago, and that was pretty good too" (Personal interview, La Pomme de Terre). The previous mixture of cantaloupe and peppercorn provides an aesthetic charter for mixing cantaloupe and basil. No set of rules predicts with any degree of certainty what goes together. The evaluation of "good" taste is not inherent in the food itself but in its social construction, which depends on the judge's membership in a community of taste. After the fact, ascertaining why certain items were defined as blending or mixing well is challenging, although one can construct rationales that justify the combinations. Since liking a flavor is, after all, a matter of preference linked to cultural capital and the flavors to which one has been exposed, "tasting good" is related as much to how one expects the food to taste—living up to an image—as to a formal standard of taste. The expectation of dishes and deviations from these expectations are often raised by cooks:

> Diane tells me how much she likes the wild mushroom tart that the kitchen has made: "It's really good. . . . It's got a really earthy flavor. It just tastes like what it is. It's like eating the woods. When someone tells you the name of a dish, it's disappointing when it doesn't taste like what you expect. This tastes like what it is."
>
> (Field notes, La Pomme de Terre)

> I ask Lew why he puts paprika on the fish; he seems surprised by my question, then responds: "It's a way to make it look good. If we didn't put it on, it looks really white. It has no color. It looks more appetizing, instead of all white."
>
> (Field notes, Stan's)

This implicit knowledge of what a dish should *be* is at the heart of understanding the "eye" or "knack" for cooking. Yet, this belief that the knowledge of how to cook is internal complicates the development of shared standards. Cooks may not recognize that their knowledge develops from the experiential side of cooking and on what they have learned from peers.

SHARED COOKING

In most large and mid-sized restaurants several cooks labor simultaneously, forging an occupational community. Cooks do not need to rely upon their personal judgments about the creation or production of a dish but can request advice from co-workers. Aesthetic judgments are potentially consensual; an ongoing process exists by which professional evaluations develop. Previous judgments, consensually arrived at, affect the evaluation of subsequent dishes.

Cooks routinely share their evaluation of dishes:

> Diane reflects on an avocado-potato soup prepared as a special: "It doesn't taste like what it is. . . . A lot of time people expect things to taste like what they think it should. If it doesn't, they won't like it, no matter how good it is." Howie comments: "It tastes like avocado and potato to me." Diane responds: "I can't really taste the potato."
>
> (Field notes, La Pomme de Terre)

Diane refers to a salmon *chaud froid:* "Good salmon. It's a nice combination," but Tim retorts: "Actually I thought the salmon was pretty shitty,
but the relish was good."

(Field notes, La Pomme de Terre)

By trading judgments, telegraphic but robust, cooks develop a sense of
others' evaluations, even though in practice they typically do not refer
to the characteristics of the dishes that allow them to reach their conclusions. They learn from a compilation of judgments over time.

Beyond these discussions cooks collectively decide in practice how
to prepare dishes. They negotiate the final outcome of some of the
dishes that they serve, especially when they have autonomy in the creation. Soups are notable for negotiation; items cooked to order on the
line are less so. In restaurants in which cooks have the authority to create new dishes, the planning and initial preparation of a dish involves
negotiation, whereas subsequent productions typically will not, unless
a problem arises. The outcome of a dish is shaped by the input of the
cooking staff:

Tim, the head chef, and Howie, the sous chef, discuss adjustments to a
strawberry sauce to be served with smoked goose. Howie finds the sauce acceptable, but Tim prefers more heavily spiced and herbed dishes. Tim suggests that the strawberry sauce needs mint. He dips a mint leaf into the
sauce and tastes [it], but decides that it is still not acceptable. Howie comments: "You got to think how it's gonna go, the mint flavors with a smoked
goose." Tim adds red wine to the sauce; then Tim adds a paste with dry
mustard and red wine that he decides is good enough but adds: "It's still
not perfect." Later I ask Howie what was wrong with the sauce, and he responds: "Nothing. It just didn't have enough oomph for him."

(Field notes, La Pomme de Terre)

As is common in hierarchical organizations, the outcome of the negotiation is shaped by structural power as well as by the opinions of these
two men who respect each other. Yet, one is obligated to decide. Aesthetic standards in organizations ultimately are directed by hierarchy.
Power and authority are also evident when the head chef is absent:
"Howie has just finished a fish terrine and says to Diane: 'Why don't
you take a taste of that terrine and see how it tastes with that [red bell
pepper sauce]?' Howie, Diane, and Denny—all taste it. Howie comments: 'It might be kinda strong.' Denny adds: 'It might be better hot.'
Howie decides: 'Tim wanted to run it cold. . . . Why don't we put a
hold on that' " (Field notes, La Pomme de Terre). Similarly cooks discuss the dishes that they are about to prepare, even when their judg-

ments do not correspond to their personal attitudes. Cooks must learn to analyze dishes to prevent their aesthetic standards, grounded in their class positions, from blocking their professional judgment, as in this discussion of steak tartare, disliked by all the participants:

MEL, the head day cook, comments: There'll be a lot of gassy people around.

PAUL, the head chef, notes: I can't eat it.

MEL adds: I don't like the capers in it.

EDDIE, the maître d', jokes about the sauce: Put a little Sterno in there. It needs something.

PAUL: It needs the meat.

Eddie tells Paul that he put in some Tabasco and pickle relish, and they agree it tastes fine.

(Field notes, Owl's Nest)

This dialogue depicts the collective shaping of dishes and helps to create a sense of what good cooking consists. While such an understanding is typically implicit, and not overtly referred to, cooks recognize that their socialization consists of learning from colleagues how to fix particular dishes. A co-worker can set the cooking standards, although the production of colleagues may also be used as negative exemplars: "Bruce describes the crepes that other cooks make: 'They'll make them lopsided. I like to see a perfect crepe. I like to hear people say [the Owl's Nest has] the best crepes in town. When you hear something like that, you put more pride into them'" (Field notes, Owl's Nest). Because of professional solidarity, and perhaps because cooks define each other as competent, negative comments are less common than positive judgments.

TALKING AESTHETIC THEORY

Although aesthetic judgments are ultimately grounded in evaluations and experiences of particulars, some cooks attempt to construct culinary theories. These "theories" are not theories in a classical, scientific sense but are extended metaphors—folk theories—that permit the cook to think about a diverse range of food products. Since these workers do not define themselves as intellectuals but emphasize their working-class origins, culinary theories are incomplete and were explicit primarily at La Pomme de Terre, the restaurant with the greatest desire to claim

haute cuisine status and whose workers had the greatest need to construct a theory of art to justify their self-conceptions (Wolfe 1976). An
explicit, verbal theory of culinary classifications is a luxury of those
with intellectual pretensions, time, and an appreciative audience.

Because of the difficulty of specifying taste and knowing in advance
which foods "go together," cooks create meaning from metaphor.
These culinary theories represent a "poetics" of cooking (Brown
1977). Metaphors allow cooks to communicate about what they think
that they are doing without explicit referents. For example, a cook
may talk about "brightening" the flavor of a dish; another dish may be
criticized for lacking "oomph."

In a more extended vein the head chef at La Pomme de Terre referred to taste as being functionally equivalent to a musical octave,
borrowing an already well-established cultural theory. He indicated
that, in some measure, he created dishes the way he imagined a com-
poser might create a symphony: "[My sous chef] was making a soup,
and he called me for assistance in finalizing the seasoning, so I thought
about it, and it was just missing the high-end taste, the flavor, it didn't
have any spark to it, so it just came to mind, boom, all of a sudden. I
thought, gee, it's kind of like a musical octave. . . . It's a good basic
analogy for preparing foods and flavor as far as I'm concerned" (Personal interview, La Pomme de Terre). Later he expands this metaphor:
"Tim says that he sees a dish like 'an octave,' in that you need elements
from all parts of the octave to give it harmony and balance. He describes how he changed the preparation of sweetbreads. Previously he
had served sweetbreads in a Madeira sauce with mustard seeds, but because it was spring, he wanted to 'lighten it up.' He decided to cook
them with shiitake mushrooms, saying that these mushrooms give the
dish a woodsy taste, and he felt that he needed something that would
balance the mushrooms and 'lighten' the dish. He finally decided to
add apples" (Field notes, La Pomme de Terre). Although this undoubt-
edly is a useful analogy for this cook, it will help other cooks little unless they are *already* aware of what is wrong and how to fix it. They
must share the dimensions of this metaphoric structure, even while
being unconscious of the implicit models. Often people simply "do"
aesthetic work without having internalized any theory of art (Sclafani
1979): formal and elaborated theories of art are a luxury of the professional aesthetician. In the first example, it is significant that this "high-
end" involves a "spark," but the content of this spark is left implicit,
part of the tacit practical knowledge that the cook must bring to the

stove. The spark might be supplied by pepper, chile, orange, chocolate, cinnamon, basil, or oregano, but it should alter the unmarked taste of the foodstuff. What this spark should be is provided by shared experiences of cooks—these people have solved problems together (Becker and Geer 1960; Becker 1982).

An aesthetic theory of cooking does not require the explicit metaphor of a music symphony to be usable; other images are found in other settings, even when the metaphors are not extensive:

> Barbara, the pastry chef, explains that she doesn't much like "decorated cakes"—that is, with flowers and strings—the traditional wedding-cake design. She tells me: "I'm really not too crazy about that. I think those cakes look too gloppy. I think it looks too much like what you go to Target (a discount department store that sells bakery products] to buy." Later she adds: "I don't like the look that's achieved by a lot of gaudy flowers. . . . I like things to be simple."
>
> (Field notes, La Pomme de Terre)
>
> Charles says to Al: "Al, can you jazz the mushrooms up a little bit." Al responds: "Yeah, I did." Al had added butter and pepper to the sautéed mushrooms.
>
> (Field notes, Stan's)
>
> I ask Herb how he goes about deciding where to place fruits on the fruit plate. He answers: "You have a dark, then a semidark, then a light [fruit]. That's what I try to do. You always want to have a balance of colors."
>
> (Field notes, Blakemore Hotel)

These examples suggest that underneath local judgments of foods and dishes, cooks maintain unstated ideologies or visions about what foods should be, drawing upon such cultural values as simplicity, jazziness, or balance, found in other aesthetic realms. These are attempts to make sense out of what might appear to customers merely idiosyncratic decisions. When coupled with collective discussions by cooks and their negotiation with each other, these images extend beyond the individual cook to influence others in kitchen, and through occupational mobility may influence co-workers elsewhere.

THE LIMITS OF CULINARY TALK

Arguing that cooks are concerned with and discuss aesthetic issues might seem odd to those who expect a richer and more elaborated discourse than that discovered in these ethnographic settings. The remarks of chefs may appear somewhat thin. It is evident from these data, and from the accounts of those who have observed or worked with cooks, that aesthetic discourse is not detailed in most kitchens—certainly in comparison with that of philosophers but even with that of head chefs or food critics in the upper reaches of culinary scenes. In a sense, these cooks are not talking about "cuisine," as elites define it, even though they are concerned with the sensory domain of food. One finds more elaborate, artistic discussion among chefs in the "better" restaurants in the major culinary centers of New York (Zukin 1993, personal communication), New Orleans, San Francisco, Paris, and Lyons. Like many occupations, culinary work is sharply segmented (Bucher 1962). Discourse is responsive to the concerns of the community and the training the discussants have received.

The cooking world in the Twin Cities cannot be said to be a fully developed "art world" (Becker 1982), and for that reason my observations are generalizable to those cooking communities that lack an "haute cuisine infrastructure."[3] Most diners wish to eat well, rather than to "think about" food. Cooks do not conceive of themselves as specializing in artistic production per se, but they are concerned with occupational aesthetics. In this they are like most occupations, in which the sensory qualities of the product or service is important. For a fully developed art world, three characteristics are necessary: an active social network, a recognized aesthetic theory, and public legitimation of the art produced. In the Twin Cities none of these characteristics was present, a reality that limited the elaborateness of the rhetoric and images available to cooks.

SOCIAL NETWORK

Among Twin Cities cooks I found little social networking necessary for the recognition of a subcultural art world. Cooks do not visit other kitchens unless the visitor is a former employee. Although cooks and chefs dine at restaurants, they do not sup in their occupational role but as customers. When there, they do not visit the kitchen or request special service. Further, when asked their favorite restaurants, cooks rarely name the recognized "best" restaurants but middle-brow restaurants. The head chef at La Pomme de Terre claims that his favorite restaurant is Stan's Steakhouse because "it's laid back and casual," insisting that he is "a normal sort of eater." Eating for this skilled chef is not a mark of identity. The chef at the Blakemore Hotel was equally revealing, naming a well-regarded hotel restaurant but explaining: "I haven't been there in years. . . . If I go [there], it's not for me. I do not go there for my enjoyment; I go there to take someone who's going to be impressed. It's for their enjoyment. I'd be just as happy to go to Mc-Donald's" (Personal interview). No cook or chef mentioned a network of cooks in the Twin Cities with whom they discuss his or her work. As I noted, the one local occupational organization, the Midwest Chefs Society, is primarily composed of those involved in trade education and institutional cooking. Only one cook at the four restaurants attended meetings of this group: a trade-school student whose instructor was then president.

The absence of informal or formal organization retarded the possibility of a more richly developed collective discussion of the "poetics of food" that transcended individual restaurants, as well as preventing cooks from self-consciously defining themselves as a group. In turn, the lack of self-consciousness of their occupational position precludes the development of such formal and informal groupings.

AESTHETIC THEORY

Cooks do have aesthetic standards, and they converse about these standards; however, they lack an intellectual grounding for these standards, and to outsiders their discourse may sound vague, as meanings are constituted by past experiences. As Becker (1982) notes, for an activity to be art, a recognition of conventions and a shared definition of art must develop. No such collective charter is evident in the Twin Cities. The discussion of the quality of a dish typically occurs in the context of that dish alone, rather than in an attempt to create a broader ideal of cooking. When I asked the head chef at The Owl's Nest about his philosophy of cooking, he responded that he wanted to do "a good basic cooking." He wanted his restaurant to be a "real good scratch house"—meaning that they would create dishes from original ingredients and not use convenience foods.

This attitude is fostered by the absence of "professional education," which might convey a philosophy. Most cooks in the Twin Cities, not "gourmets" themselves, were taught to cook in trade schools or on the job. There is no philosophical font: no courses on food theory, no books that emphasize this component of culinary work that prospective cooks are encouraged to read.

PUBLIC LEGITIMATION

In most art worlds, theory is not developed by artists themselves but by those who surround them. Critics and academics provide the intellectual grounds by which work is transformed into art and given cultural legitimation. In the culinary world such critics are rare. Although restaurant reviews are published, critics are not cultural conservators but consumer guides. No link exists from the world of cooks to the world of artistic tastemakers. The absence of public recognition is evident in the fact that neither St. Paul newspaper had a regular restaurant critic during the research. The Minneapolis paper had a part-time critic who wrote a biweekly review. When she resigned, the paper did not replace her for several months. It would have been unthinkable not to find quickly a new critic in the areas of visual art, theater, film, or television.

In sum, the absence of community, theory, and public support, coupled with the largely working-class backgrounds and trade-school training of the cooks, limits the extent of aesthetic talk within the occupation. Through shared experiences and the need to produce efficiently food that is enjoyed by clients, cooks have developed a practical language, grounded in experience—a "sociolect"—that serves their purposes, requires a "strategic vocabulary," and permits efficient work. Yet, this is language that committed food writers, upwardly mobile customers, and earnest foodies consider banal, inadequate, and lacking in poetry.

THE PHILOSOPHER IN THE KITCHEN

Although it is not particularly helpful to see cooks "guided" by a formal set of aesthetic beliefs or a clearly defined artistic ideology, these workers are sensitive to aesthetics. Food is judged not merely as a technical product but also as an aesthetic, sensory one. The recognition of joint instrumental and expressive characteristics of objects applies beyond food. All constructed objects are comparable in that they are constructed instrumentally and are to be judged, in part, on the style of the making (Fine 1992b). What is true of casseroles is true of cabinets and cars. In each case judgments are made; these have limits and are functions of the senses, of language, of the worker's habitus, and of organizational and client demands.

As competent workers, cooks require a language that permits them to complete their work smoothly and well. This strategic vocabulary must overcome the reality that sensory experiences are internal; there must be external markers—precise or metaphorical—that direct food production. While internal experiences are personal, we "externalize" these sentiments and judgments through talk, gesture, and action. These markers are grounded in the practice of cooking and in the class fraction of workers with its own norms, values, expectations, and categorizations. The family resemblances of words are known through collective action and experience.

Further, workers need language that permits them to define themselves as community members. Although cooks' language is not sufficiently developed—in the scene I studied, at least—to justify the wearing of the mantle of art, it is sufficient to lead workers to be proud and self-satisfied of their craft skills (Fine 1992b).

The senses are experienced bodily. Whatever the sociological basis of these feelings and their expression, they are inaccessible to others. Yet, this simple recognition is not sufficient. We do know something of what others feel, because of our reliance on public display. We read the selves of others through action. This display can be generated verbally, gesturally, or behaviorally, always in a form accessible to another person. The problem is to transform this individual experience into collective expression, recognizing the need for self-presentation inherent in public display. Consuming pretzels, I cannot determine if your sensation of salty is identical to my sensation of salty. All we know is that we are responding to similar stimuli, and we gain intersubjective confidence by the fact that we both liken the taste of this food to other foods that we have tasted, choose to drink water after consumption, brush off the salt, or make an appropriately "salty" face, referring to the potency of the sensation. The shared meaning of experienced events must remain somewhat uncertain—especially when it is subtle, not dramatic. The problem is more than a philosophical issue, although it has long been that; it concerns how social settings are to be understood in theory and in practice, and how interaction proceeds in kitchens, hospitals, prisons, and families.

Language creates barriers of comprehension. Western languages are not sufficiently subtle, complex, or rich in aesthetic judgment to permit a complex set of cultural meanings. Their imprecision and metaphors require us to base aesthetic talk on shared experience. The problem of talk is linked to how we share senses, providing a grounding for action. Collective action can only be assumed when the parties accept a view of their social surroundings, and when they agree on an authority system that determines who has priority in decision making or when they accept metarules of negotiating (Kleinman 1982).

To understand food, cooks construct a range of metaphors. These metaphors are not only localized to the individual speaker but also are spread within the kitchen community and, because of occupational mobility, among other restaurants. Metaphors of experience are capable of being shared. The diffusion of aesthetic evaluation extends beyond occupations, although its power is evident in such settings. When we speak of socialization, at any level, we refer not only to instruction in technical matters but also to the moral evaluation of objects and actions, which easily conflates with sensory judgments.

Definitional difficulties are inherent in languages. We must settle for family resemblances that we hope will serve us well enough, often enough. Cooking as a social scene stands not only for itself but also for other settings in which discrete actors cope with scenes that are grounded in internal judgments and subjective sensations. Aesthetic order is a domain of social order.

EIGHT

The Organization and Aesthetics of Culinary Life

Progress in civilization has been accompanied by progress
in cookery.

—Fannie Farmer

Organizational interaction is embedded within a complex set of structural and cultural relations. A kitchen does not stand apart but is integrated into a division of labor, organizational ecology, political economy, and even the world system. By describing organizational control and aesthetic production, I have attempted to demonstrate that a perspective emphasizing interpersonal interaction and the power of meaning (an interpretive sociology, grounded in symbolic interaction) can be tied to a more structural and macrosociological view of social order (Manning 1992). Culture is not an autonomous realm (Sewell 1992)—a view that too often is a failing of microcultural analysis. Organizational analysis is enriched by the incorporation of alternative perspectives, permitting the multiflavored ingredients of the social sciences to become a glorious stew. The workplace is an arena of action in which we can examine such core concepts as organization, interaction, time, emotion, community, economy, and aesthetics.

In this concluding chapter I explore the implication of these central constructs that have animated this volume. To be sure, each chapter has relied upon the description of these core concepts, but here I hope to explore their implications both within and beyond kitchen walls.

ORGANIZATION

The concept of organization is central to any understanding of human behavior. The first five chapters attempt to work upward from interaction and the person to examine how restaurants as *organizations* operate and fit into the interorganizational field and the larger economy. In turn, these systems affect the understanding of individuals and of the pattern and content of their interactions with others. Organizational domains are sensitive to the realities of meaning creation through interaction (e.g., Maines 1977; Denzin 1977; Faulkner 1983). This orientation presumes, contrary to some poststructural theories, that there is a world out there that is knowable and affects persons, and that "person" is a meaningful construct. Neither organizational structure nor persons are taken as absolute, but the reality of each helps constitute the other.

Traditionally understanding organizations has been a purview of macrosociology. This perspective is now being challenged by those, notably the new institutionalists, who disparage as misleading the divisions drawn between macrosociology and microsociology, between "culture" and "structure," and between rationality and emotional expression. From this perspective, organizations are maintained through "practical action," and groups within the organization may be loosely coupled in ways that seem disorganized or imperfectly coordinated. The structure of the organization is mediated by interactional relations and cultural images. The social world is not divided by levels of analysis, but each "level" depends on the other. The split between micro- and macroanalyses was primarily a function of an academic division of labor, which too often led to rivalry and disparagement. Microsociological presuppositions are key to an adequate macrosociology (Collins 1981), and the reverse is true as well (Fine 1991).

My data suggest that the decisions and social organization in the kitchen are channeled by the needs of actors to create pleasant and smooth workdays, and equally by the needs of organizations to operate in a highly competitive market environment, as filtered through perceptions and values of organizational decision makers. The relations of power and authority that operate within organizations have real consequences if these relationships are breached, but they do not stand apart from interaction systems. Sets of actors negotiate on the basis of their *perceptions* of the environment, but these perceptions have a direct, if imperfect, relationship to forces outside their control (e.g., customer flow or availability of capital for organizational expansion). Perceptions are never autochthonous but result from obdurate external forces. Both actors and external forces set constraints in which interaction is played out. Conditions of work, technological capacities, legitimate use of time, and relationship with management—all are tied to desires for personal satisfaction and organizational survival. Ultimately these structural elements of work are mediated by personal evaluations, but these evaluations are grounded in perceptions of an environment that has effects. While we must recognize the power of personal choices enacted in the relationships between individuals and small groups, the dimensions on which these issues are negotiated are based in a real and powerful structure of the economy and in the sweep of industrial production.

While choices are real, the *effects* of these choices affect others, altering their decision-making environment. The decisions of cooks affect servers, customers, and management. A situation can be defined as one likes, but the effects of that definition are not only of the individual's making (Fine 1992a). Providing the basis for a meaningful interactionist perspective on organizational structure is the realization that W. I. Thomas's famous dictum—the definition of the situation has the power to change reality—is true as written and false as often read (Goffman 1974), which gives too much power to the definer.

Restaurants, my empirical world, are both similar to and distinct from other types of organizations. Further ethnographic investigations, coupled with statistical and historical analyses, are needed to compare culinary settings with other systems. In particular, it is critical to recognize how those economic organizations that are small groups (single-celled) compare to other organizations that are larger and whose reticulation is greater (Gerlach and Hine 1970). Larger organizations provide a more profound challenge in that the research focus is diffused over a more extensive, more complex arena. In addition, future research should not be focused on a single occupation but should be enriched through a comparative focus. Although I have described briefly the organizational standing of dishwashers, managers, servers, and customers by limiting my primary attention to cooks, I downplayed the distinct contributions that the existence of multiple groups makes to an organizational division of labor. Further, it would have been desirable to investigate those sites and occupations that abut on these organizations—places in which one organization meets external resistance. In essence, this requires an ethnography of an organizational ecology: examining the nexus of the division of labor. A focus on input and output boundaries permits a description of how economies and social systems link.

INTERACTION

Just as restaurants are organizations, so are they interaction fields. Chapter 1 demonstrates the central position of action in the creation of restaurant meals—a perspective expanded in chapter 3, which explores the relationships among occupational groups in the kitchen. The connections among restaurant workers contribute to their experience of their employment and to their sense of identity: who they are within the workplace and what their work means to them.

While the conditions of the job contribute to satisfaction, friendships also help to determine the quality of work life. These restaurants are characterized by deep and real friendships that tether workers to the organization, and that contribute to efficient occupational performances. The reality that workers are friends means that they willingly help each other. This help supports individual workers, of course, but it also affects the organization: these ties bolster management goals. In the aftermath of a dispute within the organization, steps are often taken to heal the breach, as happened at the Owl's Nest, lest the breakdown in interaction affects the production of the kitchen. Interaction, while important to individual workers, has an effect on the system as well. Those who speak of an organization as a team focus on the smoothness of interaction and the ability of workers to create a flexible division of labor, permitting adjustments to the vagaries of circumstance.

The symbolic interactionist perspective underlines the centrality of the interactional domain for accomplishing work—an emphasis common to the writings of Anselm Strauss, Erving Goffman, Howard Becker, Everett Hughes, and Herbert Blumer, each of whom recognized the centrality of work in social life. The workplace—the kitchen—becomes a staging area in which meanings are generated, often through talk, but these meanings do not merely float in an undefined space but have effects on relationships and on patterns of action. Talk and action come to constitute the workplace. The construction of a meaningful workplace in turn shapes organizational outcomes.

The effects of organization on interaction patterns are equally real. As I have emphasized, interaction patterns are altered by forces over which individual actors have little control. For instance, the pace of work (as discussed in chapter 2), which generates patterns of interaction, is constrained by forces derived from management or externally imposed: the availability of resources provided by management (material and personnel), the work assignments of the employees (set by management but sometimes negotiated by a union or individual workers), and the customer flow (over which a frustrated management has little control). A restaurant with a kitchen staff of eight that serves one hundred people for dinner will generate dramatically distinct patterns of interaction than one with a staff of three. A restaurant that relies on microwaved products or mass-produced portions will operate under separate rules than one that believes in cooking from scratch. A busy night or season has different possibilities of action than a slow one.

In restaurants, as in other organizational environments, interaction is not an autonomous realm but is contingent upon structural forces. The workplace, because of its instrumental character and its placement within a macroeconomic order, demonstrates this constraint clearly.

As I noted when discussing organization, the selection of an organization that is functionally a small group hides some of the complexity of interaction patterns in larger organizations. Within restaurants one typically finds a single interaction system with rapid feedback loops. However, in other organizations—a factory (Dalton 1959), for instance—numerous semiautonomous interaction systems operate, which may only occasionally interface with and directly affect each other. The front office has an interaction system that, while it may occasionally have great influence over the shop floor, often operates separately. Those moments of bridging between arenas with considerable power and those with less have the ability to alter routine patterns of interaction. A decision to terminate workers or increase the rate of the line not only affects satisfaction levels and production outcomes but also affects the patterns of interaction among the participants in the relevant interaction systems. Examining these complex, reticulated interaction systems is an important direction for an organizational analysis that takes interaction seriously.

TIME

Time is both a structural variable and a key element in the lived experience of actors. As I describe in chapter 2, experiencing time cannot be disengaged from work lives. Organizations have time patterns that are characteristic. In some, such as universities, workers (professors) have considerable "free time," with discretion on how to divide that time. The fact that a professor may only spend half a dozen hours in class each week is a subject for broad public comment, but this freedom does not, of course, mean that nothing is achieved during the remaining hours. Professors have great temporal autonomy, and the ability to create temporal niches of their own choosing. This contrasts to the stereotypical factory line workers who must actively carve out "times" for themselves in the face of management demands (Bell 1984; Roy 1959–1960).

Many occupations such as cooking have variable temporal pressures. As I describe, at times during the day and on certain days, work may be impossible to regulate. The kitchen rush represents a dramatically powerful effect of temporal demand on the performance of work roles. Thankfully not all kitchen time is like the rush. On other occasions very little must be done immediately and cooks have the autonomy to decide how best to prepare for their future assignments.

Like interaction, time is not autonomous. Connections exist among external temporal demands, the doing of work, and how workers experience their tasks. Emotion is produced by temporal demands—too much work in too short a time generates anger; not enough is boring; "flow" is a result of a fit between time and attention. By controlling the relationship between task and time, organizational authority channels behavior and experience. While the kitchen rush is a particularly dramatic instance, all organizations channel "time," generating immediate emotional reactions, mediated through workers' moods. The boredom of line workers or psychoanalysts, the stress of emergency room technicians or air traffic controllers, or the exhausted exhilaration of soldiers and football players influences outcomes. These reactions result from how the sponsoring organization and the individual worker structure time.

Crucial to my argument is how demands from the organizational environment influence the temporal pattern of tasks, which in turn affects the emotional responses of workers and, through this, the outcomes of work. Although the display of this process varies depending on the organization and the type of work, the connections among demands, temporal patterns, and experience of work are a sociological reality.

Time is crucial to the practical accomplishment and lived experience of work and connects to the constructs of authority, autonomy, aesthetics, and identity. The fact that, despite pressure, cooks (and all workers) perform as competently as they do, suggests that we are not only creatures of the tool but also creatures of the moment.

EMOTION

Increasingly, organizational researchers have come to recognize that the workplace is not only an instrumental site but is also an expressive arena (Fineman 1993). As I note in my discussion of time, emotion is important to the performance of work. In occupations that have considerable contact with clients, the public performance of emotions (through emotion rules) is central (e.g., Hochschild 1983), whether that emotion is supposed to be professionally detached (Smith and Kleinman 1989), friendly (Leidner 1993), or threatening (Sutton 1991). Although these emotions may begin as performed displays, often they come to influence the way in which work is experienced.

Unlike servers and other public performers, most cooks operate in backstage venues. Their emotional reactions are little mediated by the need to impress clients, except in that general sense in which one wishes to reveal pleasant, cooperative emotional responses to one's colleagues and to be detached from the unpleasant feelings associated with stress. This performance is typically connected to standards of "professionalism." Backstage workers in practice collaborate with each other to support the emotional character of the organization and their own personal satisfactions. The display rules are displayed to an internal audience.

The reality that pressure exists to display positive emotions does not mean that positive emotions will necessarily be shown. Kitchens have the reputation for being brutal, loud places. While time pressures surely generate this emotional condition, they are not the only cause. The greatest source of friction is the differing responsibilities among occupational groups, as I describe in chapter 3. Each occupation group has its own needs and privileges. When the actions of other actors prevent meeting these needs or abrogate these privileges, hostility may result. Something similar may occur among actors in the same occupation who have different tasks, but at least in this circumstance they should be aware of the prerogatives of their colleagues, and negotiations should be smoother because of a greater knowledge of work domains.

Emotions of workers within an occupation are also linked to the satisfaction of doing the job "well." As I discuss in chapter 6, what doing a job "well" means is not a simple question but is connected to a sense of quality, mediated by the access to resources. Much emotion—

pleasure and frustration—depends on judgments of work outcomes. Workers judge themselves and their organizational support when they judge what they produce or perform; when their actions or the support they receive does not live up to their expectations, and there is no means of excusing the failure, frustration results. This emotion work in excusing or justifying failure is displayed in the comments that cooks make to others, as described in chapter 7.

Additional research should explore how self-evaluation is mediated in those occupations that regularly engage in front-stage performances. When one does not have easy access to hidden spaces (for instance, lecturers or actors), how is dissatisfaction or joy masked to maintain the appropriate emotional front? To what extent does this process of masking drain and neutralize the inapt emotion; to what extent does the emotion appear in other venues or in other forms? What is the process of emotional transformation in occupations without an accessible backstage? By examining this issue, we can see the nexus of emotional display rules and felt emotion: the former generated by an organization structure, the latter a personal experience limited by organizational requirements—their linkage represents the mediation between structures and life worlds.

COMMUNITY

Whether or not workers choose, they belong to a community. In sharing a place, they are forced to accept the presence of others. This spatial co-presence forces each to be cognizant or concerned about the other. This does not mean that they must necessarily like or support each co-worker, as abusive relations are found at work as elsewhere. Yet, workers cannot ignore those around them.

All communities develop routine expectations that organize relations among participants: norms and values. In addition, communities develop hierarchical structures that determine how rules for decision making and negotiation are generated (Levy 1982; Kleinman 1982). Participants in the community typically accept the need for some rules of ordering life, even if they do not accept the particular rules that have been established. Hierarchy is typically embraced as long as it does not excessively dampen the pleasant and effective performance of work duties or place too great a burden on one's identity as a worker.

A recognition of belonging to a community also helps workers to accept the requests from colleagues to aid in tasks set by management and the requirements of their occupational role. This desire for flexibility in the face of a division of labor justifies and encourages the development of a strong community and culture.

As noted in chapter 4, organizations can be more or less successful in the establishment of beliefs in community. Some restaurants are highly conscious of their communal character ("we are one big, happy family"), while others are more individualistic, more divisive, or less attuned to such collective rhetoric. Organizations can be seen as sites of contention as well as harmony. The *meaning* of each workplace needs to be created from local features—a group identity evident in the unique idiocultures that all small groups establish.

The cultural "lineage" of the kitchen channels those forms of behavior that can or should be performed: those meaningful to the group as well as those defined as appropriate. Work communities are cultural communities; it is through the process of "doing things together" that rules, procedures, and traditions are established (Becker 1986). In this, workplaces are similar to other interaction venues—including, notably, families—even though the level of commitment may be limited in work organizations. Culture becomes a reality for all those who are party to it.

This reality leads us to understand how the communal life of a work organization contributes to the occupational identity of the worker. To be sure, workers also develop a sense of identity from their own occupational socialization, but this socialization typically will occur within an organizational setting, often one in which several occupations come together to create a work culture. These interactions provide the worker with a sense of personal possibilities that defines his or her identity. The workplace is an arena in which selves are established individually and collectively.

Finally, smaller communities are nested in larger communities. Some organizational communities are well-organized "ecological systems," while others, such as the restaurant industry, are not. The high level of competition among restaurants, coupled with the temporal structure of kitchens and lack of occupational training ideology, makes the establishment of a tightly knit community somewhat doubtful. The absence of a vigorous, developed ideology that emphasizes a perspective that transcends individual establishments, incorporating the whole of an occupational group, may also decrease the perceived need for such collective organization. Each restaurant community copes with its own problems, in contrast to those occupations in which the problems of one establishment are linked to the problems of others. While restaurants have robust microcultures, their subculture is relatively attenuated when contrasted with other work worlds.

ECONOMY

Throughout this volume I have attempted to remember that no matter the focus on individuals and interaction we may choose, occupations and work organizations are inevitably linked to a world largely beyond their control—an economic order. The economic order, in part, affects those patterns of interaction, emotional responses, and cultural practices within the organization, just as those patterns, responses, and practices affect how the organization will be able to adjust and compete in the larger organizational field to which it belongs.

Organizations belong to a field in which some survive and some fail (a market that we might claim reflects—perhaps tautologously—the survival of the fittest). My analysis has not explored this larger, economic field, which would require using multiple ethnographic sites. In contrast, my goal has been to examine how the interaction and symbolic world of the kitchen are affected by the encouragements and constraints beyond the boundaries of the organization. My primary data were collected within the kitchen but examined in the light of the chill world outside. To survive, organizations must cope with a structured environment that demands minimized fixed, labor, and food costs, together with maximizing the number of clients and the profitability of each encounter. Meeting these goals has a direct effect on how life in the kitchen is experienced and on organization output. Efficiency typically makes work life less pleasant and more demanding, and so organization must develop ways to allow workers to feel valued and satisfied despite the removal of "benefits" such as temporal niches and resource perks.

An interactionist understanding of work is consistent with an orientation that emphasizes the position of economics and markets. The world "out there" exists, although this world is known through collective representations of it. It is *as if* it were a collective reality. In fact, this world is constituted by individuals and symbols. Then this collective representation is taken as real and is given considerable power in the creating of organizations. Individuals are wise enough to realize that they are not free from forces that they cannot control. Only a few social scientists attempt to deny what is obvious and what their informants know is true.

AESTHETICS

Cooking has had an ambivalent—and often distant—relationship to the world of art. All diners agree that the sensory characteristics of what is served matter deeply to the outcome. In that sense, as described in chapter 6, cooks have a sense of aesthetics as an integral part of their career concerns. Although that is recognized, it is equally clear that the cooking world is not a well-accepted art world as the latter is usually defined. As a result, cooks must negotiate the ways in which they are expected to take aesthetic concerns into account but simultaneously must do this with the recognition that they are industrial employees, and that their ultimate goal, if they wish to remain employed, must be to prepare food so as to be profitable and to satisfy both customers and managers. This is a delicate balance in that it involves questions of autonomy and control, craft and labor.

To some degree, every occupation must confront the relationship between the aesthetic and instrumental aspects of the job—although a different dynamic affects each occupation. The cook must adjust to those constraints that derive from the location of culinary work in the occupational order, the demands of customers, the time involved in preparation, and the cost of the ingredients. These issues were raised in chapter 5, where such concerns are analyzed in light of the restaurant's location in the marketplace.

In chapter 7, I address how, despite linguistic imprecision about sensory topics, particularly smell and taste, cooks are able to communicate effectively with each other about their experiences and judgments, making collective aesthetic activity possible. Along with understanding the possibilities of discourse, understanding the limitation of talk is central to the social construction of meaning within an aesthetic realm of knowledge. Since it is difficult—perhaps impossible—to share fully sensory experiences, especially those referring to internal impressions, cooks must rely on a set of shared references and develop a poetics of meaning that is grounded within the occupational order.

These issues need to be expanded in several directions. Viewing the occupational and organizational constraints of a single occupation is not a sufficient basis from which to generalize. While numerous investigations examine the constraints upon those occupations considered the "arts," the aesthetic components of occupations that do not have this label have not been well developed. Yet, every occupation has some connection with sensory and expression concerns. Each copes with a different set of constraints; describing these constraints allows us to expand the concept of "art world." The existence of multiple organizational constraints, perhaps involving whole industrial segments, underlines how workers must attempt to be and yet cannot be artists, because of both interactional and structural forces. All aesthetic venues are limited.

In my description of artistic talk, a closer and more detailed attention to the social construction of talk would have been desirable. My intent was not to do a conversation analysis of the talk of cooks, as practiced. However, such a detailed analysis would surely reveal much about the performance of aesthetic talk and the developing of verbal consensus. How in practice do workers create meanings that allow them to comprehend those things that have not been said, and are impossible to say, directly? Here organizational sociology and linguistics require an interface, a connection that only recently has been attempted (Boden 1994), but one that flows from my claim that structural features of occupational life are shaped by the interactional demands of workers. Organizations are constructed—in part—by talk.

The sociological treatment of the expressive side of production remains largely unmapped. A single case can only provide an outline for others to fill in. Specifically we must attend to locally based aesthetic choices. How do workers learn what is right and valued? What dimensions—instrumental and expressive—determine quality of production? How is "cultural capital" generated in work? Under what circumstances is elegant simplicity valued? When is self-conscious creation of the beautiful crucial? Issues of the aesthetics of performance and the aesthetics of material products need to be differentiated. Finally, comparative research on numerous occupations avoids the idiosyncrasies of the description of a single scene.

The expression of aesthetic choices and its relative salience depends on the work environment, the standing of the worker, and the particular work task. Workers' orientations to the expressive side of production are based on such core sociological concepts as convention, autonomy, and community; management's limitations are equally sociological, based on demands for control and efficiency deriving from instrumental requirements. Work is a minuet between expressive form and instrumental function. In this dance, as in others, he who pays the piper ultimately calls the tune.

IN SUM

Throughout this volume I have attempted to present a sustained descriptive picture of one particular and specialized occupational world: that of professional cooks. However, in this I have intended for the reader to learn about more than the local problems that this narrowly focused band of employees faces in their quotidian chores. Cooks are enmeshed in an occupational, interactional, economic, organizational, and cultural web not of their making but one that they help to shape through their responses. In this they are active creators of a socially constructed world and set of work traditions and norms, even though the world is a large and powerful reality to which they must pay heed.

In recognizing that the world is structural and meaningful, I have intended to add ethnographic substance to the theoretical confluence of a macro- and microview of organizations. The examination of organizations must be grounded in empirical observations, and it is the connections that writers make with the "world out there" that determine the viability of broad theoretical approaches. Organizational analysis is a promising arena for the joining of analyses crucial to understanding the social order. The restaurant, as an organization in which groups labor to produce physical and cultural objects, is a social system that demands multiple—and linked—interpretations. If nothing else, it provides food for thought.

APPENDIX

Ethnography
in the Kitchen

Issues and Cases

Africa assailed my senses. I smelled and tasted ethnographic
things and was both repelled by and attracted to a new spec-
trum of odors, flavors, sights, and sounds.
　　　—*Paul Stoller*, The Taste of Ethnographic Things

Every setting has quirks, tricks, surprises. That is the challenge—and
the fun—of participant observation. Veteran anthropologists who have
studied several non-Western cultures know this well. What one learned
about "getting on" in one site scarcely serves as a model for what to
do in the next. Margaret Mead's Samoans provided little guidance for
later examining the Manus of Papua New Guinea. For those mining
American middle-class sites, less intrepid spies, like myself are at least
comforted that the shared culture serves as a guide.

In studying kitchens two themes are salient: the research takes place
in an organization, and it deals with the preparation of food. The former has challenged others before me, but the latter, relatively unstud-
ied, presents novel issues.

WATCHING WORK

Observers of a work organization must recognize that workers, however fond they may be of what they do, are not present in an entirely
voluntary capacity. Employers expect workers at certain times and on
a regular schedule. Further, workers belong to a hierarchical organization that can decide, under some circumstances, to terminate the association.

Because these spaces are not public arenas, access is provided through management; as a consequence, researchers will have, even in the most optimal circumstances, a burden of trust to overcome (Burawoy 1979). Whose side are we on (Becker 1967)? As a result, who I *really* represented was an issue, although one that became muted when it grew clear that I was not reporting to management.

The most direct expression of this sentiment occurred in the kitchen at the Blakemore, which as part of a hotel chain operated under direct, external corporate control. One day early in the research one of the kitchen workers whom I had not previously met, seeing me constantly jotting in my notepad, inquired if I was conducting a time study.

More often my role emerged in the context of joking and teasing, but always with underlying concern:

> Davis, a server, jokes with me: "Who do you really work for? What hotel chain do you really work for?" Diane, one of the cooks, claims that I am a reporter for the *National Enquirer*.
>
> (Field notes, La Pomme de Terre)

> Paul, the head chef, jokes about me being a spy, adding that "he's watching to make sure we work."
>
> (Field notes, Owl's Nest)

This became salient when I observed minor deviance, especially among low-status workers, who feared my power over their careers: "Felicia, a pantry worker, eats a piece of the roast beef that had been trimmed off and giggles when she sees me watching. She says to me laughing, but nervous: 'Are you going to put this in your book?' [Felicia, I have.] Later Lee, a dishwasher, takes some of the beef and jokes to me: 'Which part will we steal today.' I am expected to legitimate their deviance, or, better, to participate in it [I do]." (Field notes, Blakemore Hotel). These workers trust that I will place myself on their side as a true, if limited, member of their group, embracing its underside. This was evident at Stan's, where cooks received beers from the bar. Once a waitress informed a cook that I noted this. He responded, "He's on our side. He's exposing the scandals of cooking" (Field notes, Stan's). As I gave them leeway, they returned the favor.

Only twice was I asked not to observe, both times during the early days of my observation. Stan's was featured on a local television show, and viewers were told that they would receive a special price on steak that weekend. The manager thought that the restaurant would be too crowded to observe. Later I was present on equally busy nights. At the Owl's Nest the head chef asked that I skip one day because a new server was being trained by observing the kitchen. However, later in the research, when another server was being trained, I was allowed to observe. I was accepted.

Although I was careful not to provide information to chefs and managers about particular workers, or even about how to improve the kitchen, these individuals had my ear when they wished and would query my general reactions. Workers might well worry about what I knew and what I might say. While I am confident that my comments did not have direct effects on individual workers or result in immediate changes in the kitchen structure, I may have oriented the concerns of managers or chefs by my presence or indirect comments.

SELF-REFLECTION AND DEPRECATION: FINE'S LAW OF SHARED MADNESS

Informants have images of themselves and their work. These self-images involve doubt, which becomes magnified when observed by an outsider. To defend themselves against the potentially critical eye of the researcher, informants typically display "role-distance" (Goffman 1961b), permitting them, in theory at least, to escape from some of the potentially negative implications of their activity. They need not fully justify their esoteric culture.

As I found among Little League baseball coaches, fantasy gamers, debate teachers, and mushroom collectors, informants suggested that they must be "crazy" to engage in their activity. This role-distance seems to be a fundamental regularity. "Fine's Law of Shared Madness" playfully proposes that in any adult research setting, informants explain that their activity is "irrational." Staff in each kitchen made similar comments:

> Howie says to me: "Everyone knows you've got to be real mental to be a cook."
>
> (Field notes, La Pomme de Terre)

> Mel, the day cook, jokes: "Did you learn that you didn't want to work in the kitchen?" A few weeks later Dan, the owner's son and the restaurant manager, jokes with me: "What have you learned? That you never want to enter the food business?"
>
> (Field notes, Owl's Nest)

Candy, one of the waitresses, jokes about my observations on one very busy
night: "Checking abnormal behavior? You'll definitely find it here. You're
standing in the right place."

(Field notes, Stan's)

Irene, a former cook, asks Keith, a current cook, about me, joking: "You're
giving him your memoirs?" Keith responds: "I'm the only guy who'll talk to
him. The book will be *Portrait of a Cook*. I'll have my name up in lights.
The movie will be filmed in an insane asylum."

(Field notes, Blakemore Hotel)

This same theme is evident among informants who saw me as a "psychologist" or "psychoanalyst," judging "are [they] crazy or sane?"
(Field notes, Blakemore Hotel). Throughout ethnography, particularly
in middle-class settings, informants desire to know "how good are we?"
"how are we doing?" and "will we pass?" (Field notes, Owl's Nest).

Some jokingly attempted to mimic the ethnographic enterprise,
sometimes discussing writing books:[1] "Gordon says to Cal and Dana:
'One day I'm gonna write a book, and then you guys are just going to
be starring in it' " (Field notes, Blakemore Hotel). Or they would observe me: "Mel and Dan kid me: 'Now we're gonna ask you questions.
What is the most interesting thing about your job?' They joke that they
will do a study of researchers" (Field notes, Owl's Nest). This partially
derives from my research style: I am overt about my presence, publicly
taking notes, believing that the novelty of my role will wear off quickly
as I am around every day. Daily research breeds familiarity, and openness is both more ethical and leads to more precise data, since memory
tricks are minimized. Yet, this strategy leads to a justifiable desire to
turn the tables.

THE PLIMPTON EFFECT

One way in which my ambiguous presence was handled was through a
continuing stream of joking, transforming me from researcher to
worker, from observer to full participant (Adler and Adler 1987): the
George Plimpton effect, after the journalist-essayist who briefly partici-
pated as a member of professional sports teams. On a few occasions I
performed such undemanding manual labor as peeling potatoes, de-
stringing beans, stirring soup, or retrieving food from shelves or coolers.

Denny, a cook at La Pomme de Terre, seriously suggests that "on your last
day here we could let you cook some. It would be like George Plimpton."

(Field notes, La Pomme de Terre)

> Toward the end of my research Paul, the head chef, asks me if I would like
> to work the window tonight, saying "You've seen enough." He has seen the
> film *Paper Lion* and wants to put me into the George Plimpton role. I am
> tempted to agree, but it is not clear whether he is joking, and we don't pur-
> sue it.
>
>   (Field notes, Owl's Nest)

Most often the attempts to involve me were jocular, indicating both
my closeness and my distance. These remarks occurred in each restaurant:

> The owner jokes to me as he is leaving for the night: "We'll make you mop
> next week. Everyone gets a job if they stay around long enough."
>
>   (Field notes, La Pomme de Terre)

> Evan jokes to me: "Why don't you take over. You've been trained in."
>
>   (Field notes, Stan's)

> Willy, the stockroom manager, jokes to Sanjay, the food and beverage man-
> ager: "[If] he stays around long enough, we're gonna put him to work."
>
>   (Field notes, Blakemore)

> Paul jokes to me as he is cutting meat: "You've watched me long enough,
> now you've got to try it."
>
>   (Field notes, Owl's Nest)

Like the desire to involve the researcher in occupational deviance, a
strong drive exists, helpful for research, to allow—or demand—the observer to participate in all aspects of the scene: in part from a desire to
help make the experience transparent and in part to cope with the frustration of seeing the researcher standing around, watching, "doing
nothing."

SHARING FOOD

One way that workers attempt to gain the allegiance of a researcher is
to provide organizational perquisites: pleasant little bribes. This is an
extension of the "gift" of information that informants give. To accept
a gift is to remain in the giver's thrall until one reciprocates. Cooks do
this with goods that technically are not theirs to give but belong to
their bosses: food. Food was continually pressed on me, and, perhaps
to my discredit, I rarely refused. During each month that I observed in
the kitchens, I gained approximately ten pounds, which I diligently attempted to lose in the two months between observations. Even had I
wished to refuse the offers, my friends were expecting me to taste their
wares, and this occasionally was a learning experience. Attempts to ply

me with food were most notable at La Pomme de Terre and the Owl's Nest, the better restaurants. Perhaps because steak is expensive and because the preparation was routine, I was not given as much at Stan's, although french fries and onion rings were offered, and when a steak was returned, it was shared. At the Blakemore food was more carefully monitored, and the better dishes were prepared in the "display kitchen." However, even there I was offered coffee, drinks, and an occasional "nibble."

The staff at La Pomme de Terre was particularly generous. During my first evening I was offered snapper Provençale, spicy sausage, lemon balm sorbet, elderberry sorbet, and chocolate cake. A few days later Davis, a room captain, gave me a large slice of cheesecake, an offer I felt rather embarrassed about. He started by asking me if I have a family. When I told him I do, he insisted I take it because they will throw it out otherwise. While they were being generous, the underlying assumption is that I would only refuse the food if I didn't like it *and them.*

The situation was more complex at the Owl's Nest, where food was supposed to be accounted for, and where staff members were expected to pay for their meals. While I was given food, it was often done with a wink and teasing remarks that I would be charged:

> Paul offers me salmon for dinner, adding "You must get hungry standing around." He adds: "Between you and me and the fence post," meaning that I should not mention his largesse.
>
> (Field notes, Owl's Nest)
>
> Bruce gives me a plate of salmon *sorbise,* and Paul jokes: "That will be ten dollars." Later he adds: "Don't steal the hash browns again."
>
> (Field notes, Owl's Nest)

These comments reflect a tension in our relationship, common in ethnography, about the researcher using and being used by informants. These cooks liked me, and I became, in some measure, a member of the group; yet, simultaneously I was and would remain an outsider, potentially affecting their lives and reputations. By bribing me and telling me about their lives, they hoped to gain my support. Because they work in scenes that they do not entirely control, and because I have access to those who control them, they were at my mercy. I, in turn, was at their mercy to the degree that I was allowed to operate, briefly and marginally, as one of them.

ETHNOGRAPHIC SENSE

As the anthropologist Paul Stoller (1989) cogently notes, contemporary Western thought has given primacy to the visual mode, particularly in academic writing (but see Corbin 1986). For those exploring distant cultures the experience of the other senses is central: "Naked children defecating into the ditches which carried the city's sewage; clouds of aromatic smoke rising from grills on which butchers roasted mouth-watering slices of mutton; dirt roads rendered impassible by rat-infested hills of rotting garbage; gentle winds carrying the pungent smell of freshly pounded ginger; skeletal lepers thrusting their stump-hands in people's faces" (Stoller, 1989, p. 3). One not only reads social structure but also hears, touches, smells, and tastes it. Yet, because of our Western training, we find that we easily misplace these skills of understanding. We are taught what to see and, implicitly, taught what we should not sense. Stoller (1989, p. 4) reflects:

> My sensual openness, however, was shortlived. I quickly lost touch with those scenes of abject deprivation which blended into those of insensitive consumption. I soon lost scent of the nose-crinkling stench of the open sewer that gave way to the aromatic aromas of roasting meat. My ears soon deafened to the moans of a sick child that were overwhelmed by the happy laughter of a healthy one. I had become an experience-hardened Africa hand. My immersion in Niger, in Africa, had been, in short, distanciated, intellectualized—taken out of the realm of sensual sentiment. The world of ethnographic things had lost its tastes.

We become so taken with the reality of the world that we have *learned to experience* that we forget to notice the world that we *are experiencing*. For this research, my attempt to remain sensitive to the challenges of senses was critical. If not as dramatic as the sewers of Niger, the kitchens of Minnesota had their share of distinct smells, touches, sounds, and tastes. The challenge was learning from these senses: to let, in the words of one cook, "the kitchen talk to you." As I describe in chapter 2, when I discuss the timing of food preparation, these senses are critical to the competent doing of cuisine. Done food has a different smell from burned or underdone food, and these smells are clues for the ethnographer.

A second element of the ethnography of senses is to avoid imposing one's own taste on one's informants. The rejection of "proper" food can be a means of differentiating insiders from outsiders. Craig Claiborne's mother ran a rooming house in Indianola, Mississippi, where the social psychologist John Dollard happened to stay while researching his admirable *Caste and Class in a Southern Town* (1949). As Claiborne (1982, pp. 32–33) recalls Dollard's tastes, "In the beginning [Dr. Dollard] criticized the cooking of the greens, complaining that there was not a vitamin left in the lot. And as a result of his well-intentioned explanations and at the base encouragement of the other boarders, my mother willingly committed one of the most wicked acts of her life. Dr. Dollard was placed at a bridge table, covered, of course, with linen and set with sterling, and he was served a mess of raw greens that he ate with considerable and admirable composure and lack of resentment." His northern taste almost prevented him from understanding the society that he had chosen to examine. As a promiscuous eater, I did not have Dollard's problem, but occasionally I would be given something to taste, because a cook wanted to know if I judged it as he did. Workers within the kitchen would no doubt gauge its quality with certainty, but I often had to guess whether the food would be judged a success or a failure. I recall particularly a highly and oddly spiced sausage served to me at La Pomme de Terre, which could be fairly described as "distinctive," a basil-cantaloupe sorbet that sticks with me still, and a beet fettucini with herbed tomato sauce that was dubbed an abject failure. An observer should not like everything but must develop tastes similar to those whom he or she is studying.

WHAT IS A COOK?

What is a cook? Who is a cook? To this point I have investigated culinary structure and interaction, without addressing the characteristics of those who labor in the kitchen or the characteristics of the specific restaurants themselves. I first describe the workers (see also Fine 1987b for a discussion of the attitudes of cooks to their profession and of their recruitment and socialization); then I turn to a detailed description of the four restaurants that I observed.

My sample is neither random nor representative. It is, in many ways, a convenience sample: four restaurants in the upper stratum of restaurants in the Twin Cities area. Yet, examining the attributes of the sample of cooks at least opens a window into an obscure social world.

GENDER

When examining census data, one discovers, surprisingly, that 57.2 percent of all cooks are female (Bureau of the Census 1984, p. 11), but this statistic is deceptive when considering restaurant life, as it includes those areas of cooking in which females predominate—institutional cooking, diners, and local cafés. Census data from the Twin Cities metropolitan area indicate that in 1980 the approximately fourteen thousand cooks, excluding short-order cooks, were almost evenly divided by gender (51 percent male versus 49 percent female). However, among the higher-status restaurants I examined, males predominated. Of the thirty cooks interviewed, only four were females (13 percent). None of these women had positions of authority. Although significant change has occurred in the past decade, in the higher-status end of the restaurant industry, males dominate. Women, while sometimes accepted (Fine 1987a), are a small minority, remaining outsiders. Although women bear the primary responsibility for cooking for the family, in institutional spaces and modest establishments, cooking that involves creativity and high-volume service, or at prestigious dining places, is typically defined as a job for men.

AGE

The census figures for 1980 reveal that cooking has one of the youngest median ages of any occupation. The median age for cooks in the Twin Cities metropolitan area was only 19.2 years, with only about one-eighth of all cooks over 30 years of age. Rather than parents cooking for their children, in restaurants the relations are reversed. This includes entry-level positions and kitchen workers at fast-food establishments. My sample was slightly older than this average but still quite young. The median age was 25, with a mean of 24.5. Only one of the cooks in the sample was older than 40 (he was 43). I asked one young cook what he felt that the general public would be most surprised by. He answered without hesitation that it would be that "people cooking are so young" (Personal interview, Stan's). Most of the cooks at Stan's, admittedly younger than at the other restaurants, were too young to drink legally. Cooking is demanding, low-wage employment, even under the most favorable circumstances; it is not surprising that few see cooking as suitable long-term employment. Kitchen labor is a transitional occupation for young men until they decide on a "real" career. Some enter management (a personal career goal for several cooks); others see cooking as temporary and transfer to other occupations.

EDUCATION AND FAMILY BACKGROUND

Only three (10 percent) of the cooks that I interviewed had college degrees; another eight (27 percent) had attended some college. Obviously the nature of the sample affects this figure considerably. Some evidence exists that as restaurant work is becoming more prestigious, the educational level of cooks and chefs may slowly be increasing (Zukin 1990). With the upgrading of the image of the cook, more cooks are recruited from the middle class, at least in better restaurants in urban centers; many of these individuals see themselves as part of the arts infrastructure and dream of opening their own establishments (Zukin 1990). My small sample includes cooks from a wide variety of class backgrounds, including children of truck drivers, postal clerks, firemen, bankers, and certified public accountants. In general, the class background tends to be from the lower middle class or upper working class, although the variability is so great that extreme caution is warranted in making generalizations.

RESTAURANT SETTINGS AND DATA SOURCES

To understand a topic ethnographically, one should select more than a single scene. Generalizability is important. Before I began this research, I had observed a hotel and restaurant cooking program at City Technical Vocational Institute (City TVI), now called City Technical College, and I was in the midst of less-intense "comparative" ethnography at Suburban Technical Vocational Institute. I wanted to understand how working-class students acquired the "cultural capital" to engage in aesthetic production (Fine 1985). I hoped to address the practical usage of aesthetic knowledge.

To gain a more complete vision of the restaurant industry, and, in particular, how students are compelled to transform their "idealism" into the real world of organizational requirements, I selected four restaurants to continue the research. At City Technical Vocational Institute the program was a long-standing one, and the four instructors had each taught at the school for a decade. I selected restaurants that had hired head chefs—or, in one case, a manager—who had attended this program.

In addition to selecting restaurants by their connection with City TVI, I also wanted to observe restaurants that employed similar numbers of cooks. I wanted each kitchen staff to be a small group. Some restaurants have extensive staffs, and others require only two or three cooks. I chose restaurants that employed approximately eight cooks, of whom three or four were on duty at any time. Finally, I desired a set of restaurants that represented diverse cooking styles. My goal was not to select the "best" restaurants in the Twin Cities or the ones with the most articulate chefs. I sacrificed artistic rhetoric for the mundane discourse found in most kitchens.

For my sample I selected a haute cuisine restaurant (La Pomme de Terre), a continental restaurant (The Owl's Nest), a steakhouse (Stan's), and a hotel kitchen (the Blakemore Hotel). These four restaurants provided a reasonable range of cooking environments. I make no claim that these four restaurants reflect a representative sample of all local restaurants; clearly they do not. They represent the upper portion of Minnesota restaurants in terms of status: they are not "ethnic," family, fast-food, or neighborhood restaurants; nor are they glorious temples of haute cuisine, such as are found in New York or New Orleans.

I approached each restaurant by contacting the man who had been trained at City TVI. At Stan's this was the manager (the owner's son), and at the other three restaurants it was the head chef.[2] After explaining that I was a professor at the University of Minnesota, had conducted related research, and had just finished my observations at City TVI, mentioning the names of the instructors, I emphasized that I was interested in understanding the work challenges faced by cooks. Cooks, like many workers, feel singularly underappreciated, and these men were flattered that an outsider, a professor, would be interested in their careers. Like many ethnographic informants, they were somewhat nervous about what I might discover, but each agreed to my presence in their kitchen for a month although they maintained the right to ask me to terminate the research temporarily or permanently. I eventually became friends with each of them.

After receiving their approval, I arranged to speak to the manager or owner.[3] I emphasized that I had the chef's approval and explained that I would not evaluate their restaurant, either for them or for publication. I wished to stand quietly in the kitchen, watching and learning.

I indicated that if they felt that my presence interfered with the running of their business, they could ask me to leave. The owner at La Pomme de Terre quickly agreed, as did the manager at the Owl's Nest (the son of the owner). The food and beverage manager at the Blakemore requested a formal letter stating the goals of my research. When I presented that documentation, he agreed readily.

Upon receiving the approval of the manager, I selected a day to begin my research. I chose a time that would not be busy, so that I could meet with each cook and explain my research goals. I informed them that they did not have to participate if they did not wish, but no one refused. All those whom I asked to be interviewed agreed. Like the head chefs, they were flattered that someone of "importance" was interested in their lives.[4]

During my stay at the restaurant, I attempted to be present six days each week (three were open seven days a week), and I attempted to stagger my observation times, so that I witnessed the kitchen at each time of the day. I also attempted to be present for special events and on particularly busy evenings. In each kitchen I found a place to observe that avoided traffic and afforded a good view. While I did not often help with the kitchen work, on occasion I did small tasks when asked. I avoided times of the year that would be particularly busy (November or December) or especially slow (July or August), in order to capture the normal routine of cooking.

I spent a month observing in the kitchen of each restaurant and then interviewed all the full-time cooks for a total of thirty in-depth interviews. Each interview lasted from one to three hours and covered the cook's background, recruitment to cooking, attitudes toward work and the restaurant, and the aesthetics of cooking. Most interviews were conducted in the respondent's home, but a few took place in quiet areas of the restaurant or in other public places. Details of the research are included in table 1.

TABLE 1   RESEARCH PARAMETERS

	La Pomme	Owl's Nest	Stan's	Blakemore
No. of days observing	26	22	28	29
No. of hours observing	71	83	47	54
No. of interviews	7	7	7	9
Months in kitchen	Sept./Oct.	May/June	Jan./Feb.	March/April

Each restaurant is unique. Although these restaurants differ from each other in their production dynamics and social placement, I have avoided treating them separately, ignoring their idiosyncratic dynamics. I doubt the utility of a single case study. Stan's differs from La Pomme in much more than the cuisine—to contrast a "typical" gourmet restaurant with a "typical" steakhouse would mislead. A set of similar cases are required for a meaningful contrast between steakhouses and gourmet restaurants or, for that matter, between hotel kitchens and freestanding restaurants. My interest was not in how any of these idiosyncratic establishments operate but the social processes that link all restaurants. Despite my caution in using each individual restaurant to stand for a restaurant "type," the interested reader deserves a description of each restaurant.

LA POMME DE TERRE

La Pomme de Terre had the reputation of being one of the finest, most creative haute cuisine restaurants in the Twin Cities area. Some restaurant reviewers, perhaps tinged by local boosterism, claimed that La Pomme de Terre was the best restaurant between Chicago and California. Perhaps. Partisans of other restaurants in the Twin Cities might dispute whether La Pomme de Terre is the best restaurant in the Twin Cities, but no one would doubt that at the time of the research it had an enviable reputation. Each night the restaurant offered two fish specials, occasionally a meat special, two soups, and several sorbets and desserts. These specials included such comestibles as beef Wellington with wild mushrooms, monkfish in a peach beurre blanc, cumin-lamb sausage, or sole turban. The restaurant was known for high prices although by no means as high as those of restaurants on either coast. In the mid-1980s, one could eat well at La Pomme de Terre for under forty dollars per person.

The head chef, Tim, was born and raised near Sioux Falls, South Dakota, the child of a middle-class, midwestern family. At fifteen he was hired at a local truck stop, first washing dishes and then cooking. Evaluating job possibilities after high school, Tim relocated to the Twin Cities to learn to cook at City TVI. After TVI he worked at a "home-style" restaurant, several country clubs, a Chinese restaurant, finally landing an entry-level job at La Pomme de Terre. Along the way he had decided that he wanted to be a gourmet chef, even though his previous employment had not prepared him for this goal. Tim was both hardworking and creative, and spent much time in La Pomme's kitchen, learning all that he could from the European-trained head chef. A few years later that chef left in a personality conflict with the owner, and Tim was asked to run the kitchen, in part, he claims, because he was cheap labor. This proved to be a great challenge for an unknown chef, then in his midtwenties. Tim triumphed in his new position, and the restaurant enhanced its reputation.

The restaurant itself was located on the ground floor of an elegant apartment building, lately turned into condominiums. One must walk through the lobby to reach the restaurant. While the lobby is pleasant, it is often deserted during the dinner hour. This odd location, with its low overhead, permits the restaurant to survive, serving fewer than one hundred customers on busier nights and perhaps two dozen customers when slower. The restaurant was open for lunch and dinner during the week, dinner on Saturday, and brunch on Sunday. The brunch was eventually canceled.

The kitchen was quite spacious, particularly compared to the two other freestanding restaurants. Cooks worked in a large, bright, airy rectangular room, with space for movement and separate areas for pastry work and salad preparation. The waiters and dishwashers worked on the other side of this large room and rarely interfered with the cooks. The dining room was decorated in muted tones of gray and cream, understated and tasteful.

La Pomme de Terre was owned and operated by a husband and wife; the husband had been a marketing vice-president for a large corporation before deciding to enter the restaurant business in the late 1970s. At the time of the research he was planning to open other restaurants in the Twin Cities. La Pomme de Terre is located within a short walk of some of the premium cultural attractions of the Twin Cities, within an area that has an artistic, yuppie, and gay ambiance.

One of the restaurant's major problems was that it did not have a liquor license permitting it to serve hard liquor, although it did maintain an excellent wine cellar, especially well stocked with California vintages. As a consequence, La Pomme lost some business clientele.

In addition to the head chef, the restaurant employed a sous chef, a day cook, and a pastry cook; three other cooks prepared salads, soups, or worked the ovens and grills, depending on need. Of these seven employees, two were women. One of these cooks was fully accepted (see Fine 1987a), but the other was marginal to the kitchen community. This woman had not been formally trained as a cook but had been a schoolteacher who had switched careers. Because of her knowledge of food and her enthusiasm, Tim had decided to hire her but soon regretted the decision. According to him, she never acquired the skills of a professional cook and was terminated.

The cooks employed by La Pomme de Terre were, perhaps not surprisingly, more interested in food as art and more committed to the aesthetic presentation of foodstuffs than cooks at the other restaurants. Tim claimed to look less for impressive résumés than for those who were creative and hardworking, and who, he felt, had a drive to succeed. Within a few years after my observations, at least two of the cooks had become head chefs in important Twin Cities restaurants, and the pastry chef was well-known in the Twin Cities for her remarkable creations.

The servers were all male with the exception of one female. The servers—and, to a degree, the cooks—had more cultural capital than the staff at the other restaurants. In general, the staff worked well together and would occasionally go drinking after a hectic weekend evening.

THE OWL'S NEST

Like La Pomme de Terre, the Owl's Nest was blessed and cursed by its location. The restaurant, opened in 1964, was situated on a main thoroughfare connecting Minneapolis and St. Paul, a street of car lots, decaying businesses, second-tier shopping centers, pornography boutiques, Asian groceries, and various minor public offices. Its location, approximately five minutes from the state capitol and ten minutes from downtown St. Paul, coupled with its patina of 1960s elegance and low overhead, permitted success. The Owl's Nest was a continental restaurant from a period when that term implied a luxurious dinner for many midwesterners. Prior to my observations, the head chef, who had previously worked in a large hotel kitchen, had revised the menu, adding more fish dishes to replace the beef that was increasingly out of fashion. Paul, the head chef, explained that about 70 percent of the orders were seafood. The prices were comfortably high, as they catered to a class of well-to-do businessmen, often on expense accounts. Luncheon was the most profitable meal, although they were open evenings Monday through Saturday. The Owl's Nest was best known for their Caesar salad, prepared tableside by a male house captain, London broil, and the various fresh-fish dishes, such as walleyed pike *aux fines herbes* or sautéed scallops *meunière*. The restaurant also had an adequate wine list and bar service.

The Owl's Nest had been operated for twenty years by the same family, and for many years it was one of the two or three most elegant restaurants in the Twin Cities. During my research its former competitors were closing for lack of customers. Its plush, dark, clubby interior contrasted with the airy openness and postmodern bricolage coming into vogue. Yet, in light of its goals the Owl's Nest was well respected. Its clientele included the political and business elite of the state, and its entrance was filled with framed certificates, indicating its multiyear status as a Holiday Award recipient. It was not a place dear to the artistic and cultural elites, who were more likely to patronize La Pomme de Terre or a local bistro. Despite snide comments by this elite this once-stylish restaurant served the needs of its upper-middle-class business clientele with well-prepared continental dishes.

Paul, the head chef, was a child of middle-class St. Paul parents. After graduating from high school, he attended City TVI, where his brother teaches. He thought that he would enjoy working with food, even though he hadn't had a cooking job, and he enrolled in the restaurant program. Most of his career was spent in a hotel kitchen—of a hotel in the same chain as the Blakemore. There he was eventually promoted to sous chef but decided to leave the hotel when management offered to promote him to executive chef without any increase in salary. In time he took the proffered position but was unhappy with the arrangement. When he received a call from the owner of the Owl's Nest, he accepted the offer, at a higher salary. He had been at the Owl's Nest for about eighteen months at the time of my observations.

Paul's staff consisted of six other cooks and two regular pantry workers. Trained at City TVI, Paul was a strong believer in vocational education, and five of his cooks had graduated from those programs. All cooks were men, but one of the pantry workers was female. Desserts were not created in the restaurant but purchased from outside vendors.

In general, the staff was friendly although there was friction during my observation because of the temper of one cook and problems with a lack of space in the kitchen and a confusion of organizational responsibility. Eventually Paul held a kitchen meeting to thrash out differences, which seemed to have a positive effect, at least temporarily. The cooks had to work in a very narrow area, with stoves close together. The cook who worked the window was in charge of the grill and would continually interfere with the cook on the stove and the one doing preparation work. This was complicated by the fact that the pot-men and the pantry workers operated in the same narrow area. For reasons of space it was almost impossible for the servers to enter the kitchen for any purpose, except at slow times. Most communication was through a small window on one side of the dining room. The majority of the servers were female although the house captains were male.

The owner and particularly his son, who managed the restaurant, were often present, and while they afforded the head chef considerable leeway, their presence was notable. The son was on good terms with the cooks and would occasionally take them fishing.

STAN'S

Thank you, God, for blessings
That often come our way,
The things we take for granted
But don't mention when we pray.

And thank you, God, for all the folks
Who stop to eat and share,
Who give us all a chance to serve
And show how much we care!
        —printed on Stan's menu

During the food revolution of the 1980s, steakhouses were not exactly trendy, particularly those like Stan's that aspired to little more than providing simple, hearty pleasure, without becoming a bizarre theme park. Stan's affected no Western motif, no hyper-macho bric-a-brac. It was, and is, a plain, comfortable restaurant without a conscious sub-text. On a busy night Stan's might serve over six hundred customers in its rabbit warren of rooms. Many customers were middle-aged, lower middle class, and frequently from the unpretentious neighborhood in which Stan's was located. Stan's was known throughout the Twin Cities as a very good, moderately priced establishment, not as elegant as some local steakhouses but a restaurant that had won multiple awards for the quality of its meat. During the period in which I observed, Stan's was featured on a local entertainment show, and viewers were offered a special deal on steak if they would mention the show. For the next week the restaurant was mobbed.

Stan's was comfortable with its simple decor, long bar, community of young and older waitresses (there were no male servers), and regular customers. While open for lunch and dinner from Monday to Friday, and dinner on Saturday, its Sunday-afternoon "dinner" (3:00 P.M.– 10:00 P.M.) was distinctive, catering to the "cardiac crowd." Here senior citizens ventured out for a special afternoon meal. On Sundays, orders of steak gave way to chicken or fish. Beef cuts included New York strip, sirloin, baby back ribs, hamburger, and butterfly-cut steak. These were supplemented with fried chicken, scallops, salmon steak, french fries, and onion rings. Most entrees during the early to mid-1980s sold for under ten dollars.

Stan's had been open since the 1940s and was operated by the same family for nearly twenty years. The owners were actively involved in operating the restaurant, which made the structure of Stan's quite different from La Pomme de Terre and the Owl's Nest. On a day-to-day basis Stan's was run directly by the manager, the owner's son, a City TVI graduate. This structure is reflected in that the "official" title of the lead chef was "head cook" although Doug called himself "chef." Doug shared responsibility for ordering food with Charles, the owner's son. It was Charles, and his father, who selected the menu and prices.

Doug's only restaurant experience, other than cooking at the state fair, was at Stan's. He had worked at Stan's for nearly fifteen years, starting as a cook's helper, later doing dishwashing and busing. At that time his grandmother worked at the restaurant, so he had an in. He had had no dreams of cooking, but as he described it, "I found I like this work fairly well, and it didn't disagree with me" (Personal interview, Stan's). He did not plan to leave Stan's. Doug had had no formal culinary training and had no plans to get any. The other cooks were young men with the exception of one older woman, a longtime employee who helped Doug at lunchtime.

The cooks who worked on the weekends and in the evenings were good friends, mostly in their late teens or early twenties, and would occasionally party together, sometimes with waitresses or dishwashers. Some of these men had TVI training, but few saw cooking as a permanent occupation. The kitchen was structured so that typically three or four cooks were on duty at any time, with one operating the fryer, a second the grill, and a third the ovens. Working the grill was more desirable than the other two positions. Unlike the other restaurants, the cooks at Stan's were hired as dishwashers or busboys, and when there was an opening for a cook, a higher-paid occupation, they made a casual switch. Unlike other restaurants, sharp divisions did not exist among the staff, other than the fact that the occupations were gendered: women were servers, and males cooked, bused, washed dishes, and poured drinks at the bar.[5] There was an easy exchange relationship, and cooks received an occasional beer in return for the odd steak.

The main kitchen area was rectangular with a large metal table in the middle of the floor. The cooks and servers worked on opposite sides of the room. When ready, dishes were placed on shelves above the table. Because of the large number of customers, coupled with the need for turnover in the restaurant and the close proximity of servers and cooks, friction occasionally emerged as servers would demand or wheedle their dishes from cooks who felt overworked and underpaid in contrast to the waitresses, who received good tips. Because of the fryer and the grill, Stan's kitchen was the most "fragrant" and the greasiest. While I observed in the middle of a Minnesota winter, I heard that during the summer the kitchen could be unbearable.

THE BLAKEMORE

Hotel kitchens often do not get much respect; such was certainly the case at the Blakemore Hotel. One of a chain of hotels in the Twin Cities, the restaurants at the Blakemore were not judged to be among the premier dining places in the cities, even by hotel standards. The hotel was relatively new, located downtown, catering primarily to business travelers. Its location was not propitious for success, as it was within several blocks of several other hotels, including a second hotel of the same chain. The Blakemore was the smaller and less prestigious of the two.

The Blakemore operated a coffee shop, a restaurant with a display kitchen, a banquet service, and room service. The coffee shop was open for breakfast and lunch seven days a week; the restaurant was open for lunch and dinner from Monday through Saturday. On holidays such as Easter or Mother's Day the restaurant opened for a Sunday brunch. The restaurant—an airy, flower-filled area off the lobby, partitioned from hotel traffic—maintained an open "presentation kitchen" in which food was prepared to order for the entertainment of customers. Most food was typical hotel fare—updated examples of the hotel plates that William Foote Whyte (1948) saw prepared in Minneapolis in the 1940s: veal marsala, stuffed trout, shrimp Provençale, and rack of lamb. Prices were generally comparable to the Owl's Nest, with those of most entrées ranging from ten to fifteen dollars. During my observation, business in both the coffee shop and the restaurant was disappointingly slow, frequently with fewer than three dozen customers a night. The kitchen staff had recently been cut, eliminating the popular sous chef. The main source of business, other than breakfast in the coffee shop, was the banquet service. Most nights the kitchen prepared at least one banquet for up to three hundred customers. The hotel served traditional banquet foods such as baked chicken, broccoli, and baked potatoes. Most desserts were provided by outside suppliers. Unlike other restaurants, the Blakemore frequently relied on prepared foods such as a mousse mix, instant mashed potatoes, or precooked chicken Kiev.

The structure of this hotel kitchen was more bureaucratic than the other restaurants. Sharply drawn lines of authority existed, leading from the hotel manager to the food and beverage manager to the executive chef. A separate employee was in charge of the storeroom, and foods had to be signed out to maintain cost control. Workers were expected to punch in and were not paid for overtime unless it was formally approved, which was rare in this period of budget cutting. There was relatively little contact between the cooks, servers, and potwashers-dishwashers: each group maintained its own social system. The servers were female, the potwashers-dishwashers and cooks mostly male.[6] As at the Owl's Nest and Stan's, employees at the Blakemore were unionized, but at no other restaurant was there an equivalent level of strain between the kitchen workers and management. Most workers were alienated from their work and indicated little organizational loyalty. In addition, although some personal friendships existed among the staff, the level of community found at the other three restaurants was not present at the Blakemore.

The Blakemore's kitchen was huge and much space was unused. This spatial structure separated workers from each other and decreased communication. While the space might have seemed luxurious, and necessary for banquet preparations, it had a deleterious effect on kitchen functioning.

The executive chef, Denver, was raised in the Twin Cities and attended the University of Minnesota long enough to get a two-year Associate of Arts degree. After becoming frustrated at the university, he decided to try City TVI. He had no occupational goals but knew a friend who had enjoyed the cooking program, and so he decided to enroll. When we met, he had been cooking professionally for ten years, mostly in hotel kitchens, catering, and country clubs. Occupational mobility was such that by the time that Denver was in his early twenties, he was a chef, and he continued to change positions as new opportunities arose. He had recently finished a stint as executive chef at a motel, during which he had received an offer from the Blakemore, a larger hotel.

Unlike the chefs at the other three restaurants, Denver was neither well liked nor respected by his staff. Several cooks had been on staff before he was hired, and they preferred the sous chef who had been recently laid off. The basic complaints of his eight-person staff was that Denver was rarely around when needed, and that he didn't help as much as they wished. His claim was that he was hired as *executive* chef and did not have responsibility for line cooking. He did help some but not enough to gain the allegiance of his staff, several of whom were bitter about his "laziness." The Blakemore was not a happy kitchen, as Denver didn't much like his superiors and wasn't sure that he would remain or be allowed to remain. The cooks were dispirited about the workload. For its part, management was disappointed by the performance of the restaurant, which was barely breaking even, despite the cutbacks. It was not surprising that shortly afterward, a new chef was hired, and soon after the chain sold the hotel to another chain.

Notes

INTRODUCTION

1. There is by now a significant literature on how diet is linked to ideological structures (Turner 1982; Levenstein 1988; Fiddes 1991), including those of class, ethnicity, and gender.

2. In this I have not been alone. Maines (1988) argues that there has always been an organizational core to interactionist theory (e.g., Blumer 1990). While this might extend the emphasis of interactionist writing and the challenge of interactionist theory to conventional sociology, it is true that from the writings of Roy (1952, 1954) and Dalton (1959), there has been an abiding interest in examining the social lives of organizations and in how these lives fit into the larger surround.

3. This setting proved particularly apt for the development of this analysis because of the looseness and uncertainty of techniques for treating patients. Several ideologies competed against each other in these settings. Because of the difficulty in judging certainty of outcome, it is easier to see negotiation on psychiatric wards than on cardiac wards, but some negotiation occurs there as well.

4. DeVault (1991) cogently notes that within the family, women serve as the provisioning specialists, as "care" is part of their responsibilities.

5. Some consider the publication of Taillevent's cookbook *Le Viandier* to mark the beginning of cooking as we know it (Willan 1977, p. 9).

6. The history of taverns and coffeehouses is a related subject. While liquid comestibles were provided, they served similar functions by providing public spaces in which groups could meet. As with establishments that served food, those that served drinks were heavily stratified by class. Taverns, as male enclaves, reflected the gendered structure of society, increasing gender-based solidarity (Brennan 1988, p. 8).

7. Hughes (1971, p. 298) suggests that labeling one's work an industry is an attempt to gain status for that workplace; he notes the attempt of junk dealers to label themselves "the salvage industry."

8. Restaurants along major highways seem to provide contrary evidence, but here the issue revolves around when drivers wish to eat. At that point they will choose the nearest suitable establishment.

9. This obviously will apply somewhat more to those restaurants that self-consciously attempt to make a cultural statement. The primary goal of other restaurants is more humble: to serve food to a local clientele and, in the process, generate profits.

10. A similar dynamic explains the decision of the owner of La Pomme de Terre (one of my ethnographic sites) to open his restaurant. He was an executive in a local corporation, and disillusioned by the quality of food available in the Twin Cities, he felt that he could do better. While he was not a cook, he considered himself a gourmet.

1. LIVING THE KITCHEN LIFE

1. In this book I use the word *servers* to indicate those who might otherwise be termed *waiters* or *waitresses*. In most restaurants one gender or the other predominates in the service staff. I find the gender-neutral terms *waitron* or *waitperson* gangly and discordant.

2. To sheet pan a steak is to bake it on a sheet pan.

3. Craig Claiborne comments about his friend and collaborator, Pierre Franey: "I have known and interviewed countless chefs over the years but I have never known any chef with such an extraordinary capacity to improvise and rectify when working in the kitchen as Pierre Franey. He is a veritable Merlin when it comes to changing failed sauces into triumphs, in knowing precisely how to make a culinary catastrophe into a thing of genius. It may be as seemingly simple as turning a curdled hollandaise into a masterpiece of silken homogeneity or whisking in a little cold water to revitalize and reconstitute a mayonnaise" (Claiborne 1982, p. 215).

4. Cooks on display have the challenging Goffmaniacal task of looking like cooks while cooking. As a result, they are far less efficient than their colleagues who cook behind closed doors, and often they are helped by those behind the doors.

5. One cook, who was the head chef at a health food restaurant, made the opposite case: "I have a good stomach. . . . In fact I take a definite perverse pleasure when I run into an irate customer who found a hair in the food. I tend to be, you know, diplomatic about it, but inwardly I'm laughing that he's offended by a hair" (Personal interview, Minneapolis).

6. Americans seem more fastidious about bodily fluids than are their European counterparts and do not spit on cutlery or reuse unwashed dishes; yet, in American restaurants dirty serving cloths and touching food are common.

7. "Scored off" refers to the technique whereby steaks are placed on the grill in order to put grill marks on them. After that, the steaks are baked, which is easier for cooks.

8. There is some anecdotal evidence that this same emphasis on cooperative teamwork is not found in the great European kitchens. One German chef is quoted about his work in America: "I learned a great deal in America, especially how to treat people. I learned respect for those who worked with me. In Europe there is little comprehension of what Americans call teamwork" (Wechsberg 1980, p. 36).

9. Cooking, like other occupations, is internally divided, with segments of the industry valued differently (Bucher and Stelling 1977). One goal of socializers is to direct the "right" students to the "right" section of the industry while providing some indication of the forthcoming public responses (Manning and Hearn 1969). This connects to theories of "social reproduction," as mediated by an internal occupational hierarchy. The culinary elite has always had high status, and this exalted views of chefs may be spreading among the population, particularly with the development of city centers by those with cultural capital, such as yuppies and gentrifiers (Zukin 1990, p. 1). Not all cooks agree that attitudes have changed. For some of these working-class males in the Twin Cities, for instance, cooking is viewed by friends and relatives as an occupation "for girls." In most working- and middle-class homes wives cooked, and husbands ate.

10. As a function of societal values and economic necessities, these age ranges are subject to change. In France during the nineteenth century, children as young as ten were hired in kitchens (Charpentier and Sparkes 1934, p. 16).

11. In a few instances cooks became servers, and the reverse happened at La Pomme de Terre, but this was only true for those who had been previously trained in the kitchen. Anyone with good manners and personal presentation could become a server. There is also some evidence that there may be movement from various performing arts into restaurant work, particularly, though not exclusively (Wygan 1981, p. 23), for servers (Zukin 1990).

12. This is modified by the fact that cooking students may have been employed by restaurants in the evening or on weekends, or may have had "real-world" cooking training before they entered trade school.

2. COOKS' TIME

1. The interest in the sociological structure of time is largely a development of the past two decades despite some earlier works (Sorokin and Merton 1937; Hawley 1950; Gurvitch 1964).

2. By "temporal niche" I refer to a slice of time, cut from the rest of work, in which a worker or group of workers has autonomy in the use of that period. This is a component of the "active worker" (Hodson 1991). A classic instance of a temporal niche is "banana time" (Roy 1959–1960).

3. With exceptions, cooks are told explicitly or there is a notation on the ticket indicating when the dish is needed. For example, at the Owl's Nest servers wrote "downtown" on the ticket when they needed an order as soon as possible; otherwise, cooks assumed that the dish was required twenty minutes after the ticket was submitted.

4. No work is totally unpredictable; emergency room medics expect to work more on Saturday nights than on Tuesday mornings.

5. "Ivory" refers to an ivory salmon. "Downtown" means "immediately." A "top" is a top sirloin. The shrimps are baked; the steaks, cooked medium.

6. For example, at Stan's during a rush, moderately burned au gratin potatoes were served, whereas at quieter periods they would not have been.

7. When cooks feel they can take no more, they may snap and throw something:

GAF: What do you think an outsider would be most upset by?

GENE: Sometimes the actions of the cooks. The swearing. Sometimes you get frustrated, and you throw something against the wall, and you snap when you throw something.

GAF: What has been thrown?

GENE: Steaks, potatoes—all kinds of things. If a steak's too well done, I see Al do it and I've done it, and you throw the whole thing in the wastebasket, plate and all. You swear and rant and rave, and later you pick it out and throw it in the dishwasher. It's just one of those surges that you get.

(Personal interview, Stan's)

8. Fish has a much narrower temporal window than steak, which can vary by several minutes. The cooking time of some soups, on the other hand, can be varied by hours without much affecting the taste.

9. Some occupations have their problems compounded by the demand for emotion work (Hochschild 1983; Leidner 1993) by the client or organization. Front-stage occupations like flight attendants, servers, prostitutes, and family physicians have a greater need for emotional impression management than such backstage occupations as cook, writer, or night custodian (Hood 1988).

3. THE KITCHEN AS PLACE AND SPACE

1. A novice walking into a restaurant kitchen may be struck by the gargantuan size of some of the equipment. I took particular notice of this in the hotel kitchen, where huge kettles were used to make soup.

2. Only at Stan's Steakhouse did cooks use restaurant knives.

3. Occasionally cooks mention the danger of injury from slippery floors or from heavy lifting.

4. In these restaurants there were also house managers, captains, busboys, bookkeepers, parking valets, and bartenders. I will not discuss these occupations in this analysis.

5. Stan's Steakhouse did not have an employee called "chef"; they employed a "head cook." This man had the day-to-day responsibilities of running the kitchen, but the owner (and his son) was more involved in the management of the kitchen than was true at other restaurants. At the Blakemore Hotel the chef also had somewhat diminished responsibility, reporting to the hotel's house manager. Still, although the supervision was closer, the chef had responsibilities similar to those found at the other restaurants with the notable exception that major changes in the menu were often suggested by the management of the hotel chain.

6. The distinction between cook and chef seems more firmly drawn in European restaurants, which parallels the more structured class distinctions existing

there. As one American head "chef" who has worked in European haute cuisine restaurants commented: " 'I consider myself a good professional cook, but not a chef. Not after working with the great chefs.' He tells a story about Didier Oudill, an assistant to Paul Bocuse in one cooking seminar and a formidable chef himself, meeting a young woman who introduced herself as a chef in a Napa Valley restaurant. Gesturing toward Bocuse across the room, Didier said, 'I am a cook. He is the chef' " (Bates 1984, p. 32). This compares to a comment made to me by a cook at the Owl's Nest: "Bruce tells me that he thinks of himself as the 'assistant chef' although he says that his actual title is vague. He adds: 'Or I could be sauté cook. We all like to consider ourselves chef in some way or other. . . . I don't consider myself a true chef until I'm in Dick's position with all that pressure' " (Field notes, Owl's Nest). The line between cook and chef is not always certain. Many American cooks, however, desire to be considered a "chef," with its attendant status, but recognize that the difference lies in more responsibility, rather than in greater creativity or expertise.

7. To some extent this extensive division of labor persists in the best French restaurants. A top New York chef notes: "Take Guerard. He does 65 meals a night with 17 people in the kitchen. In America if you're serving 75, you have six to eight in the kitchen" ("Great French-American Chef's Debate" 1984, p. 19). At La Pomme de Terre, which served 65–75 dinners on weekend nights, only four cooks were on staff. Its owner once explained that what distinguished his establishment from the "best" American restaurants was that it didn't have the manpower to do "the touches"—the little decorative things that made a dinner truly remarkable.

8. One day the Blakemore chef was helping in the pantry area. The following humorous colloquy occurred; the humor is based on the extreme role reversals expressed:

MELISSA, joking to Denver, the chef:	Make another special.
DENVER:	Yes, ma'am.
MELISSA:	Make it correctly this time.
BERNICE, after Denver makes rainbow jello:	You do it pretty well.
DENVER, joking:	I make the best blue-cheese dressing.
MELISSA:	Like your tuna salad.

(Field notes, Blakemore Hotel)

Although Denver had problems with some of his cooks, his pantry workers were much more satisfied, in part because they expected less from him.

9. Most dishwashers at Stan's were young men who worked at the restaurant on a temporary basis to earn money for school.

10. As one cook noted, "It's a thankless task. . . . I just try to buy them a can of pop every now and them. When you say something nice to Ray, he's on top of the world" (Field notes, Owl's Nest). The sense that merely saying a nice word or giving a soft drink is sufficient indicates this patronizing attitude, and it probably is a fairly accurate assessment.

11. This analysis does not really apply to Stan's, where there were relationships of more equal-status among the cooks, busboys, and dishwashers. At Stan's it was common for a young man to start as a dishwasher, then become a busboy, and then a cook.

12. The gender composition of the serving staff varies by restaurant. In general the higher the status of the restaurant, the more male servers (and cooks and dishwashers)—a rule generalizable to the gender composition of many occupations. At Stan's and the Blakemore, servers were female. At La Pomme de Terre all servers but one were male. At the Owl's Nest about three-quarters of the servers were female. Most servers were young adults, but some older women worked at Stan's and the Blakemore. Servers had widely varying educational backgrounds, but those at La Pomme de Terre were the best educated. In contrast to the common belief that many servers are gay, only two were alleged homosexual (one male and one female) although other Twin Cities restaurants reportedly hire a higher percentage of homosexual servers.

13. Mars and Nicod (1984, pp. 45–47) suggest that tension is more likely to be found in lower-status establishments. My data do not allow me to judge this hypothesis, but on the basis of the information available, it seems supported: there was less tension between cooks and servers at La Pomme de Terre than at Stan's.

14. Such a desire to serve more food is not appropriate everywhere. In fact, at a restaurant such as La Pomme de Terre moderate-sized portions may be considered more appropriate; whereas at the steakhouse and at family restaurants generally, more is better.

15. A large majority of cooks felt that servers should share some portion of their tips, but not all felt this way. One said, "The tip, I think, is considered part of the waitress's wage. I wouldn't take part of somebody else's wage" (Personal interview, Stan's).

16. At La Pomme de Terre servers attempted to downplay personal uncertainty and interpersonal friction by having all servers pool their tips. Otherwise, in this restaurant with few tables and high tabs per customer, a difference in the number of customers could mean substantial differences among the take-home pay of the various servers. Pooling tips avoids this although potentially some servers might shirk work.

4. THE COMMONWEALTH OF CUISINE

1. The French are known for these doings, under conditions that others would find erotically challenging: "Pierre brought his girlfriend, Olympe, from Paris. 'She was a waitress at one of the restaurants where we worked,' Pierre whispered slyly. 'I made love to her in the cold room between the carcasses of beef. One day, the chef opened the door and said, "Oh, excuse me," and slammed the door at once. He was a good chef' " (De Groot 1972, p. 244).

2. In his study of brewery workers Molstad (1986, pp. 230–31) describes that to relieve the pain of boredom, these men throw bottles for the simple enjoyment of hearing them explode.

3. The existence of pranks and practical jokes has been documented at elite

restaurants as well. For example, in one world-class restaurant in Lyons: "André walks across the kitchen carrying a tower of empty aluminum cake pans. Pierre, at the butcher's block, flashes out his foot and trips him. The deafening crash of the pans sets the whole kitchen to a roar of laughter" (De Groot 1972, p. 246).

4. Such episodes are also found in other occupational spheres. Much is done to patients when under anesthesia, which typically, though not always, can be made right before the patient blissfully awakens.

5. Consider this French-Swiss example of tight networking: "Girardet doesn't say much about his astonishing experience at the Troisgros's, but apparently it was there that he saw the light—or was struck by lightning. He drove back to Crissier and decided to try to cook in the new exquisite manner, refined and 'simple.' After a few hard years of trial and error he managed to do it. Now a third-generation Troisgros works as pâtissier in Girardet's kitchen" (Wechsberg 1977, p. 25).

6. Elite networks are stronger than those that are not, because of their greater interpersonal contact. This is also the case in some ethnic restaurant communities, such as the Macedonian community in Toronto: "To find a restaurant whose owner was moving out or to find a suitable place for a new restaurant, Macedonians relied a great deal on interpersonal relations with other Macedonians. During meetings of friends and relatives after work, information about daily happenings were exchanged. Changes in the neighborhood of one's work place were reported, and this often included information about new or old restaurants" (Herman 1978, p. 36). The denser the social network and the greater the openness, the more the social network can be used for job mobility.

5. THE ECONOMICAL COOK

1. Most freestanding restaurants are not opened by aspiring gourmets. Most are simple affairs in structure and cuisine, often attempts by middle-class citizens to become their own boss. The gourmet restaurant, however defined, is a small, if prominent, segment of the market.

2. Desens (1979, p. 60) writes about these complaints, justifying the connection to multinationals: "The objection raised by some people to the methods of the CIA [Culinary Institute of America] is that the school is perhaps too closely linked to the giants of the industry—the Marriotts, the ITT Sheratons, the Hiltons. Understandably and necessarily so, for the big chains offer most of the jobs in the industry as well as the money for grants and endowments."

3. The depths of dislike for customers among some in the restaurant industry can be intense. One co-owner of an haute cuisine restaurant remarked: "I have to listen to urologists and bulldozer operators telling me things about food. After eleven years, your opinion of the public is low. I used to think anyone eating reasonably well-prepared food will know he's eating it, but I move through the dining room sometimes and it's depressing. For some people, we could just as well open a can. They are so used to artificial flavors that when you give them actual food they don't know what it is. They look at fresh whipped cream with suspicion" (McPhee 1979, p. 90).

4. Hotels are less dependent on regular customers, and during my month of observation, I was not aware that any customer received special treatment by the kitchen. No doubt officials of that chain received special treatment if they chose to eat in the restaurant.

5. Public fights between cooks and customers, while rare, have occurred. I was told that the hot-tempered former chef at La Pomme de Terre would occasionally argue with sinning customers (Field notes, La Pomme de Terre), just as a professional athlete will occasionally argue with his or her "fans."

6. Manhattan executive chefs or pastry chefs may earn up to $100,000 per year (Zukin 1990, p. 12), but even this figure, much higher than elsewhere, puts them far below the top of other "artistic" or "professional" occupations, except perhaps academics.

7. In contrast, the owner of La Pomme de Terre, even though he was well liked, was criticized for his occasional "stupid ideas." One cook told me, "He's never worked in a kitchen, and he comes up with these ideas of how we're supposed to work. He can't possibly know" (Personal interview, La Pomme de Terre).

8. Restaurants differed in the amount of functional control that the owner-manager exerted in the kitchen. The control was greatest at the hotel and the steakhouse. In the former, there was a string of managers who visited the kitchen and had the authority to make decisions—from the food and beverage manager to various levels of hotel management. At Stan's, Charles, the culinary-trained son of the owner, actually ordered meat for the restaurant, and he reviewed many important decisions that would have been the chef's responsibility elsewhere.

9. I was told that this is a particular source of conflict. As one cook informed me: "The owners get their nose in the kitchen; they don't know what to order; they order too much. . . . You've got Charles who's making phone calls from his office downstairs ordering stuff that Doug doesn't know about. I've seen a lot of friction between those two. Doug doesn't say nothing. I think the head chef in the kitchen, let him try to run it his way" (Personal interview, Stan's).

6.   AESTHETIC CONSTRAINTS

1. The study of aesthetics has been filled with conflicting assumptions and opinions. Philosophers rarely choose to examine situations in which aesthetic decisions are made in the messy reality of everyday life, and they suggest that aesthetic judgments transcend the production of an aesthetic object and its socially situated character (e.g., Diffey 1984; Hincks 1984). These explanations, which focus on qualities of mind (Aldrich 1966; Stolnitz 1960) or the qualities of an object (Beardsley 1958) that produce the recognition that one has had an aesthetic experience (Wolff 1983; Shepard 1987), downplay the sociological interest in the interactional, relational, or institutional features of aesthetic evaluation (see Dickie 1974; Danto 1981).

2. Wishing to see how such choices are constrained and utilized, I bracket the origin of aesthetic choices. My concern is not to trace the dynamics by

which particular judgments become seen as "aesthetic" but to examine only those choices that have been accepted by a group of workers. Nor am I concerned with the qualities of the object involved. Griswold (1986) argues that the aesthetic involves both elegance and beauty to produce a response. While I use Griswold's distinction to focus on the characteristics of objects, my definition emphasizes the relationship between actors and objects.

3. Sociologists of aesthetics interested in comparative research must confront two basic presuppositions: (1) that all occupations have aesthetic components, and that sensory issues are a part of all work; and (2) that occupations vary in the consciousness and centrality of these aesthetic issues to the work. Because my research is grounded on a single occupational case study, I can do no more than suggest the plausibility of these claims.

4. "Occupational triumphs" consist of occasions in which workers feel that they have operated to the limits of their jobs—they are "pushing the envelope." Working within the rules, they have transcended them, demonstrating in their own minds at least that they are not "mere" workers but "true artists," "true professionals," or the like. They have produced, not just an object, but a memory that they can narrate to convince others of their virtues, even under a set of constraints and normal operating procedures.

5. My argument is that Kant's idea of free judgments of taste is unlikely to be made in most practical aesthetic worlds; rather, aesthetic judgments have a relational character. We judge things in relationship or in comparison to other objects. At some level we are deciding not whether something is "good," but whether it is good for its kind (Kant 1952; Shepard 1987).

6. Comparative data indicate that this is not unique to this scene; for example, Walker and Guest (1951, p. 60) describe the similar attitudes of auto workers.

7. Market niches are in part a function of conscious decisions by managers and chefs to capture audiences. In this they create an establishment that will provide an experience that appeals to a potential pool of clients. Some niches are carved by customers who discover establishments; then managers must insure that they continue to meet the desires of these clients.

8. This is a problem faced by portrait painters who give up their artistic autonomy to the client. The client feels that he or she has the right to determine his or her personal likeness (see Stewart 1988; Wisely 1992).

9. The sole turban, as prepared at La Pomme de Terre, is essentially a fishy charlotte russe. Layers of sole are placed on the edge of a circular mold, with the inner part filled with a fish mousse.

10. For those with a sentimental attachment to happy endings, within a few years this young man had become head chef at an outstanding, creative restaurant in the Twin Cities. By then he had learned to control his employer's costs.

11. Pierre Bourdieu (1984) uses food consumption in France as an indication of the cultural capital of the eater, but it is also true that food production is an indicator of the cultural capital of the cook. We are known by what we eat, but we are also known by what we cook. The more sophisticated cooks—better trained, raised in more "sophisticated" homes, or driven by the goals of

their restaurant—are more attuned to the dishes that represent "haute cuisine" and demonstrate the existence of cultural capital.

12. We have no equivalent term for crafts, but the occupational autonomy among craftsworkers points to the same issue.

7. THE AESTHETICS OF KITCHEN DISCOURSE

1. By flavor I refer to the combination of taste and smell.

2. A recent news report suggests that just such a course has been developed in French schools. Educators there believe that students have lost the appreciation of flavor.

3. One reader of this chapter noted that even in the best circumstances, cooks must fight for aesthetic status. "Cuisine" in France is usually categorized as "artisanship," rather than "art." The sources of culinary theory are typically a few important critics, published in major media outlets, such as Le Reynière in *Le Monde*. This reader proposed the interesting thought experiment of how the Minnesota restaurant world could be made into an "art world." Would awards be enough? What about state subsidies? Classes in college? Restaurants with elite boards of trustees?

APPENDIX

1. Tim, the head chef at La Pomme de Terre, was particularly interested in my research because he had been seriously thinking of writing a book. He had planned to compile a book of recipes that would be autobiographical. He pressed me about how publishers work and about the audience for my book.

2. Stan's was the second steakhouse I contacted. I had called, and then met, a City TVI–trained chef at another steakhouse and obtained his approval for my research. He informed me that he would have to clear it with his manager, which he assured me would pose no problem. Later when I called him, he told me that the manager was afraid that my presence might be disruptive. This underlines the rule that a researcher should never let anyone else make his or her case.

3. At Stan's I had gained the approval of the manager first and then spoke with the head "cook," who had less authority than the chefs at the other restaurant. While he had the power to reject my proposal, the support of his manager made this less likely. In turn, I had to be careful to establish good relations with him, so I would not appear to be an agent of his manager.

4. Sometimes ethnographers forget about their status with some working-class people. I was surprised to learn at the Blakemore that one of the pantry workers whom I had met and chatted with was so impressed that she had talked with a "professor" that she called her best friend, who also worked at the restaurant, at 1:00 A.M. (after work) to describe her meeting. My status was, no doubt, magnified by the reality that some of these employees (especially pantry workers or washers) had low educational achievement, and some were developmentally disadvantaged.

5. The servers at Stan's also prepared the salads, and desserts were purchased from vendors outside the restaurant.

6. Two of the cooks at the Blakemore were female. These were two of the better cooks but also the most dissatisfied. Neither felt that she had any real chance for advancement in the hotel kitchen. Both felt that the hotel and the managers discriminated against women in subtle or overt ways.

References

Abbott, Andrew.
  1988.   *The System of Professions*. Chicago: University of Chicago Press.
Ackerman, Diane.
  1990.   *A Natural History of the Senses*. New York: Random House.
Adams, Robert M.
  1986.   "The Nose Knows." *The New York Review of Books* (November 20): 24–26.
Adler, Patricia and Peter Adler.
  1987.   *Membership Roles in Field Research*. Newbury Park, Calif.: Sage.
————.
  1990.   *Backboards and Blackboards: College Athletes and Role Engulfment*. New York: Columbia University Press.
Adler, Peter.
  1978.   *Momentum*. Beverly Hills: Sage.
Aldrich, Howard, B. Rosen, and W. Woodward.
  1986.   "The Impact of Social Networks on Business Foundings and Profit: A Longitudinal Study." *Frontiers of Entrepreneurial Research* 3: 154–68.
Aldrich, Virgil.
  1966.   *Philosophy of Art*. Englewood Cliffs, N.J.: Prentice-Hall.
Alhusen, Dorothy.
  1927.   *A Book of Scents and Dishes*. London: Williams and Norgate.
Anderson, E.N. and M.L. Anderson.
  1988.   *The Food of China*. New Haven: Yale University Press.
Archer, Margaret.
  1988.   *Culture and Agency*. Cambridge: Cambridge University Press.

Arian, Edward.
  1971.   *Bach, Beethoven, and Bureaucracy.* University, Ala.: University
               of Alabama Press.
Arnold, Thurmond.
  1937.   *The Folklore of Capitalism.* New Haven: Yale University Press.
Aron, Jean-Paul.
  1975.   *The Art of Eating in France.* New York: Harper and Row.
Baldamus, Wilhelm.
  1961.   *Efficiency and Effort.* London: Tavistock.
Bales, Robert Freed.
  1970.   *Personality and Interpersonal Relations.* New York: Holt,
               Rinehart and Winston.
Barber, Bernard.
  1965.   "The Sociology of the Professions." Pp. 15–34 in Kenneth S. Lyon,
               ed., *The Professions in America.* Boston: Houghton Mifflin.
Bates, Carolyn.
  1984.   "Spécialités de la Maison: California." *Gourmet* (December):
               30–40, 187–189.
Bates, Marston.
  1968.   *Gluttons and Libertines.* New York: Random House.
Beardsley, M.C.
  1958.   *Aesthetics: Problems in the Philosophy of Criticism.* New
               York: Harcourt Brace.
Becker, Howard S.
  1960.   "Notes on the Concept of Commitment." *American Journal of
               Sociology* 66: 32–40.
  ———.
  1963.   *Outsiders.* New York: Free Press.
  ———.
  1967.   "Whose Side Are We On?" *Social Problems* 14: 239–47.
  ———.
  1970.   "The Nature of a Profession." Pp. 87–103 in *Sociological
               Work: Method and Substance.* Chicago: Aldine.
  ———.
  1974.   "Art as Collective Action." *American Sociological Review* 39:
               767–76.
  ———.
  1976.   "Art Worlds and Social Types." *American Behavioral Scientist*
               19: 703–18.
  ———.
  1982.   *Art Worlds.* Berkeley: University of California Press.
  ———.
  1986.   *Doing Things Together.* Evanston, Ill.: Northwestern Univer-
               sity Press.
Becker, Howard S. and James Carper.
  1956.   "The Elements of Identification with an Occupation." *Ameri-
               can Sociological Review* 21: 341–48.

Becker, Howard S. and Blanche Geer.
    1960.   "Latent Culture: A Research Note." *Administration Science
                 Quarterly* 5: 304–13.
Becker, Howard S., Blanche Geer, Everett C. Hughes, and Anselm L. Strauss.
    1961.   *Boys in White: Student Culture in Medical School.* Chicago:
                 University of Chicago Press.
Belasco, Warren J.
    1989.   *Appetite for Change: How the Counterculture Took on the
                 Food Industry, 1966–1988.* New York: Pantheon Books.
Bell, Michael.
    1976.   "Tending Bar at Brown's: Occupational Role as Artistic Perfor-
                 mance." *Western Folklore* 35: 93–107.

    ———.

    1984.   "Making Art Work." *Western Folklore* 43: 211–21.
Bennett, Bev.
    1982.   "Editor's Eyes Open to Trends in the Food Industry." *Chicago
                 Sun-Times* (May 21): 2.
Bergson, Henri.
    1910.   *Time and Free Will.* London: George Allen and Unwin.
Bernstein, Basil.
    1971.   *Class, Codes and Control.* London: Routledge.
Bernstein, Stan.
    1972.   "Getting It Done: Notes on Student Fritters." *Urban Life and
                 Culture* 1: 275–92.
Berry, Naomi.
    1979.   "Young Chefs of Paris." *Gourmet* (November): 35–39, 150, 158.
Bigus, Otis E.
    1972.   "The Milkman and His Customer: A Cultivated Relationship."
                 Urban Life and Culture 1: 131–65.
Bishop, James M.
    1979.   "Institutional and Operational Knowledge in Work: A Sensitiz-
                 ing Framework." *Sociology of Work and Occupations* 6:
                 328–52.
Blau, Judith.
    1984.   *Architects and Firms.* Cambridge: MIT Press.
Blumer, Herbert.
    1969.   *Symbolic Interactionism.* Englewood Cliffs, N.J.: Prentice-Hall.

    ———.

    1990.   *Industrialization as an Agent of Social Change.* New York: Al-
                 dine de Gruyter.
Boden, Deirdre.
    1994.   *The Business of Talk.* Cambridge, Eng.: Polity Press.
Borman, Kathryn.
    1991.   *The First 'Real' Job: A Study of Young Workers.* Albany:
                 SUNY Press.
Bosk, Charles.
    1979.   *Forgive and Remember.* Chicago: University of Chicago Press.

Bourdieu, Pierre.
1984.   *Distinction: A Social Critique of the Judgment of Taste.* Cambridge: Harvard University Press.
Bowden, Gregory Houston.
1975.   *British Gastronomy: The Rise of Great Restaurants.* London: Chatto and Windus.
Bowman, John.
1983.   "Making Work Play." In Gary Alan Fine, ed., *Meaningful Play, Playful Meaning.* Champaign, Ill.: Human Kinetics Press.
Braude, Lee.
1975.   *Work and Workers: A Sociological Analysis.* New York: Praeger.
Brennan, Thomas.
1988.   *Public Drinking and Popular Culture in Eighteenth-Century Paris.* Princeton: Princeton University Press.
Brillat-Savarin, Jean-Anthelme.
1970 [1825]. *The Philosopher in the Kitchen.* London: Penguin.
Brown, Richard H.
1977.   *A Poetic for Sociology.* Cambridge: Cambridge University Press.
Bryant, Carol A., Anita Courtney, Barbara A. Markesbery, and Kathleen M. DeWalt.
1985.   *The Cultural Feast: An Introduction to Food and Society.* St. Paul: West Publishing.
Bryant, Clifton D. and Kenneth B. Perkins.
1982.   "Containing Work Disaffection: The Poultry Processing Worker." Pp. 199–213 in Phyllis L. Stewart and Muriel G. Cantor, eds., *Varieties of Work.* Beverly Hills: Sage.
Bucher, Rue.
1962.   "Pathology: A Study of Social Movements within a Profession." *Social Problems* 10: 40–51.
Bucher, Rue and Joan Stelling.
1977.   *Becoming Professional.* Beverly Hills: Sage.
Buckley, Peter.
1982.   "Food for Thought." *Republic Scene* (May): 42–49, 92.
Burawoy, Michael.
1979.   *Manufacturing Consent.* Chicago: University of Chicago Press.
Bureau of the Census.
1984.   *1982 Census of Retail Trade: United States.* Washington, D.C.: U.S. Department of Commerce.
Burros, Marian.
1986.   "What Makes André Soltner Tick? His Restaurant, Lutèce." *New York Times* (October 29): 23, 25.
Burton, Robert.
1976.   *The Language of Smell.* London: Routledge.
Busch, Lawrence.
1980.   "Structure and Renegotiation in the Agricultural Sciences." *Rural Sociology* 45: 26–48.

Busch, Lawrence.
    1982.   "History, Negotiation, and Structure in Agricultural Research." *Urban Life* 11: 368–84.
Butler, Suellen R. and James K. Skipper, Jr.
    1980.   "Waitressing, Vulnerability, and Job Autonomy: The Case of the Risky Tip." *Sociology of Work and Occupations* 7: 487–502.
Butler, Suellen R. and William E. Snizek.
    1976.   "The Waitress-Diner Relationship: A Multimethod Approach to the Study of Subordinate Influence." *Sociology of Work and Occupations* 3: 209–22.
Cain, William S.
    1978.   "History of Research on Smell." Pp. 197–229 in Edward C. Carterette and Morton P. Friedman, eds., *Handbook of Perception*, vol. 6A. New York: Academic Press.
Caldwell, Mary.
    1986.   "Food Imitates Art." *Cook's Magazine* (May-June): 38–48, 80.
Carr-Saunders, A. P. and P. A. Wilson.
    1933.   *The Professions*. Oxford: Oxford University Press.
Chang, Kwang-chih, ed.
    1977.   *Food in Chinese Culture: Anthropological and Historical Perspectives*. New Haven: Yale University Press.
Charpentier, Henri and Boyden Sparkes.
    1934.   *Life à la Henri*. New York: Simon and Schuster.
Christopherson, Richard.
    1974.   "Making Art with Machines: Photography's Institutional Inadequacies." *Urban Life and Culture* 3: 3–34.
Cicourel, Aaron.
    1974.   *Cognitive Sociology*. Cambridge: Cambridge University Press.
Claiborne, Craig.
    1982.   *A Feast Made for Laughter: A Memoir with Recipes*. New York: Holt, Rinehart and Winston.
Clark, Burton R.
    1972.   "The Organizational Saga in Higher Education." *Administrative Science Quarterly* 17: 178–84.
Clark, Priscilla.
    1975.   "Thoughts for Food, I: French Cuisine and French Culture." *The French Review* 49: 32–41.
————.
    1975.   "Thoughts for Food, II: Culinary Culture in Contemporary France." *The French Review* 49: 198–205.
Clark, Robert, ed.
    1990.   *Our Sustainable Table*. San Francisco: North Point Press.
Collins, Randall.
    1981.   "On the Microfoundations of Macrosociology." *American Journal of Sociology* 86: 984–1014.

Colomy, Paul and J. David Brown.
    1995.   "Progress in the Second Chicago School." In Gary Alan Fine, ed.
               A Second Chicago School? Chicago: University of Chicago Press.
Colvin, S.
    1910.   "Fine Arts." Pp. 355–75 in *Encyclopaedia Britannica,* 11th ed.,
               vol. 10. Cambridge, Eng.: University Press.
"The Cook's Interview: Anne Willan."
    1985.   *Cook's Magazine* (September-October): 18–19.
"The Cook's Interview: Richard Olney."
    1986.   *Cook's Magazine* (May-June): 21–22.
Corbin, Alain.
    1986.   *The Foul and the Fragrant.* Cambridge: Harvard University
               Press.
Corbin, Juliet and Anselm L. Strauss.
    1993.   "The Articulation of Work through Interaction." *The Socio-
               logical Quarterly* 34: 71–83.
Coser, Lewis, Charles Kadushin, and Walter W. Powell.
    1982.   *Books.* New York: Basic.
Cosman, Madeleine Pelner.
    1976.   *Fabulous Feasts: Medieval Cookery and Ceremony.* New York:
               Braziller.
Cottrell, W.F.
    1939.   "Of Time and the Railroader." *American Sociological Review*
               4: 190–98.
Crocker, E.C.
    1945.   *Flavor.* New York: McGraw-Hill.
Csikszentmihalyi, Michael.
    1975.   *Beyond Boredom and Anxiety.* San Francisco: Jossey-Bass.
Curtin, Deane W. and Lisa M. Heldke, eds.
    1992.   *Cooking, Eating, Thinking: Transformative Philosophies of
               Food.* Bloomington: Indiana University Press.
Dalton, Melville.
    1948.   "The Industrial Ratebuster." *Applied Anthropology* 7: 5–18.
    ———.

    1959.   *Men Who Manage.* New York: Wiley.
Danto, Arthur C.
    1964.   "The Artworld." *Journal of Philosophy* 61: 571–84.
    ———.

    1981.   *The Transfiguration of the Commonplace.* Cambridge: Har-
               vard University Press.
Davis, Fred.
    1959.   "The Cabdriver and His Fare." *American Journal of Sociology*
               63: 158–65.
Dawe, Alan.
    1978.   "Theories of Social Action." Pp. 362–417 in Tom Bottomore
               and Robert Nisbet, eds. *A History of Sociological Analysis.*
               New York: Basic.

Deal, T.E. and A. Kennedy.
    1982.   *Corporate Cultures: The Rites and Rituals of Corporate Life.* Reading, Mass.: Addison-Wesley.
De Groot, Roy.
    1972.   "Have I Found the Greatest Restaurant in the World?" *Playboy* (April): 107, 116, 244–49.
Demerest, Michael.
    1980.   "A Virtual Victory for the U.S." *Time* (November 17): 87.
Denzin, Norman K.
    1977.   "Notes on the Criminogenic Hypothesis: A Case Study of the American Liquor Industry." *American Sociological Review* 42: 905–20.

————.

    1984.   *On Understanding Emotion.* San Francisco: Jossey-Bass.
Desens, Carl.
    1979.   "A Look inside the CIA: A Toque-and-Dacquoise Story." *International Review of Food and Wine* (May): 19–20, 60.
DeVault, Marjorie.
    1991.   *Feeding the Family: The Social Organization of Caring as Gendered Work.* Chicago: University of Chicago Press.
Dickie, George.
    1974.   *Art and the Aesthetic: An Institutional Analysis.* Ithaca: Cornell University Press.
Dickinson, Hilary and Michael Erben.
    1984.   " 'Moral Positioning' and Occupational Socialization in the Training of Hairdressers, Secretaries and Caterers." *Journal of Moral Education* 13: 49–55.
Diffey, T.J.
    1984.   "The Sociological Challenge to Aesthetics." *British Journal of Aesthetics* 24: 168–71.
Dimaggio, Paul.
    1977.   "Market Structure, the Creative Process, and Popular Culture." *Journal of Popular Culture* 11: 436–52.
Dimaggio, Paul and Walter W. Powell.
    1983.   "The Iron Cage Revisited: Institutional Isomorphism and Collective Rationality in Organizational Fields." *American Sociological Review* 48: 147–60.

————.

    1991.   Introduction. Pp. 1–38 in Walter W. Powell and Paul Dimaggio, eds., *The New Institutionalism in Organizational Analysis.* Chicago: University of Chicago Press.
Ditton, Jason.
    1979.   "Baking Time." *Sociological Review* 27: 157–67.
Dollard, John.
    1949.   *Caste and Class in a Southern Town.* New York: Harper.
Donovan, Frances.
    1920.   *The Woman Who Waits.* Boston: R. G. Badger.

Douglas, Mary.
    1966.   *Purity and Danger: An Analysis of the Concepts of Pollution and Taboo*. London: Routledge.
Douglas, Mary.
    1974.   "Food as an Art Form." *Studio International* (September): 83–88.
————.
    1984.   *Food in the Social Order: Studies of Food and Festivities in Three American Communities*. New York: Russell Sage Foundation.
Dundes, Alan.
    1972.   "Seeing Is Believing." *Natural History* (May): 8–12, 86–87.
Elias, Norbert.
    1978.   *The History of Manners*. New York: Urizen.
Engel-Frisch, Gladys.
    1943.   "Some Neglected Temporal Aspects of Human Ecology." *Social Forces* 22: 43–47.
Enloe, Cynthia.
    1989.   *Bananas, Beaches and Bases*. Berkeley: University of California Press.
Epstein, Jason.
    1993.   "A Taste of Success." *The New Yorker* (April 19): 50–56.
Etzioni, Amitai, ed.
    1969.   *The Semi-Professions and Their Organization*. New York: Free Press.
Fantasia, Rick.
    1988.   *Cultures of Solidarity*. Berkeley: University of California Press.
Farberman, Harvey.
    1975.   "A Criminogenic Market Structure: The Automobile Industry." *Sociological Quarterly* 16: 438–57.
Faulkner, Robert.
    1971.   *Hollywood Studio Musicians*. Chicago: Aldine.
————.
    1974.   "Coming of Age in Organizations: A Comparative Study of Career Contingencies and Adult Socialization." *Sociology of Work and Occupations* 1: 131–73.
————.
    1983.   *Music on Demand: Composers and Careers in the Hollywood Film Industry*. New Brunswick, N.J.: Transaction.
Fiddes, Nick.
    1991.   *Meat: A Natural Symbol*. London: Routledge.
Fine, Gary Alan.
    1979.   "Small Groups and Cultural Creation: The Idioculture of Little League Baseball Teams." *American Sociological Review* 44: 733–45.
————.
    1982.   "The Manson Family as a Folk Group: Small Groups and Folklore." *Journal of the Folklore Institute* 19: 47–60.

————.

1983.   *Shared Fantasy: Role-Playing Games as Social Worlds.*
             Chicago: University of Chicago Press.

————.

1984.   "Negotiated Orders and Organizational Cultures." *Annual Re-
             view of Sociology* 10: 239–62.

————.

1985.   "Occupational Aesthetics: How Trade School Students Learn
             to Cook." *Urban Life* 14: 3–31.

————.

1986.   "Friendships in the Workplace." Pp. 185–206 in Val Derlaga
             and Barbara Winstead, eds., *Friendship and Social Interaction.*
             New York: Springer-Verlag.

————.

1987a.   "One of the Boys: Women in Male-Dominated Settings." Pp.
             131–147 in Michael S. Kimmel, ed., *Changing Men: New Di-
             rections in Research on Men and Masculinity.* Newbury Park,
             Calif.: Sage.

————.

1987b.   "Working Cooks: The Dynamics of Professional Kitchens."
             Current Research on Occupations and Professions 4: 141–58.

————.

1987c.   *With the Boys: Little League Baseball and Preadolescent Cul-
             ture.* Chicago: University of Chicago Press.

————.

1990.   "Organizational Time: The Temporal Experience of Restau-
             rant Kitchens." *Social Forces* 69: 95–114.

————.

1991.   "On the Microfoundations of Macrosociology: Constraint and
             the Exterior Reality of Structure." *Sociological Quarterly* 32:
             161–77.

————.

1992a.   "Agency, Structure, and Comparative Contexts: Toward a Syn-
             thetic Interactionism." *Symbolic Interaction* 15: 87–107.

————.

1992b.   "The Culture of Production: Aesthetic Choices and Constraints
             in Culinary Work." *American Journal of Sociology* 97:
             1268–94.

————.

1992c.   "Wild Life: Authenticity and the Human Experience of 'Nat-
             ural' Places." Pp. 156–75 in Carolyn Ellis and Michael G. Fla-
             herty, eds., *Investigating Subjectivity.* Newbury Park, Calif.:
             Sage.

Fine, Gary Alan and Nora L. Ross.

1984.   "Symbolic Meaning and Cultural Organization." Pp. 237–56
             in Samuel Bachrach and Edward Lawler, eds., *Perspectives in
             Organizational Sociology,* vol. 4. Greenwich, Conn.: JAI Press.

Fineman, Stephen.
    1993.   Introduction. Pp. 9–35 in Stephen Fineman, ed., *Emotion in Organization*. London: Sage.
Finkelstein, Joanne.
    1986.   "Dining Out: The Self in Search of Civility." In Norman K. Denzin, ed., *Studies in Symbolic Interaction,* vol. 6. Greenwich, Conn.: JAI Press.
———.
    1989.   *Dining Out: A Sociology of Modern Manners.* New York: New York University Press.
Finlay, William.
    1988.   *Work on the Waterfront.* Philadelphia: Temple University Press.
Fisher, M.F.K.
    1976.   "The Gastronomical Me." Pp. 351–572 in *The Art of Cookery.* New York: Vintage.
Flaherty, Michael.
    1987.   "Multiple Realities and the Experience of Duration." *The Sociological Quarterly* 28: 313–26.
Forrest, John.
    1988.   *Lord, I'm Coming Home: Everyday Aesthetics in Tidewater, North Carolina.* Ithaca: Cornell University Press.
Freeman, John and Michael Hannon.
    1983.   "Niche Width and the Dynamics of Organizational Populations." *American Journal of Sociology* 88: 1116–45.
Friedson, Eliot.
    1970.   *Professional Dominance: The Social Structure of Medical Care.* New York: Atherton.
Fuchs, Victor R.
    1968.   *The Service Economy.* New York: National Bureau of Economic Research.
Gans, Herbert J.
    1974.   *Popular Culture and High Culture.* New York: Basic.
Garfinkel, Harold.
    1967.   *Studies in Ethnomethodology.* Englewood Cliffs, N.J.: Prentice-Hall.
Garnier, Maurice.
    1973.   "Power and Ideological Conformity: A Case Study." *American Journal of Sociology* 79: 343–63.
Gerlach, Luther and Virginia Hine.
    1970.   *People, Power, Change: Movements of Social Transformation.* Indianapolis: Bobbs-Merrill.
Giddens, Anthony.
    1984.   *The Constitution of Society.* Berkeley: University of California Press.
Gillon, John.
    1981.   *Le Menu Gastronomique: An Interpretation of Nouvelle Cuisine.* Edinburgh: Macdonald.

Glaser, Barney and Anselm L. Strauss.
  1967.   *The Discovery of Grounded Theory*. Chicago: Aldine.
Goffman, Erving.
  1961a.   *Asylums*. Garden City, N.Y.: Anchor Books.
———.
  1961b.   *Encounters*. Indianapolis: Bobbs-Merrill.
———.
  1963.   *Behavior in Public Places*. New York: Free Press.
———.
  1974.   *Frame Analysis*. Cambridge: Harvard University Press.
———.
  1981.   *Forms of Talk*. Philadelphia: University of Pennsylvania
               Press.
Gonos, George.
  1977.   " 'Situation' versus 'Frame': The 'Interactionist' and the 'Struc-
               turalist' Analyses of Everyday Life." *American Sociological Re-
               view* 42: 854–67.
Gopnik, Adam.
  1992.   "Just Desserts." *The New Yorker* (October 19): 128.
Gordon, Steven.
  1981.   "The Sociology of Sentiments and Emotion." Pp. 562–92 in
               Morris Rosenberg and Ralph H. Turner, eds., *Social Psychol-
               ogy: Sociological Perspectives*. New York: Basic.
Gouldner, Alvin.
  1954.   *Wildcat Strike*. Yellow Springs, Ohio: Antioch Press.
Granovetter, Mark.
  1974.   *Getting a Job*. Cambridge: Harvard University Press.
"The Great French-American Chef's Debate."
  1984.   *Cook's Magazine* (September-October): 18–19.
Greenwood, Ernest.
  1957.   "The Attributes of a Profession." *Social Work* 2: 44–55.
Grimshaw, Allen D.
  1981.   *Language as Social Resource*. Stanford: Stanford University
               Press.
———.
  1989.   *Collegial Discourse: Professional Conversation among Peers*.
               Norwood, N.J.: Ablex Publishing.
Griswold, Wendy.
  1986.   *Renaissance Revivals*. Chicago: University of Chicago Press.
Gross, Edward.
  1958.   *Work and Society*. New York: Crowell.
Grzyb, Gerard J.
  1990.   "Deskilling, Decollectivization, and Diesels." *Journal of Con-
               temporary Ethnography* 19: 163–87.
Guilbaut, Serge.
  1984.   *How New York Stole the Idea of Modern Art*. Chicago: Uni-
               versity of Chicago Press.

Gurvitch, Georges.
    1964.   *The Spectrum of Social Ties*. Dordrecht, Neth.: D. Reidel.
Haas, Jack.
    1972.   "Binging: Educational Control among High-Steel Ironwork-
               ers." *American Behavioral Scientist* 16: 27–34.

———.

    1974.   "The Stages of the High-Steel Ironworker Apprentice Career."
               Sociological Quarterly 15: 93–108.
Haas, Jack and William Shaffir.
    1982.   "Ritual Evaluation of Competence: The Hidden Curriculum of
               Professionalization in an Innovative Medical School Program."
               Work and Occupations 9: 131–54.
Hall, Trish.
    1985.   "Who Matters Most to Any Restaurant? Hint: Not the Chef."
               Wall Street Journal (April 10): 1, 23.
Hanke, Robert.
    1988.   "Mass Media and Lifestyle Differentiation: An Analysis of
               Changes in the Public Discourse about Food." Unpublished
               manuscript.
Hannon, Michael and John Freeman.
    1989.   *Organizational Ecology*. Cambridge: Harvard University Press.
Harper, R., E.C. Bate Smith, and D.G. Land.
    1968.   *Odour Description and Odour Classification: A Multi-Discipli-
               nary Examination*. New York: American Elsevier Publishing.
Hawley, Amos.
    1950.   *Human Ecology*. New York: Ronald Press.
Hayano, David.
    1982.   *Poker Faces*. Berkeley: University of California Press.
Herbodeau, Eugene and Paul Thalamas.
    1955.   *George Auguste Escoffier*. London: Practical Press.
Herman, Harry V.
    1978.   *Men in White Aprons*. Toronto: Peter Martin.
Hewitt, John and Randall Stokes.
    1975.   "Disclaimers." *American Sociological Review* 40: 1–11.
Herzfeld, Michael.
    1992.   *The Social Production of Indifference: Exploring the Symbolic
               Roots of Western Bureaucracy*. Chicago: University of Chicago
               Press.
Hincks, Tony.
    1984.   "Aesthetics and the Sociology of Art." *British Journal of Aes-
               thetics* 24: 341–54.
Hirsch, Paul.
    1972.   "Processing Fads and Fashions: An Organization-Set Analysis
               of Cultural Work." *American Journal of Sociology* 77:
               639–59.
Hirshorn, Paul and Steven Izenour.
    1979.   *White Towers*. Cambridge: MIT Press.

Hochschild, Arlie.
   1983.   *The Managed Heart.* Berkeley: University of California Press.
Hodson, Randy.
   1991.   "The Active Worker: Compliance and Autonomy at the Work-
              place." *Journal of Contemporary Ethnography* 20: 47–78.
Hollander, Edwin P.
   1958.   "Conformity, Status, and Idiosyncrasy Credit." *Psychological
              Review* 65: 117–27.
Hollingshead, August.
   1939.   "Behavior Systems as a Field for Research." *American Socio-
              logical Review* 4: 816–22.
Hood, Jane.
   1988.   "From Night to Day: Timing and the Management of Custo-
              dial Work." *Journal of Contemporary Ethnography* 17:
              96–116.
Hosticka, C.J.
   1979.   "We Don't Care about What Happened, We Only Care about
              What Is Going to Happen: Lawyer-Client Negotiations of Re-
              ality." *Social Problems* 26: 599–610.
Howe, Louise Kapp.
   1977.   *Pink Collar Workers.* New York: Avon.
Hughes, Everett C.
   1971.   *The Sociological Eye.* Boston: Little, Brown.
Hutter, Mark.
   1969.   "Summertime Servants: The Schlockhaus Waiter." Pp. 203–25
              in Glenn Jacobs, ed., *The Participant Observer.* New York:
              Braziller.
Isenberg, Arnold.
   1954.   "Critical Communication." Pp. 131–46 in William Elton, ed.,
              Aesthetics and Language. Oxford: Basil Blackwell.
Jacobs, Jay.
   1980.   *Winning the Restaurant Game.* New York: McGraw-Hill.
   ——— .
   1982.   "Spécialités de la Maison: New York." *Gourmet* (December):
              4, 6, 8.
Jefferson, Gail.
   1979.   "A Technique for Inviting Laughter and Its Subsequent Ac-
              ceptance/Declination." Pp. 79–96 in George Psathas, ed.,
              Everyday Language: Studies in Ethnomethodology. New York:
              Irvington.
Julian, Sheryl.
   1986.   "New England Schools for Chefs-to-Be." *Boston Globe* (Octo-
              ber 22): 37, 41, 42.
Kamens, D.H.
   1977.   "Legitimating Myths and Educational Organization: The Rela-
              tionship between Organizational Ideology and Formal Struc-
              ture." *American Sociological Review* 42: 208–19.

Kant, Immanuel.
    1952.   *Critique of Aesthetic Judgment.* Oxford: Oxford University
            Press.
Kaplan, Max.
    1960.   *Leisure in America: A Social Inquiry.* New York: Wiley.
Karen, Robert L.
    1962.   "Some Factors Affecting Tipping Behavior." *Sociology and So-
            cial Research* 47: 68–74.
Kealy, Edward R.
    1979.   "From Craft to Art: The Case of Sound Mixers and Popular
            Music." *Sociology of Work and Occupations* 6: 3–29.
Kimball, Christopher.
    1985.   "The Cook's Interview: Jeremiah Tower." *Cook's Magazine*
            (January-February): 18–19.
Kleinfield, N. R.
    1991.   "The Countdown in One Kitchen." *New York Times* (January
            11): C1, C24.
Kleinman, Sherryl.
    1982.   "Actors' Conflicting Theories of Negotiation: The Case of a
            Holistic Health Center." *Urban Life* 11: 312–27.

——.
    1984.   *Equals before God.* Chicago: University of Chicago Press.
Koenig, Rhoda.
    1980.   "Of Temperamental Waiters and Volatile Chefs: How to Han-
            dle the Staff." *New York* (February 18): 46.
Kraft Foodservice Division.
    n.d.   *Hail to the Chief!* Chicago: EBO Productions.
Lakoff, George and Mark Johnson.
    1980.   *Metaphors We Live By.* Chicago: University of Chicago Press.
Lamont, Michèlle.
    1989.   "The Power-Culture Link in a Comparative Perspective." Pp.
            131–50 in Craig Calhoun, ed., *Comparative Social Research,*
            vol. 11. Greenwich, Conn.: JAI Press.
Lauer, Robert.
    1981.   *Temporal Man.* New York: Praeger.
Leidner, Robin.
    1993.   *Fast Food, Fast Talk: Service Work and the Routinization of
            Everyday Life.* Berkeley: University of California Press.
Levenstein, Harvey.
    1988.   *Revolution at the Table: The Transformation of the American
            Diet.* New York: Oxford University Press.

——.
    1993.   *Paradox of Plenty: A Social History of Eating in Modern
            America.* New York: Oxford University Press.
Levy, Judith.
    1982.   "The Staging of Negotiations between Hospice and Medical In-
            stitutions." *Urban Life* 11: 293–311.

Liebling, A.J.
    1986.   *Between Meals: An Appetite for Paris.* San Francisco: North
                 Point Press.
Lloyd, Timothy and Patrick Mullen.
    1987.   "In Your Blood: Traditions of Commercial Fishermen." Un-
                 published manuscript.
Locke, John.
    1700 [1975]. *An Essay Concerning Human Understanding.* Oxford:
                 Clarendon Press.
Lohof, Bruce.
    1979.   "Hamburger Stand: Industrialization and the American Fast-
                 Food Phenomenon." *Journal of American Culture* 2: 515–33.
Lyman, Stanford and Marvin Scott.
    1970.   *The Sociology of the Absurd.* Pacific Palisades, Calif.:
                 Goodyear.
Lynxwiler, John, Neal Shover, and Donald Clelland.
    1983.   "The Organization and Impact of Inspector Discretion in a
                 Regulatory Bureaucracy." *Social Problems* 30: 425–36.
MacClancy, Jeremy.
    1992.   *Consuming Culture: Why You Eat What You Eat.* New York:
                 Henry Holt.
Maines, David.
    1977.   "Social Organization and Social Structure in Symbolic Interac-
                 tionist Thought." *Annual Review of Sociology* 3: 235–59.

    ———.

    1982.   "In Search of Mesostructure: Studies in the Negotiated Order."
                 Urban Life 11: 267–79.

    ———.

    1987.   "The Significance of Temporality for the Development of Soci-
                 ological Theory." *The Sociological Quarterly* 28: 303–11.

    ———.

    1988.   "Myth, Text, and Interactionist Complicity in the Neglect of
                 Blumer's Macrosociology." *Symbolic Interaction* 11: 43–58.
Manfredi, John.
    1982.   *The Social Limits of Art.* Amherst: University of Massachusetts
                 Press.
Manning, Peter K.
    1992.   *Organizational Communication.* New York: Aldine de
                 Gruyter.
Manning, Peter K. and H.L. Hearn.
    1969.   "Student Actresses and Their Artistry: Vicissitudes of Learning
                 a Creative Trade." *Social Forces* 48: 202–13.
Mars, Gerald and Michael Nicod.
    1984.   *The World of Waiters.* London: George Allen and Unwin.
Marshall, Gordon.
    1986.   "The Workplace Culture of a Licensed Restaurant." *Theory,
                 Culture, and Society* 3: 33–47.

Martin, Joanne.
   1992.   *Cultures in Organizations: Three Perspectives.* New York: Ox-
                ford University Press.
Martorella, Roseanne.
   1982.   *The Sociology of Opera.* South Hadley, Mass.: Bergin.
Mast, Sharon.
   1983.   "Working for Television: The Social Organization of TV
                Drama." *Symbolic Interaction* 6: 71–83.
Matza, David.
   1964.   *Delinquency and Drift.* New York: Wiley.
McCartney, William.
   1968.   *Olfaction and Odours: An Osphresiological Essay.* Berlin:
                Springer-Verlag.
McPhee, John.
   1979.   "Profiles: Brigade de Cuisine." *The New Yorker* (February 19):
                49–99.
Mead, George Herbert.
   1934.   *Mind, Self, and Society.* Chicago: University of Chicago Press.
————.
   1938.   *The Philosophy of the Act.* Chicago: University of Chicago
                Press.
Meara, Hannah.
   1974.   "Honor in Dirty Work: The Case of American Meat Cutters
                and Turkish Butchers." *Sociology of Work and Occupations* 1:
                259–83.
Mechling, Elizabeth W. and Jay Mechling.
   1983.   "Sweet Talk: The Moral Rhetoric against Sugar." *Central
                States Speech Journal* 34: 19–32.
Melbin, Murray.
   1987.   *Night as Frontier: Colonizing the World after Dark.* New
                York: Free Press.
Mennell, Stephen.
   1985.   *All Manners of Food: Eating and Taste in England and France
                from the Middle Ages to the Present.* Oxford: Basil Blackwell.
Mennell, Stephen, Anne Murcott, and Anneke H. van Otterloo.
   1992.   *The Sociology of Food: Eating, Diet, and Culture.* London:
                Sage.
Mesler, Mark.
   1989.   "Negotiated Order and the Clinical Pharmacist: The Ongoing
                Process of Structure." *Symbolic Interaction* 12: 139–57.
Miller, Daniel.
   1978.   *Starting a Small Restaurant.* Harvard, Mass.: Harvard Com-
                mon Press.
Mintz, Sidney W.
   1985.   *Sweetness and Power: The Place of Sugar in Modern History.*
                New York: Viking.

Mitchell, Timothy J.
   1986.   "Bullfighting: The Ritual Origin of Scholarly Myths." *Journal of American Folklore* 99: 394–414.
Moir, H.C.
   1936.   "Some Observations on the Appreciation of Flavour in Foodstuffs." *Chemistry and Industry* 55: 145–48.
Molstad, Clark.
   1986.   "Choosing and Coping with Boring Work." *Urban Life* 15: 215–36.
Moore, Wilbert.
   1963.   *Man, Time, and Society.* New York: Wiley.
Morrisroe, Patricia.
   1984.   "Restaurant Madness." *New York* (November 26): 46–49.
Mukerji, Chandra.
   1976.   "Having the Authority to Know." *Sociology of Work and Occupations* 3: 63–87.

———.
   1978.   "Distinguishing Machines: Stratification and Definitions of Technology in Film School." *Sociology of Work and Occupations* 5: 113–38.
Mulkay, Michael and Elizabeth Chaplin.
   1982.   "Aesthetics and the Artistic Career: A Study of Anomie in Fine-Art Painting." *The Sociological Quarterly* 23: 117–38.
Nathan, John and Elizabeth Sahatgian.
   1984.   "Whither the Great American Food Fad?" *Cuisine* 13: 56–60, 90–99.
Neapolitan, Jerry.
   1986.   "Art, Craft, and Art/Craft Segments among Craft Media Workers," *Work and Occupations* 13: 203–16.
Nilson, Linda B.
   1979.   "An Application of the Occupational 'Uncertainty Principle' to the Professions." *Social Problems* 26: 570–81.
Nisbett, R.E., C. Caputo, P. Legant, and J. Marecek.
   1973.   "Behavior as Seen by the Actor and as Seen by the Observer." *Journal of Personality and Social Psychology* 27: 154–64.
Oldenberg, Ray.
   1988.   *The Great Good Place.* New York: Praeger.
Olesen, Virginia.
   1992.   "The Sociology of Hospitality." Paper presented to the SSSI/Stone Symposium, February, Las Vegas, Nevada.
Orwell, George.
   1933.   *Down and Out in Paris and London.* New York: Harcourt Brace.
Ouchi, William G.
   1981.   *Theory Z.* Reading, Mass.: Addison-Wesley.

Ouchi, William G. and Alan L. Wilkens.
    1985.   "Organizational Culture." *Annual Review of Sociology* 11:
               457–83.
Overington, Michael A.
    1977.   "Kenneth Burke as Social Theorist." *Sociological Inquiry* 47:
               133–41.
Paget, Marianne.
    1988.   *The Unity of Mistakes: A Phenomenological Interpretation of
               Medical Work.* Philadelphia: Temple University Press.
Palmer, C. Eddie.
    1983.   " 'Trauma Junkies' and Street Work." *Urban Life* 12: 162–83.
Pangborn, R.M.
    1960.   "Taste Interrelationships." *Food Research* 25: 245–56.
Parkin, Wendy.
    1993.   "The Public and the Private: Gender, Sexuality and Emotion."
               Pp. 167–89 in Stephen Fineman, ed., *Emotion in Organiza-
               tions.* London: Sage.
Parsons, Talcott.
    1939.   "The Professions and Social Structure." *Social Forces* 17: 457–67.
Patnode, Randall.
    1983.   "Food for Nought." *The Bloomsbury Review* (November):
               17–18.
Paules, Greta Foff.
    1991.   *Dishing It Out: Power and Resistance among Waitresses in
               a New Jersey Restaurant.* Philadelphia: Temple University Press.
Paz, Octavio.
    1972.   "Eroticism and Gastrosophy." *Daedalus* 101: 67–85.
Peters, Thomas J. and R. H. Waterman, Jr.
    1982.   *In Search of Excellence.* New York: Harper and Row.
Peterson, Richard A.
    1979.   "Revitalizing the Culture Concept." *Annual Review of Sociol-
               ogy* 5: 137–66.
Pettigrew, Andrew.
    1979.   "On Studying Organizational Culture." *Administrative Science
               Quarterly* 24: 570–81.
Pfeffer, Jeffrey and Gerald R. Salancik.
    1978.   *The External Control of Organizations: A Resource Depen-
               dence Perspective.* New York: Harper and Row.
Phizacklea, Annie.
    1990.   *Unpacking the Fashion Industry.* London: Routledge.
Pillsbury, Richard.
    1990.   *From Boarding House to Bistro: The American Restaurant,
               Then and Now.* Boston: Unwin Hyman.
Polanyi, Michael.
    1958.   *Personal Knowledge.* Chicago: University of Chicago Press.
Pollner, Melvin.
    1987.   *Mundane Reason.* Cambridge: Cambridge University Press.

Prendergast, Christopher and J. David Knottnerus.

1990.   "The New Studies in Social Organization: Overcoming the Astructural Bias." Pp. 158–85 in Larry T. Reynolds, ed., *Interactionism: Exposition and Critique,* 3d ed. Dix Hills, N.Y.: General Hall.

Prus, Robert.

1987.   "Developing Loyalty: Fostering Purchasing Relationships in the Marketplace." *Urban Life* 15: 331–66.

————.

1989.   *Pursuing Customers: An Ethnography of Marketing Activities.* Newbury Park, Calif.: Sage.

Prus, Robert and Styllianoss Irini.

1980.   *Hookers, Rounders, and Desk Clerks.* Toronto: Gage.

Putnam, Linda L. and Dennis K. Mumby.

1993.   "Organizations, Emotion, and the Myth of Rationality." Pp. 36–57 in Stephen Fineman, ed., *Emotion in Organizations.* London: Sage.

Revel, Jean-Francois.

1982.   *Culture and Cuisine: A Journey through the History of Food.* Garden City, N.Y.: Doubleday.

Riesman, David.

1951.   "Toward an Anthropological Science of Law and the Legal Profession." *American Journal of Sociology* 57: 121–35.

Ritzer, George.

1993.   *The McDonaldization of Society.* Thousand Oaks, Calif.: Pine Forge.

Robbins, Maria P.

1984.   *The Cook's Quotation Book.* New York: Penguin.

Roethlisberger, F.J. and W.J. Dickson.

1939.   *Management and the Worker.* Cambridge: Cambridge University Press.

Root, Waverly and Richard de Rochemont.

1976.   *Eating in America: A History.* New York: Morrow.

Rosch, Elizabeth.

1978.   "Principles of Categorization." Pp. 27–48 in Elizabeth Rosch and B.B. Lloyd, eds., *Cognition and Categorization.* Potomac, Md.: Erlbaum.

Roth, Julius.

1974.   "Professionalism: The Sociologist's Decoy." *Sociology of Work and Occupations* 1: 6–51.

Roy, Donald.

1952.   "Quota Restriction and Goldbricking in a Machine Shop." *American Journal of Sociology* 57: 427–42.

————.

1954.   "Efficiency and the Fix: Informal Intergroup Relations in a Piecework Machine Shop." *American Journal of Sociology* 60: 255–66.

———.
1959–1960. "Banana Time: Job Satisfaction and Informal Interaction."
           Human Organization 18: 156–68.
Rubinstein, Jonathan.
1973.   *City Police*. New York: Farrar, Straus, and Giroux.
Sacks, Harvey.
1974.   "An Analysis of a Joke's Telling in Conversation." Pp. 37–53
           in Richard Bauman and Joel Sherzer, eds., *Explorations in the
           Ethnography of Speaking*. Cambridge: Cambridge University
           Press.
Sanger, Marjory Bartlett.
1980.   *Escoffier: Master Chef*. New York: Farrar, Straus, and Giroux.
Sardi, Vincent and Richard Gehman.
1953.   *Sardi's: The Story of a Famous Restaurant*. New York: Henry
           Holt.
Sass, Lorna J.
1977.   "Serve It Forth: Food and Feasting in Late Medieval England."
           Pp. 22–26 in Jessica Kuper, ed., *The Anthropologists' Cook-
           book*. New York: Universe Books.
Schiller, Barry Myron.
1972.   "Prestige Markets and Status Conventions: The Case of Select
           American Restaurants." Ph.D. diss., University of Southern
           California.
Schmelzer, Claire D. and James R. Lang.
1991.   "Networking and Information Sources of Independent Restau-
           ranteurs." *Hospitality Research Journal* 14: 327–39.
Schroedl, Alan.
1972.   "The Dish Ran Away with the Spoon: Ethnography of Kitchen
           Culture." Pp. 177–89 in James P. Spradley and David M. Mc-
           Curdy, eds., *The Cultural Experience*. Chicago: Science Re-
           search Associates.
Schudson, Michael.
1989.   "How Culture Works: Perspectives from Media Studies on the
           Efficiency of Symbols." *Theory and Society* 18: 153–80.
Schwartz, Barry.
1975.   *Queuing and Waiting*. Chicago: University of Chicago Press.
———.
1983.   "The Whig Conception of Heroic Leadership." *American Soci-
           ological Review* 48: 18–33.
Schwartzman, Helen.
1987.   *Transformations*. New York: Plenum.
Sclafani, Richard J.
1979.   "Artworks, Art Theory, and the Artworld." *Theoria* 39:
           18–34.
Scott, Marvin and Stanford Lyman.
1968.   "Accounts." *American Sociological Review* 33: 46–62.

Scott, W. Richard.
    1992.   *Organizations: Rational, Natural and Open Systems.* 3d ed. Englewood Cliffs, N.J.: Prentice-Hall.
Searle, John.
    1969.   *Speech Acts.* Cambridge: Cambridge University Press.
Seckman, Mark A. and Carl J. Couch.
    1989.   "Jocularity, Sarcasm, and Relationships: An Empirical Study." *Journal of Contemporary Ethnography* 18: 327–44.
Sewell, William.
    1992.   "A Theory of Structure: Duality, Agency, and Transformation." *American Journal of Sociology* 98: 1–29.
Shelton, Allen.
    1990.   "A Theater for Eating, Looking, and Thinking: The Restaurant as Symbolic Space." *Sociological Spectrum* 10: 507–26.
Shepard, Anne.
    1987.   *Aesthetics.* Oxford: Oxford University Press.
Smircich, Linda
    1983.   "Concepts of Culture and Organizational Analysis." *Administrative Science Quarterly* 28: 339–58.
Smith, Allen C., III and Sherryl Kleinman.
    1989.   "Managing Emotions in Medical School: Students' Contacts with the Living and the Dead." *Social Psychology Quarterly* 52: 56–69.
Smith, Solomon X.
    1984.   "A Bell Unrung." *City Pages* (May 30): 13.
Smith, Vicki.
    1991.   *Managing in the Corporate Interest: Control and Resistance in an American Bank.* Berkeley: University of California Press.
Snow, David and Leon Anderson.
    1987.   "Identity Work among the Homeless: The Verbal Construction and Avowal of Personal Identities." *American Journal of Sociology* 92: 1336–71.
Sorokin, Pitirim and Robert Merton.
    1937.   "Social Time: A Methodological and Functional Analysis." *American Journal of Sociology* 42: 615–29.
Statistical Abstracts 1990.
    1990.   Washington, D.C.: Department of Commerce.
Stearns, Peter N.
    1987.   "The Problem of Change in Emotions Research: New Standards for Anger in Twentieth-Century American Childrearing." *Symbolic Interaction* 10: 85–99.
Stebbins, Robert A.
    1970.   "On Misunderstanding the Concept of Commitment: A Theoretical Clarification." *Social Forces* 48: 526–29.
———.
    1979.   *Amateurs.* Beverly Hills: Sage.

Stenross, Barbara and Sherryl Kleinman.
   1989.   "The Highs and Lows of Emotional Labor: Detectives' En-
               counters with Criminals and Victims." *Journal of Contempo-*
               rary Ethnography 17: 435–52.
Stern, Jane and Michael Stern.
   1991.   *American Gourmet.* New York: HarperCollins.
Stewart, Doug.
   1988.   "For a Portraitist, Making Faces Is a Hard Day's Fight."
               Smithsonian (July): 43–50.
Stinchcombe, Arthur.
   1959.   "Bureaucratic and Craft Administration of Production: A Com-
               parative Study." *Administrative Science Quarterly* 4: 168–87.
Stoller, Paul.
   1989.   *The Taste of Ethnographic Things.* Philadelphia: University of
               Pennsylvania Press.
Stolnitz, Jerome.
   1960.   *Aesthetics and Philosophy of Art Criticism.* Boston: Houghton
               Mifflin.
Strauss, Anselm L.
   1978.   *Negotiations.* San Francisco: Jossey-Bass.
———.

   1991.   *Creating Sociological Awareness: Collective Images and Sym-*
               bolic Representations. New Brunswick, N.J.: Transaction.
Strauss, Anselm L., Leonard Schatzman, Rue Bucher, Danuta Ehrlich, and
Melvin Sabshin.
   1964.   *Psychiatric Ideologies and Institutions.* Glance, Ill.: Free Press.
Strauss, Anselm L., Leonard Schatzman, Danuta Ehrlich, Rue Bucher, and
Melvin Sabshin.
   1963.   "The Hospital and Its Negotiated Order." Pp. 147–69 in Eliot
               Freidson, ed., *The Hospital in Modern Society.* New York: Free
               Press.
Sutton, Robert I.
   1991.   "Maintaining Norms about Expressed Emotions: The Case of
               Bill Collectors." *Administrative Science Quarterly* 36: 245–68.
Sutton, Robert I. and Anat Rafaeli.
   1988.   "Untangling the Relationship between Displayed Emotions and
               Organizational Sales: The Case of Convenience Stores." *Acad-*
               emy of Management Journal 31: 461–87.
Swidler, Ann.
   1986.   "Culture in Action." *American Sociological Review* 51:
               273–86.
Sykes, A.J.M.
   1966.   "Joking Relationships in an Industrial Setting." *American An-*
               thropologist 68: 188–93.
Symons, Michael.
   1983.   "An 'Abominable' Cuisine." *Petits Propos Culinaires* 15:
               34–39.

Tharp, Paul.
  1980.   "So You Want to Open a Restaurant." *New York* (February
               18): 37–48.
Thompson, E.P.
  1967.   "Time, Work-Discipline, and Industrial Capitalism." *Past and
               Present* 38: 56–97.
Tiger, Lionel.
  1985.   *China's Food*. New York: Friendly Press.
Tolbert, Frank X.
  1983.   *A Bowl of Red*. Garden City, N.Y.: Dolphin Books.
Tomlinson, Graham.
  1986.   "Thought for Food: A Study of Written Instructions." *Symbolic Interaction* 9: 201–16.
Turner, Bryan.
  1982.   "The Government of the Body: Medical Regimens and the
               Rationalization of Diet." *British Journal of Sociology* 33:
               254–69.
Van Maanen, John and Edgar Schien.
  1979.   "Toward a Theory of Organizational Socialization." Pp.
               209–64 in B. M. Staw, ed., *Research in Organizational Behavior*, vol. 1. Greenwich, Conn.: JAI Press.
Vickers, Zeta M. and Stanley S. Wasserman.
  1980.   "Sensory Qualities of Food Sounds Based on Individual Perceptions." *Journal of Texture Studies* 10: 319–32.
Waldemar, Carla.
  1985.   "Hail to the Homegrown Chef." *Mpls-St. Paul* (October):
               151–54.
Walker, Charles R. and Robert H. Guest.
  1951.   *The Man on the Assembly Line*. Cambridge: Harvard University Press.
Waters, Alice.
  1990.   "The Farm-Restaurant Connection." Pp. 113–22 in Robert
               Clark, ed., *Our Sustainable Table*. Berkeley: North Point
               Press.
Wechsberg, Joseph.
  1975.   "Profiles: La Nature des Choses." *The New Yorker* (July 28):
               34–48.
———.
  1977.   "Giradet of Switzerland." *Gourmet* (December): 24–26, 128.
———.
  1980.   "Three Chefs in Germany." *Gourmet* (January): 24–37.
———.
  1985.   *Blue Trout and Black Truffles*. Chicago: Academy Chicago
               Publishers.
Wheaton, Barbara Ketcham.
  1983.   *Savoring the Past: The French Kitchen and Table from 1300 to
               1789*. Philadelphia: University of Pennsylvania Press.

Whyte, William Foote.
    1946.   "When Workers and Customers Meet." In William Foote
                 Whyte, ed., *Industry and Society*. New York: McGraw-Hill.
    ———.
    1948.   *Human Relations in the Restaurant Industry*. New York: Mc-
                 Graw-Hill.
    ———.
    1949.   "The Social Structure of the Restaurant." *American Journal of
                 Sociology* 54: 302–10.
Wilensky, Harold.
    1964.   "The Professionalization of Everyone." *American Journal of
                 Sociology* 70: 137–58.
Willan, Anne.
    1977.   *Great Chefs and Their Recipes*. New York: McGraw-Hill.
Winegar, Karin.
    1982.   "Edible Art." *Mpls-St. Paul* (November): 171–72.
    ———.
    1985.   "The Burning Desire to Eat Spicy Food." *Minneapolis Star and
                 Tribune Sunday Magazine* (January 20): 13–15, 18.
Wisely, Nancy.
    1992.   "Making Faces: A Sociological Analysis of Portraiture." Ph.D.
                 diss., University of Minnesota.
Wittgenstein, Ludwig.
    1968.   *Philosophical Investigations*. Translated by G.E.M. Anscombe.
                 New York: Macmillan.
    ———.
    1978.   *Remarks on Colour*. Edited by G. E. M. Anscombe and trans-
                 lated by Linda L. McAlister and Margarete Schattle. Berkeley:
                 University of California Press.
Wolfe, Alan, ed.
    1991.   *America at Century's End*. Berkeley: University of California
                 Press.
Wolfe, Tom.
    1976.   *The Painted Word*. New York: Bantam.
Wolff, Janet.
    1983.   *Aesthetics and the Sociology of Art*. Boston: Allen and Unwin.
Woodward, Joan.
    1965.   *Industrial Organization: Theory and Practice*. London: Oxford
                 University Press.
Wygan, Camilla.
    1981.   "Thanks to the Culinary Institute . . ." *Taste* 10: 20–32.
Yoels, William C. and Jeffrey Michael Clair.
    1994.   "Never Enough Time: How Medical Residents Manage a Scarce
                 Resource." *Journal of Contemporary Ethnography* 23: 185–213.
Zelinsky, Wilbur.
    1985.   "The Roving Palate: North America's Ethnic Restaurant
                 Cuisines." *Geoforum* 16: 51–72.

Zerubavel, Eviatar.
    1979.   *Patterns of Time in Hospital Life: A Sociological Perspective.*
                 Chicago: University of Chicago Press.
Zukin, Sharon.
    1989.   *Loft Living: Culture and Capital in Urban Change.* New
                 Brunswick, N.J.: Rutgers University Press.
    _____.
    1990.   "New Cusine as a Landscape of Cultural Consumption." Un-
                 published Manuscript.
    _____.
    1991.   *Landscapes of Power.* Berkeley: University of California Press.

Index

Gary Alan Fine is Professor of Sociology at the University of Georgia and the author of ten previous books. Photo by John Sheretz.

Compositor:	ComCom
Text:	10/13 Sabon
Display:	Sabon
Printer:	Haddon Craftsmen
Binder:	Haddon Craftsmen